Customer Data
Integration

Customer Data Integration

Reaching a Single Version of the Truth

JILL DYCHÉ
EVAN LEVY

WILEY

John Wiley & Sons, Inc.

Copyright © 2006 by John Wiley & Sons, Inc. All rights reserved.

Published by John Wiley & Sons, Inc., Hoboken, New Jersey.

Published simultaneously in Canada.

For general information on our other products and services, or technical support, please contact our Customer Care Department within the United States at 800–762–2974, outside the United States at 317–572–3993 or fax 317–572–4002.

Wiley also publishes its books in a variety of electronic formats. Some content that appears in print may not be available in electronic books.

For more information about Wiley products, visit our Web site at *http://www.wiley.com*.

Library of Congress Cataloging-in-Publication Data:

Dyché, Jill.
  Customer data integration : reaching a single version of the truth / Jill Dyche, Evan Levy.
    p. cm.
  Includes index.
  ISBN-13: 978–0–471–91697–0 (cloth)
  ISBN-10: 0–471–91697–8 (cloth)
  1. Customer relations—Data processing. 2. Data warehousing. I. Levy, Evan. II. Title.
  HF5415.5.D95 2006
  658.8′120285—dc22   2006013003

Printed in the United States of America

10 9 8 7 6 5 4 3 2 1

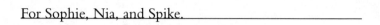

For Sophie, Nia, and Spike.

Contents

Foreword

Customer data is the most basic raw material required for building customer relationships. Ironically, while the raw material itself has never been in greater supply, converting it into usable customer information and insight has never been more challenging.

CRM has been defined in many ways, but the very words *customer relationship management* imply that a company is thinking about and acting toward its customers individually, one customer relationship at a time—in essence, taking customer-specific action by *treating different customers differently.* (After all, the term isn't *market relationship management* or *segment relationship management.*) Of course, as more companies adopt CRM as a business strategy, more customers will demand that all businesses should do it. Any company that values long-term customer relationships will learn quickly that customers want four basic things:

1. They want you to know who they are and to remember them from one event or transaction to the next, no matter what part of the selling organization is engaged. They want you to stop asking the same questions over and over.

2. They want you to remember what they need or what their specific preferences are. They want you to stop asking the same questions over and over.

3. They want a reliable and convenient way of communicating with you. They want to be able to tell you things about themselves and know you will respect that information and remember it. They want you to stop asking the same questions over and over.

4. They want you to provide a product or service that meets their specific needs and their specific definition of value, and to anticipate what they may want next, when, for how much. Above all—they want you to stop asking the same questions over and over.

Providing individualized service the way customers want it is surely one of the oldest strategies for commercial success, but today's computer technologies have given businesses of all kinds an unprecedented ability to keep track of and interact with their many customers, individually and cost-efficiently. In effect, companies can now process individual customer inputs cost-efficiently, across millions of customers measured one customer at a time, allowing them to maintain an individualized and profitable relationship with each one.

Even on a fully allocated basis, it costs less than a penny to handle one incremental automated customer interaction on a high-volume, commercially capable Web site. The Internet, in other words, has quite suddenly siphoned off a great deal of the friction encountered when executing commercial interactions and transactions. This has generated a level of transparency sufficient that customers can find out everything they need to know to make the best decisions, if they want to. And, of course, we've seen a phenomenal increase in the volume and velocity of interactions between customers and companies, and in the blizzard of customer data generated.

Companies everywhere are now awash in customer data—swimming in it, barely able to stay afloat. Names, titles, billing addresses, shipping addresses, e-mail addresses, phone numbers. Householding data, affiliated companies, associated parties. Credit card numbers, payment records, invoicing requirements, due dates, receivables dates. Products purchased, sizes, colors, transactions, and interactions. Services commissioned, complaints handled, referrals, inquiries, channel partner information, specifications, requirements, warranty and repair records, delivery options. You can try to organize it and simplify it, but the sheer volume of customer-oriented data collected and recorded by companies today is, well, mind-numbing.

Businesses do have a specific objective for this customer data. They have a purpose for it. They want to be able to retrieve it at will, analyze it, and use it to make better business decisions, execute better communication programs, deliver better customer service, and operate their businesses more cost-efficiently. They want to use the data to *understand* their customers better—not just *all* their customers, and not just the *average* customer, but *each* customer. They want to strengthen and deepen their relationships with individual customers, treating each one in the way that's best for that particular customer.

Why does this matter? Because nothing less is at stake than *all* of a company's revenue, today and tomorrow. Customers are the only source of revenue any company has. Products don't pay us money. Neither do brands. Only customers do. And so, whatever industry we list when we file corporate income tax returns, we are *really* in the business of finding, getting, and keeping the most valuable customers in our industry, and then maximizing the value that we can realize from each one. There's only one way to do that: maximize our value *to each customer.* The only way we can do *that* is take each customer's point of view. And the only way to do *that* is to turn the incoming tide of data into usable, coherent information.

Companies crave the understanding promised by their vast oceans of customer data, because customers represent any firm's most precious value-creating asset, and should not be frittered away through uninformed decisions or incompetent service delivery. Making the right decisions and delivering the right service can dramatically increase the value created by these financial assets. A company whose decision-making DNA is geared up to use customer information will be eager to generate as much value as possible from each customer, maximizing its Return on Customer[SM 1] to ensure that its customers create value not just in the form of this quarter's earnings, but also in the long run, to preserve and enhance the value of the enterprise.

The problem at most firms is that these oceans of customer data lie about in randomly distributed, separate and uncoordinated electronic reservoirs, often poorly maintained or updated. Formats are different, data specifications are different, and the data reservoirs themselves are often placed within different organizational jurisdictions, subject to different rules, available on different terms to different organizational actors. The data in the reservoirs can be subject to different hierarchical and organizational constraints.

- A pharmaceutical firm's sales force may call on general practitioners who are members of a broader health provider organization or network, and who have relationships with individually identified patients as well as specific pharmacists.

- An insurance company may have several agents selling to the same business client, and some of those policies could be provided by reinsurers. The customer might have different beneficiaries across policies.

- A business services firm may track the different divisions and purchasing units at an enterprise client, as well as the various decision makers and influencers who play roles within these divisions, linking this information as appropriate to specific reseller and service partner records.

- There may be multiple identified individuals within a single household, one of whom has recently gone bankrupt, but all of whom are now subject to increased financial risk.

- A phone company may need to make a decision regarding a customer's value, but the only consolidated data on the customer is 90 days old. It may be able to determine whether the customer disconnected service last month, but what it really needs to know is whether the customer has disconnected within the last few hours. It needs to know not only the customer's credit score, but his relevant characteristics and preferences, and it needs this data immediately, before it assigns someone to call him back to try to reinstate him as a customer.

Over the years there have been many attempts to help companies organize the raw material of customer data. The fact is, however, that it is still a nearly insurmountable obstacle for most firms to make enough order out of this chaos to gain substantial leverage from the volumes of customer data they all have readily available.

This is where customer data integration (CDI) comes in. CDI represents a new set of technologies designed to help companies turn the raw material of customer data into usable, reliable customer information—and to do this cost-efficiently and conveniently. CDI technologies automate the access, reconciliation, quality checking, and correlation of customer data from many different operational systems without requiring that the data be copied onto (yet another) database platform. Using CDI, a business gets individual customer data from its various sources and correlates it in real time.

CDI alleviates a lot of the brute-force work of data reconciliation, which at many firms involves hard-coded extraction programs and other custom applications. It automates the difficult and time-consuming work, eliminating both the need to apply the heavy lifting of massive data manipulation *and* the time delay inherent in scheduled runs and batch processing.

CDI can help you spend your time making business decisions about how best to treat different customers and how to help make sure they are helping you create the maximum value for your firm, rather than trying to pin down which particular system contains the best customer data for making the decision.

And that, in turn, will allow you to concentrate on strengthening your customer relationships, rather than trying to understand why the billing records don't jive with the service log.

Don Peppers
Martha Rogers, Ph.D.

ENDNOTE

1. Return on Customer[SM] *and* ROC[SM] *are registered service marks of Peppers & Rogers Group.*

Introduction

In 2000, one of the coauthors of this book, Jill Dyché, wrote a book called *e-Data*. While certainly exploiting the "e" that prefaced almost everything in those days, *e-Data* focused less on "electronic" data and more on "enterprise" data. The book explained how smart companies could leverage data across their various siloed systems to make better business decisions. The book profiled companies like Hallmark, Bank of America, and Twentieth Century Fox—all of which were integrating data on data warehouses to differentiate themselves and improve their business operations.

The Internet had claimed its place as a bona-fide business phenomenon. The dot-com explosion had provided executives with a brand new vocabulary. They were focused on complementing their companies' traditional brick-and-mortar storefronts with e-commerce capabilities. Meanwhile, information technology (IT) departments were trying to Web-enable just about everything.

At the same time, another business movement was also afoot: customer relationship management (CRM). Companies were realizing that their burgeoning e-channels were changing how they interacted with their customers. The competition, as the well-worn aphorism went, was only a mouse-click away. Customer relationship management vendors were sprouting up like so many saplings in a forest of enterprise software firms, and executives began shedding their budget constraints and frolicking amidst the fertile landscape of vendors.

Trouble was, the companies that had invested in CRM technology naïvely believed that they could "install" CRM. Flip a switch, the logic went, and we can automate our customer relationships. "CRM out-of-the-box!" crowed one vendor. Would it were that easy.

Most companies didn't reap what they'd sown. Executives began asking questions about drawn-out implementation time frames and payback. Industry analysts fueled the disappointment, igniting the debate on scary statistics about CRM failures. In 2001, Gartner reported that it expected an increase in CRM failure rates from its current estimate of 65 percent to 80 percent. Bain and Company reported that out of 451 executives surveyed about their satisfaction with new technology initiatives, CRM ranked at the bottom. Other surveys bemoaned the high cost of CRM implementation. Analysts and consultants took to finger-wagging their clients about creating CRM strategies and securing executive sponsorship at the get-go. The refrain of "people, process, and technology" rang hollow as project managers began reluctantly to "descope" their CRM efforts.

By late 2002, the industry gurus began realizing that the unfulfilled dream of customer information on demand had less to do with lack of process or organizational rigor and more to do with the availability of data. Integration became the *cause celebre*. "Integration is the dominant technical obstacle to CRM progress," Forrester Research crowed. Responding to a Morgan Stanley Dean Witter survey that asked chief information officers what their "top strategic project" was for the coming year, integration was the number one response. ("E-business" was number two.)

By then, Jill's second book, *The CRM Handbook*, had been published. The case studies in the book featured the likes of Hewlett Packard, Verizon, Eddie Bauer, and Harrah's Entertainment—companies that had deployed customer management initiatives in a deliberate, requirements-driven way, and were generating some well-deserved buzz. The projects themselves were vastly different, but the common denominator was that the executives charged with getting CRM right understood that integrated data wasn't a luxury—it was a mandate. "We needed to stop wasting money on duplicate yet disconnected efforts that ultimately clouded the CRM landscape," said Beth Leonard, Verizon's then-vice president of database marketing.

The discussion in the CRM community thus turned to data. Data modelling and design were hot topics, as was data quality. "We didn't know our data was dirty!" was the surprisingly surprised refrain from IT practitioners whose missed deadlines and cost overruns were attracting the attention of executives. Peeling back the layers of their aging legacy systems, companies realized that customer data was redundant, contradictory, meaningless, missing, and ubiquitous. And it still is. Thus the third book—the one that you're reading now.

WHO SHOULD READ THIS BOOK

The aim of this book is twofold. Our first goal is to define customer data integration (CDI)—describe what it is and why it's a critical solution to customer-focused business programs. We'll put it in context with other emerging trends like master data management (MDM) and data governance, and distinguish it from other technologies you might already have in-house. Our second goal is to describe how CDI works. Our hope is that this will inform decisions you'll make around vendor selection, data management, CDI development, and usage. We think that the promise of CDI is nothing less than making your company—on both the business and IT fronts—more agile.

Because this book explains the "whys"—why customer data integration is so important for business strategy and growth—it can be read by executives and managers seeking to launch a CDI project or justify CDI to their organizations. Included in this group will be:

- Executive managers, including chief executive officers, chief operating officers, chief strategy officers, or any other executive who needs comprehensive customer information in order to provide business insight.
- Privacy professionals, including chief privacy officers, who have a mandate to individualize constituents on behalf of their companies.
- Marketing executives, including marketing vice presidents, directors, product managers, and anyone else who needs to target the right customers and prospects for meaningful interactions.
- Program managers who are responsible for customer-focused initiatives like CRM, target marketing, voice-of-the-customer projects,

market research, and customer surveys. Most of these initiatives require customer detail that can be delivered through CDI.

- Sales managers and field salespeople, for whom customer relationships can mean the difference between a good year and a bad year. These professionals need to understand customers as individuals.

- Financial analysts who need to understand not only company performance, but the contribution of customers to their company's bottom line.

- Customer support managers and representatives. Simply put, they need to know who they're talking to. Customer data integration helps determine "who's who"—an important capability, especially when you've got the customer on the telephone.

Information technology professionals responsible for implementing CDI will also find value in these pages, particularly as they embark on what may well be their first CDI journey. These professionals might include:

- Chief information officers or chief technology officers who need to deliver the technology to implement CDI or who may be interested in how CDI differs from their other strategic technology initiatives.

- Information technology project managers who will be tasked with choreographing the resources and activities of a CDI project and thus should understand its various components and success factors.

- Information technology architects who need to support the introduction of new CDI technologies and thus understand where and how CDI fits into their companies' existing technology infrastructures.

- Data administrators and data stewards responsible for customer reference data or MDM. As a delivery vehicle for integrated data, CDI should be well understood by these data professionals.

- Information technology practitioners who need to cut through the complexity inherent in data integration. Often, CDI is new to even experienced developers, and thus the concepts and development processes may be new to them. This list includes programmers, database administrators, and network administrators.

Other professionals—many of whom may straddle the fence between the business and IT—will also benefit from reading this book, including:

- Industry consultants who need to understand the specific vertical applications for CDI
- IT consultants who might specialize in data-enabling solutions such as data warehousing, business intelligence tools, CRM software, or enterprise application packages, all of which might benefit from the newly reconciled data CDI offers
- Systems integrators who need to understand CDI product and architectural details as they relate to their clients' specific technology needs
- Software vendors who might be interested in understanding how CDI functionality complements their product offerings
- Hardware vendors who might consider positioning their products as CDI platforms

HOW TO READ THIS BOOK

This book can be read in a linear fashion, chapter by chapter. Alternatively, individuals with specialized areas of interest might choose to go directly to the chapters that interest them. In either case, the material in each chapter can stand on its own with minimal context from the other chapters. It is recommended that everyone read Chapters 1 and 2 to get a sense for the business problems CDI addresses, and to understand how it differs from other data-enabling solutions currently available.

Following is a description of each chapter and its audience focus:

Chapter	Description	What You Will Learn
1. Executives Flying Blind	With all the buzz around CRM, executives know less than they ever did about what makes their customers tick—or not.	*What the business issues are behind the need— more urgent than ever— for information about what our customers want from our companies, and vice versa.*

Chapter	Description	What You Will Learn
2. Master Data Management and Customer Data Integration Defined	There's a lot of noise around what CDI is, as some vendors hang the shingle and others claim they've done it all along.	*Formal definitions and comparisons of CDI and MDM and an explanation of their boundaries.*
3. Challenges of Data Integration	If it were easy, we'd all have done it by now. Here are the barriers and challenges around CDI that continue to vex the companies that need it so badly.	*There are some common "gotchas" on CDI projects that represent the major roadblocks to success. Learn from the early adopters, many of whom failed in their first forays because of the challenges described here.*
4. "Our Data Sucks!": The (Not So Little) Secret about Bad Data	The impact of inaccurate, bad, and missing data transcends CDI and arguably has far-reaching effects on how companies operate. Almost all of the CDI solutions on the market have data quality built in, so it's an essential topic.	*Data quality is more than a goal—it's a process and a corporate culture. Here are some critical success factors for ensuring that your CDI effort is synonymous with "good data."*
5. Customer Data Integration Is Different: A CDI Development Framework	CDI implementation involves a specialized implementation process that probably differs from your company's tried-and-true system development lifecycle. These differences are described here.	*In order to deliver CDI successfully the first time out, you should understand what the steps are and why they're unique. You'll also learn what you can adapt from other projects, and what you might have to create from scratch.*
6. Who Owns the Data Anyway?: Data Governance, Data Management, and Data Stewardship	Data ownership is an area fraught with confusion and politics. Here's how you can put some policies in place in order to start managing data as an asset.	*It's not easy to create new job roles. It's even harder to change existing ones. You'll learn how to put a structure around data governance and establish roles to*

Chapter	Description	What You Will Learn
		ensure the quality and availability of customer data.
7. Making Customer Data Integration Work	There are different types of CDI. They have their own processing and architectural characteristics. This chapter explains how CDI works and what you should know to determine where it fits.	*Understanding a bit about CDI functionality can help you choose the solution that's right for your company and retrofit that solution into your existing IT environment.*
8. Making the Case for Customer Data Integration	Most companies require some sort of cost-benefit analysis, and CDI can be expensive and resource-intensive. Or not. But one thing's for sure—you won't get a blank check for CDI. Here's how to justify the need.	*You're probably going to have to explain why your company needs CDI. Here are some tips for doing this right the first time—while not stepping on anyone's toes.*
9. Bootstrapping Your Customer Data Integration Initiative	This chapter explains how to avoid the most common CDI mistakes and launch your initial project for optimal results.	*Knowing the questions to ask to gauge your "readiness" level for CDI is a great start. Knowing what to do to prepare is even better.*
Glossary	Any new movement worth its buzz adapts a vocabulary or creates a new one. Here's a little of both.	*You'll have a trusty reference guide for new terms, buzzwords, and three-letter acronyms at the ready.*

You'll find a list of "manager do's and don'ts" at the end of each chapter. Each list summarizes some of the points made in the chapter for executives who might be skimming certain sections, and provides some experience-based tactics for putting some of the chapter's concepts into practice. Since much of this book provides some real-life lessons learned, we think the accompanying scenarios, checklists, and questionnaires should help readers evolve the CDI vision in their own workaday worlds.

More importantly, we've interviewed seasoned managers across industries about their CDI journeys, the challenges they confronted, and what the successful delivery meant at their companies. They told us their stories, and shared the wins and the "gotchas." In the spirit of "a picture is worth a thousand words," we think the case studies featured throughout this book teach valuable lessons you can use to avoid the mistakes of those who have gone before you—or compare yourself against CDI best practices. And be on the lookout for the "What Works: Tips from the Experts." We think you'll find some golden nuggets.

Acknowledgments

There are a lot of drops of water in a reservoir. The individuals listed here represent a veritable wellspring of fresh ideas and expertise, which we are grateful to them for sharing.

Our friends in the vendor community have been a tremendous resource for us. The vendors listed here all walk the CDI walk, and have real, bonafide customers using their products to do the hard work of customer data integration and master data management. We thank Gina Sandon and Bill Conroy from Initiate Systems; Bob Hagenau and Karen Styres of Purisma; and Karen Leightell of IBM. Siperian's Anurag Wahedra and Ken Hoang engaged early to help shape our CDI paradigm. Arvind Parthasarathi from Informatica; Scott Schumacher and Sean Cassidy at Initiate Systems; Dave Butler at Oracle; and John Radcliffe from Gartner all provided important feedback on our initial drafts and served as sounding boards for our theories.

Of course, we're thrilled with our Foreword writers, Don Peppers and Martha Rogers. We have traveled in the same circles as Don and Martha and know that many of our projects at Baseline have involved the tactics of implementing their vision. It's fulfilling to know that CDI is so symbiotic with the concepts of one-to-one marketing and Return on Customer^{SM}.

We also thank Teradata's Kim Dossey and Informatica's Shauna O'Boyle for putting us in touch with some key experts. Susan Spencer from Spencer Communications had tenacity to spare. David Loshin at Knowledge Integrity did QA on our quality content. CRM guru Cathy Burrows from RBC Centura pointed us toward some best practices—it takes one to know one. Beth Leonard and Linda McHugh made sure that, where data management and governance are concerned, our words reflected our deeds. And a hearty shout-out to Tamara Dull and Susan Welton of Noetix, who built us a handy dashboard, stalwarts of the consolidated app world that they are.

Hooray to our case study subjects for telling their CDI stories—and revealing their battle scars. Thanks also to the many practitioners and executives who have made comments during our conference presentations and seminar talks, and who approached us afterward to share their own experiences and insights.

Katie Fabiszak from DataFlux shines forth amidst this constellation of friends and colleagues. Katie had a vision for the role that CDI would play in the marketplace—a vision that's been borne out in the months since our first meeting. Katie and DataFlux President Tony Fisher have been intrepid supporters of our work. Thanks, too, to Joyce Norris-Montanari for connecting us.

We're grateful to Sheck Cho, our editor at Wiley, for his patience and clarity, and to Julie Platt at SAS for encouraging us to put pen to paper in the first place.

We collaborated on this book in fits and starts, in airport lounges and remote hotel rooms, with both dial-up and broadband, often from opposite sides of the globe. We'd like to thank Gordon Levy, David Rankell, and Tiffany Sainton for their ongoing and ever-nimble support during a crazy few months, as well as Bryan Rockoff, Kim Stanick, and John Earle for picking up the leadership reigns at some critical times.

Last but not least, we'd like to thank all our colleagues at Baseline Consulting, mostly for your patience with us as we extracted ourselves from our day-to-day responsibilities to write this book, but also for contributing your knowledge about the steps involved in delivering integrated data at our clients. "We couldn't have done it without you" is an understatement.

Jill Dyché
Evan Levy

Executives Flying Blind

You can't understand the future without knowing something about the present. Knowing the characteristics of your customers, partners, and suppliers—who they are, where they are, how they interact with your company, and how you support them—can shape every aspect of your company's strategy and operations, right down to the individuals you target and the products you pitch.

As customer relationship management (CRM) enters the mainstream, companies continue to struggle with finding, gathering, and integrating information about their customers. Unlike other business challenges that require automation, integrating customer data isn't an obvious call for brute force programming—it's clearly a problem for management.

What executives don't know can not only hurt them, it could send them to jail. In the "information age," there are fewer excuses for ignorance, especially when it comes to corporate performance. But there are also significant barriers to knowledge, and these barriers haven't been toppled by the latest juggernaut of packaged software solutions like CRM. In this chapter, we examine what's holding companies back from understanding their customers at a holistic level. Customer information isn't destiny, but it's close.

SLOUCHING TOWARD CUSTOMER FOCUS

Nothing has as much impact on a company's operations as an executive who declares a new strategic direction. Such declarations were common in the early 2000s, when many CEOs proclaimed that their companies would henceforward become "customer focused."

Of course, major strategy shifts invited analysis of how the company did business prior to its becoming customer focused. Many companies paid large consulting firms big bucks to help them migrate from a state of "customer aware" to the nirvana of being "customer intimate." While the distinction itself was up for debate, what was clear was that executives had to reexamine how their firms were building products, managing business operations, and interacting with customers.

Mature companies understood that in order to reach customer-centricity, they needed to understand who their customers were. More to the point, they needed to engage in an ongoing dialog with customers and continue to track their interactions and responses. This in turn allowed businesspeople across the company to understand who their good customers were, what made them good customers, and how to motivate other customers to share some of those traits. They needed to understand customers' various demographics, income levels, existing product mixes, tenure, and the tried-and-true "recency, frequency, and monetary" analysis[1] that could all foretell purchase behaviors. In doing so, managers were finally heard admitting that no two customers were the same.

Companies that had been product-centric since their inception had to endure significant changes to business processes, technologies, job roles, and their very corporate cultures in an effort to become customer-centric. The trouble was that executives expected their organizations to turn on a dime.

Such lofty expectations took the form of new business discussions that informed a new crop of strategic goals. One of those discussions centered on the emerging concept of one-to-one marketing. Made popular by the best-selling book *The One-to-One Future* by Don Peppers and Martha Rogers, as well as their subsequent writings, one-to-one marketing brought the term *mass customization* into the popular business lexicon, and set the expectation that every customer was unique and thus should be communicated and sold to accordingly.

Part of one-to-one marketing meant engaging customers on a one-to-one basis, not only "pushing" communications out to them via direct mail and Web messages, but recording their comments via surveys, solicitation of feedback, and even ad-hoc customer conversations. As much as companies needed to start accessing customer information, they also needed to begin recording information about customers in a proactive and sustained way.

Integrated data is increasingly on people's radar, especially management's. Of the information technology (IT) professionals surveyed by Baseline Consulting at the end of 2005, over half claimed that their companies lacked a single, authoritative customer system of record.[2] Ironically, 77 percent of respondents said that their company executives considered having a "single version of the truth about customers" to be an important issue.

Irrespective of the industry, data integration can have a huge impact. The U.S. Transportation Security Administration (TSA), a division of Homeland Security, had struggled to deploy its Secure Flight program. The program, which was issued a budget of $81 million for 2006, was meant to prequalify air passengers for faster security screening. This not only means cross-checking passenger information against the data on terrorist watch lists, but combining up-to-the-minute traveler data with established information about terrorists. Secure Flight was controversial because of the privacy concerns, but the technical challenges of mapping real-time passenger data with historical records ultimately grounded it for good. The TSA shut down the program in order to audit its IT systems.

As customer data continues to be distributed across a variety of internal and external data sources, more people are recognizing the need to bring it together. And it's usually these same visionaries who confront how hard that is to do. In survey after survey[3] across all the challenges IT executives face, integration is routinely cited as one of the biggest. Not surprisingly, the research firm IDC predicts that the market for data integration tools and services will reach $13.6 billion by the year 2008.

> *Simply put, companies' ability to communicate with and support their customers is only as effective as their access to consistent and accurate customer data.*

Simply put, companies' ability to communicate with and support their customers is only as effective as their access to consistent and accurate customer data.

MANAGEMENT MANDATES
CUSTOMER INTIMACY

Customer-focused business trends incite drastic and far-reaching business programs. Executives whose company strategies had previously been entrenched in research and development (R&D) and supply chains were suddenly putting the customer in the middle of every conversation. There were a lot of anecdotes about how far this went. For example, as part of his newfound customer-centricity, the CEO at one of our clients declared a new company-wide policy: if you're in a meeting and within five minutes a customer isn't mentioned, you're free to leave the meeting.

Executives are transcending the tired edicts of the late 1990s ("The Customer is King!") and advocating more tactical, measurable customer-focused programs in order to drive smarter marketing and higher revenues. The following list of customer-focused business trends represents the core set of initiatives that helped set the stage for many companies' newfound customer-focused projects. Not coincidentally, they also prompted escalating requests among businesspeople for integrated customer data:

- **Personalization.** The emergence of one-to-one marketing combined with a new customer awareness in advertising and brand management circles sparked fresh attention around personalization, the tactic of customizing both written and online communications according to the attributes and behaviors of individual customers or customer groups. Personalization transcended the customized letterhead salutation, relying on customer information like past purchases, sales rep name, or number of customers in a household. These details would then be mentioned in conversations—both by phone and via live Web chat—or in marketing materials and even tailored sales collateral. The desired outcome was for personalized interactions to result in higher response rates.[4]

- **Competitive analysis.** With their newfound goal of customer-centricity, companies slowly came to terms with the fact that they were competing with other companies—not for superior products or more pervasive branding—but for customers. This meant a new pressure to understand what competitors were doing and which customers they might be targeting. One Baby Bell we worked with in the late 1990s invested millions of dollars in several campaigns to entice new residential customers. Meanwhile, a competing national carrier was laying fiber-optic cable directly underneath the city streets of the Baby Bell's headquarters. The national carrier's cover was blown by the local press, but the Baby Bell ignored the news. The national carrier subsequently launched a campaign to lure away corporate customers, with huge consequences for the Baby Bell.

- **Customer segmentation.** The one-to-one movement made customer segmentation—traditionally based on simplistic attributes like geography—a dirty word. The premise was that the more specific a company's characterization of customers, the better its chances for communicating with smaller groups of customers. Marketing vice presidents saw one-to-one marketing as a way to narrow their customer segments by behaviors and preferences, so that the "households in the Midwest" segment became "empty-nesters in suburban Chicago whose next sequential purchase will be a home equity line of credit." The more detail the company had about its customers, the more precise the segments could be. With the growing volumes of granular information and advanced data mining technologies, companies are treating their highest-value customers as so-called segments of one.

- **Cross-selling and up-selling.** Cross-selling—that is, selling a different product or service to an existing customer—got traction from various research studies that declared that it was more cost effective to sell products and services to existing customers than to cast the net for new ones.[5] Hence, executives in sales, marketing, and customer support, and even chief strategy officers, put cross-selling in their strategic crosshairs. The problem was that in order to cross-sell a new product, or to up-sell a better one, companies had to understand the products the targeted customer had already. This meant, at the very least, integrating customer information with product purchase and payment history. In more mature environments, it meant companies running sophisticated product profitability algorithms or propensity-to-buy models. Whatever the specific requirement, the company's success with cross-selling and up-selling was directly proportional to the variety of detailed data it kept about its customers.

- **Return on marketing investment.** The wake-up call of customer focus meant that large, infrequent mass marketing campaigns were to be replaced with more targeted and more frequent campaigns to smaller customer groups. In some companies, this temporarily raised the cost of marketing, and executives began demanding return-on-investment figures from their marketing staff. Return on marketing investment (ROMI) offers a structured way to quantify the cost and return of individual marketing campaigns in order to pinpoint unsuccessful promotions, leverage the characteristics of successful ones, and refine campaigns to be more successful—and more cost effective—over time.[6] ROMI also allowed companies to evaluate different marketing ideas based on their anticipated financial returns.

- **Employee productivity.** In the early part of the twenty-first century, executives turned their heads toward cost savings as a means of satisfying surly shareholders. Creating a business case for all new IT initiatives went from desirable to mandatory at most large companies.

CASE STUDY: ROYAL BANK OF CANADA

Back when Ted Brewer and his team were planning their first CDI (customer data integration) project, the acronym hadn't been invented. There were few if any CDI vendor solutions available. Brewer, vice president of customer information management, had seen the bank's organizational infrastructure change since he joined Royal Bank of Canada (RBC) in 1978, but the business focus around the customer has grown more and more refined with time.

"In 1999 we were well on our way toward relationship management," Brewer recalls. "In fact, we were already thinking about developing client strategies beyond clients' relationship with the bank. We wanted to formulate programs around their total relationship with the organization. So we decided to build a utility to help us corroborate and reconcile all those relationships."

Brewer's customer information management group is a center of excellence that reports into a key business area: Canadian Personal and Business (CPB), which encompasses multiple RBC companies. In addition to retail banking, CPB spans Action Direct, RBC's discount brokerage firm; Dominion Securities, its full-service brokerage firm; and RBC's insurance organization. The utility, called Enterprise Customer Registry (ECR), reads daily data off the operational systems of these organizations and links customer records using their individual customer information source data.

ECR reads the individual customer information files and reconciles their customer identifiers using a unique matching key. "Once that unique ECR number is available, we can load that data onto our data warehouse and profile to our hearts' content," says Brenda Kydd, Senior Manager of Information Management Infrastructure and Governance. "This lets us learn more about building true cross-enterprise strategies and value propositions." ECR also "closes the loop," updating the data marts in the respective business areas with newly reconciled information for further analysis at the organizational level.

The results have been quantifiable and significant. Toni Molinaro, project manager for client relationship initiatives, explains one of RBC's key discoveries. "We've found that most of our Action Direct clients are referred through our retail bank. ECR showed us a high match rate between the two organizations. In fact, 85 percent of Action Direct clients are also banking clients." The Customer Information Management team has confirmed other cross-selling successes among various RBC companies.

Since cross-selling had been on the radar of executive management, Brewer's team didn't spend much time pitching a CDI value proposition. "When you have the CEO of the company talking about representing the client relationship from an enterprise perspective, not a lot of people argue," says Kydd. "We simply explained ECR's capabilities and assured stakeholders that we wouldn't be usurping their data. No one balked."

Indeed, rather than having to convince the various organizations, one at a time, to buy into the ECR project, Brewer assured them that their existing data and technology would remain untouched. ECR was delivered to the various companies as a service, ultimately sparking their curiosity and engaging them in analyzing information about their customers from across various business areas.

With the various lines of business on board and executive sponsorship secured, what were the organizational challenges that have become such a hot button in CDI circles? The answer at RBC is: there weren't many. Martin Lippert, the company's chief information officer (CIO), recently summed it up by telling *CIO* magazine: "We have a culture that recognizes that what's in the information vault is as critical to us as what's in the money vault."

Brewer's team has been living this adage. "This isn't about software," he confirms. "It's really about information, and the change management and process management necessary to enable it. The most important pieces were developing the business architecture, understanding the business rules, and avoiding a lot of disruption. ECR didn't cause the businesses any angst. That's what made it work."

DATA BACK IN THE LIMELIGHT

Ask any CEO about an integrated customer view, and odds are he or she will know what you're talking about. In fact, most CEOs can probably even cite the consequences of not having that view or the benefits of having it. Consider the three real-life business scenarios in this chapter.

Each of the scenarios described in this chapter represents either a hazard or an opportunity for the company in question. The common denominator is the ongoing struggle to harness and manage the information they have about their customers.

To top it off, customers are more demanding than ever. They understand as well as the companies they do business with that the competition is only a phone call or a mouse click away. And they've done business with enough companies who have delighted them to understand what being delighted or even satisfied really means. Companies are increasingly at the mercy of savvy, time-strapped customers with more than enough choices about whom to do business with.

Executives are coming to realize that, for many different reasons, their firms have multiple systems housing customer data. With customer data in different silos, the customers themselves had effectively been siloed. This realization takes many forms, none of them pretty. One director of marketing at a large cosmetics company recently explained it this way:

CASE STUDY: SCENARIO I

A high-tech company has a strategy of growth through acquisition. The company has been buying smaller competitors for the last several years and is thus growing into existing locations and geographies, consolidating offices, merging into new locations, and acquiring and shedding employees.

Each of the acquired companies has its own list of customers, and shares at least a handful—but more often hundreds or thousands— of customers with their new parent company. Those lists are constantly growing and merging. But no one's actually combined the lists into a single "master" customer list. The parent company's CIO understands that such an activity is fraught with cost and politics. So the company continues to maintain separate customer databases across its subsidiaries and affiliates. The overcharges, duplicate billings, rerouted mailings, and incoming trouble tickets continue to increase.

I already knew that marketing wasn't the only department that had hung the CRM shingle. Customer support was doing its own CRM project, but I figured they needed different information than we did, so I didn't think much of it.

But last year as we were preparing to launch a major new line, I met with the VP of customer support, who told me that his reps were entering information about every retailer that called our 800 number. We had information about retailers, too. But when we compared reports, our lists were totally different. Which one was the right one? Of course, I swore ours was right and he swore his was right. Now we're behaving like we're in two different companies.

It's bigger than just a problem with duplicate customer records—though that in itself is a growing phenomenon as businesses evolve. Having different versions of customer data has been a common problem at companies since the introduction of the relational database, which was easier to implement than its hierarchical and network predecessors, rendering databases easier for laypeople in the business to create without having to rely on their

IT counterparts. This "democratization" of databases contributed to the proliferation of redundant and contradictory data across companies.

> *The proliferation of duplicate, erroneous, unsynchronized, or just plain missing information is getting worse.*

The proliferation of duplicate, erroneous, unsynchronized, or just plain missing information is getting worse. And the resulting mistakes—from duplicate catalog mailings to misidentified hospital patients to individuals on "watch lists" slipping through the cracks—can have significant tangible and intangible costs.

Why the crisis in customer information?

Proliferation of Data Sources

Over the last 15 years or so, database technologies have advanced to the point where providing information to businesspeople has become easier. In the past, a company's customer database would often represent data that was replicated from the billing or general ledger systems likely to reside on large, expensive mainframes. Yesterday's monolithic mainframes have

---

CASE STUDY: **SCENARIO 2**

You work for a formerly small drug company which, because of several new medicines that have recently been approved by the U.S. Food and Drug Administration (FDA), has experienced booming growth and a host of large corporate customers. With the onslaught of new accounts, your sales management has become overwhelmed with territory reassignment and account reconciliation. No one knows the difference between "parent company" and "billing entity." Not to mention that salespeople in certain geographic regions are laying claim to the same physicians and account reps are cannibalizing each other's sales initiatives. With most of the hospitals and HMOs having dozens of subsidiaries, account assignment is easier said than done.

ceded to more flexible systems and tools. But companies are arguably no closer to controlling and managing their data.

The Data Warehousing Institute reports that a mere 11 percent of companies have consolidated their data across the enterprise.[7] Clearly, integrating data silos is harder than everyone thinks.

These days, anything from a mainframe to a desktop spreadsheet can be a source of data to one or more users or systems. Start poking around a company of any size, and you'll inevitably find a host of "skunkworks" databases that have been developed on the sly in order to support the workaday demands of well-meaning business users.

Add to that the introduction of so-called packaged applications. Such packaged software represents the alternative to costly and time-consuming custom code that has plagued IT organizations for years and been responsible for so much red ink. Packaged applications offer off-the-shelf functionality that IT developers can supplement using easy-to-learn system development kits. The transition of functionality from "from scratch" to "out-of-the-box" has been a productivity boon to IT organizations.

However, what's good news for development productivity has become bad news for maintenance. Packaged applications from new sales force automation (SFA) tools to enterprise resource planning (ERP) software have spread like wildfire. The time companies have saved in development is now being spent maintaining, enhancing, tracking, and synchronizing these new systems. The likelihood of the packaged application becoming a data silo increases in lock-step with the number of enhancements.

Information technology managers have been very proactive in understanding that the bevy of new systems being introduced into their organizations require data. Project plans account for the fact that, at some point, the new SFA system will need to pull in data from other systems in order to provide centralized contact tracking, pipeline management, and reporting functions, as in Exhibit 1.1.

However, less well understood is the reality that, in addition to needing information from other systems to work, the new application also *generates* new data. Often, the original data sources can also be the destinations for new data produced by the nascent application or system. Other systems in the company, such as the billing system or the general ledger system,

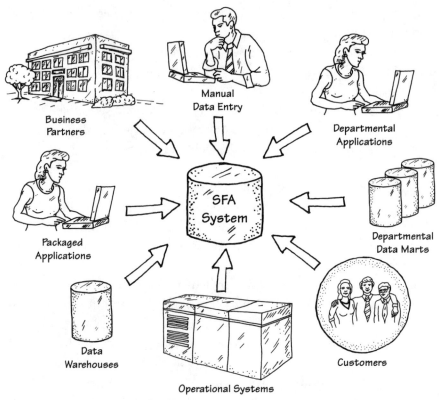

Business Partners

Manual Data Entry

Departmental Applications

Packaged Applications

SFA System

Departmental Data Marts

Data Warehouses

Operational Systems

Customers

EXHIBIT 1.1 **New Systems Require Data**

might use new sales orders in their processing, closing the loop between the source and destination systems.

Most companies implicitly treat their data as if it's linear or unidirectional. It comes in through, say, the order entry system and eventually gets parked into a downstream database that functions like a corporate cul-de-sac of information. Occasionally, a business user will have trouble finding a set of customer records and someone in IT will need to write a custom program to extract data from a proprietary system.

The truth is that every company has what we call a *data supply chain*. The term *supply chain* conjures up visions of a life-cycle for a product as it travels from parts acquisition through assembly and on to distribution and sales. The analogy is an apt one for data. As Exhibit 1.2 shows, data actually travels

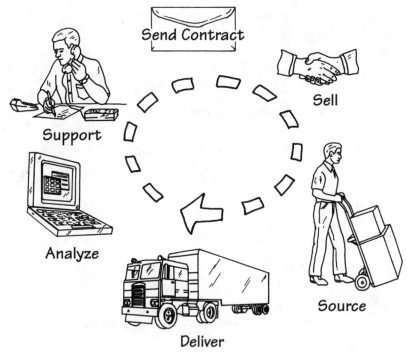

EXHIBIT 1.2   Corporate Data Supply Chain

across the company and is touched by many systems, applications, organizations, and knowledge workers.

The awareness that data isn't static within the organization—indeed, it has a life-cycle—is a big leap for many organizations, but one that more and more are starting to make as they recognize the opportunities for reuse and economies of scale inherent in data integration. The same data element can make its way to almost every organization in your enterprise.

Remember Edward Lorenz and chaos theory? Lorenz said: "When a butterfly flutters its wings in one part of the world, it can eventually cause a hurricane in another." It's interesting to quantify how many business users e-mail their favorite spreadsheets to other business users. The implication here is that any event, no matter how seemingly insignificant, can have far-reaching implications.

> *The same data element can make its way to almost every organization in your enterprise.*

Ideally, the same version of data passes through the various organizations and business processes uncorrupted. (In Chapter 4 we'll discuss the point that the extent to which a data element is processed by a system or updated by a human is the extent to which it's likely to become corrupted over time.) Companies can put the right infrastructure in place to support the sustainability of their master data, meaning that over time a single version of each customer, order, product, or supplier is available to every individual and system at any time. The practice of synchronizing data across the enterprise is called master data management, and we'll formally introduce it in Chapter 2.

Infoglut

Not only are there more data sources than ever before, there's simply more data. A 2003 University of California, Berkeley, research study[8] found that five exabytes of data were generated in the prior year. That's the equivalent of 800 megabytes of data for every human being on the planet. The study reported that new information grew at the rate of 30 percent a year between 1999 and 2002. And the data volumes just keep on growing.

New reasons for this explosive growth are everywhere. From Web logs that track every click on every page to Radio Frequency Identification (RFID) tags that can track a product or shipment across the supply chain to unstructured data from e-mails and video, every piece of data is grabbed and stored. Whether the data is kept in customer databases, Web logs, or on large storage area networks, the explosion in data volumes is hitting businesses hard. Most companies use a range of technology solutions to solve their data management and storage needs. Large mainframes, midrange systems, packaged applications, and even PC spreadsheets are considered important data sources for a wide range of business processes.

Vendors of data warehouses and storage area networks are convincing their customers to store more data for longer periods of time, citing the decreasing cost of disk space and increasing processing power and advocating the need for real-time data access. It's no longer uncommon for corporate databases to reach dozens of terabytes in size. There are a few companies with hundreds of terabytes of data. According to one research study, the size of the world's largest databases has tripled every two years since 2001.[9]

Aside from the decreasing technology costs, there are bona fide business reasons for storing greater quantities of data. The ability to track and monitor a customer's every transaction—whether on its Web site, in its stores, or through its call center—can help a company better understand customer needs and preferences. The data must be stored not only to support the processing needs of systems like CRM and ERP systems—which themselves are often accompanied by massive databases—but to represent historical transaction activities. Many companies have a policy of storing three or more years of transaction history online so that they can mine that information to understand customer behaviors before their next innovation.

Regulatory and compliance legislation ups the ante for data storage. For instance, Health Insurance Portability and Accountability Act (HIPAA) legislation forces health care organizations to keep patient records for at least seven years. AMR Research predicted that in 2005 companies would shell out $15.5 billion on compliance programs.[10] While most of that money has so far gone toward hiring new staff to support compliance, at least a portion of that money will surely be used to capture and store data in support of historical tracking, as well as formalize and automate data security policies.

Ultimately, this infoglut costs companies money. The investment is not only in technology upgrades to support the ever-growing need for storage and access, but in the increasing maintenance of the solutions necessary to provide the data. "Every dollar I spend maintaining and patching my existing systems is one less dollar I have to invest in new, enabling technologies," a drug company CIO recently confided to us.

It's no wonder that when executives were asked in a recent Accenture survey to cite the biggest problem in forecasting sales, the most popular response was "time required to collect data."[11] Similarly, 58 percent of respondents cited "time it takes to collect the data" as one of their three biggest concerns.

Advent of External Data

Add to the growing data sources and volumes the fact that companies are buying their data from third-party providers like consumer list providers and credit bureaus, and we have a veritable triple-whammy of data growth.

The more data companies have about their customers, it seems the more they want.

Many firms are simply missing basic name and address information from their customer lists. This data can be purchased from companies like Experian and Acxiom in order to augment existing customer lists. In many cases companies may buy external data as a comparison "baseline" against their own consumer data, testing their data against the baseline data at regular intervals in order to monitor accuracy or track address or demographic changes.

Other companies purchase additional data to mitigate risk. For instance, understanding a consumer's credit history can help a company determine the risk of giving that consumer a loan or establishing a line of credit. Many companies purchase consumer data to use as part of target marketing campaigns, which, when successful, generate more revenue than what they cost. Research has shown that highly targeted e-mails generate better responses than those aimed at more general segments. For most companies with even basic customer databases, the days of expensive and risky "spray and pray" marketing are over. Marketing departments have replaced gut-feel decision making with campaigns based on careful, fact-based analysis on large sets of customer data.

Even companies with mature customer data can enrich it with additional external data, purchased from third-party sources, in order to gain additional knowledge about their customers. Data such as annual household income or car make and model can be purchased from these third-party data providers for a price. Thus, companies have more complete information about their customers, which they can use to perform more accurate segmentation or analysis work.

Regulatory Compliance

We'll discuss compliance again in this book, but we're citing it here as another reason customer data volumes are escalating at such a quick clip. The essence of most of the current crop of regulatory measures is accurate and timely reporting of information. Thus, they require companies to not only have that information, but to be able to trace the history of various transactions involving their constituencies. For instance, the Sarbanes-

Oxley Act (SOX) requires the electronic certification of data at various processing points, as well as the capability to provide an audit trail. This means being able to track point-in-time data across its life-cycle. Thus, data location, collection, and tracking are mandates for SOX compliance.

HIPAA requires health care providers to adopt privacy and security standards for patient data. Patients must be able to access—and make corrections to—their own medical records. This means that patient activity and care history should be readily available when needed, rendering the need for additional online storage of this critical information.

The Gramm-Leach-Bliley Act, which regulates the exchange of customer financial records and is also known as the Financial Services Modernization Act, requires that companies be able to identify individual customers yet not use or distribute their personal information without permission.

These and other regulations have heightened the pressure on companies to capture and identify information about their customers in a sustained way, but at the same time keep ever more complete data about these customers as individuals.

The pressure to monitor and track business activities is not only external, but also internal. In a recent Deloitte study,[12] 73 percent of respondents, comprised of executives and board members, claimed that they were under increasing pressure to measure nonfinancial performance indicators for their companies. The need for integrated data across business domains is ever more critical in an environment where executives and board members are faced with growing expectations for accountability. In order to be accountable, company managers need complete and accurate information. And they need lots of it.

WHAT WE DON'T KNOW CAN HURT US

More data. More users. More platforms. More business questions. No wonder companies can't get their arms around information! The results of an Accenture survey published in *Customer Interface* magazine found that 56 percent of executives said that their businesses would grow from 1 to 20 percent if they could gain access to comprehensive customer data.[13]

It takes executives a little while and often some business pain in the form of fines or worse—the threat of jail time—to deconstruct their new business

CASE STUDY: SCENARIO 3

You work for an HMO and are challenged with the issue of patient
compliance. HMOs and other health care providers often struggle
convincing patients to fill their medication prescriptions. Providers
have found that patient compliance is directly correlated to lower
costs and better outcomes, so you want to make sure your patients
follow doctors' orders. However, it's imperative that the pharmacist
understand the patient's other medications to prevent unpleasant
side effects of incompatible drugs being taken together. Looking at
the wrong patient record at the wrong time could literally mean life
or death.

drivers back to the need for data. But when they do, they understand that, without clean, complete, and auditable data, there's a lot they can't do.

This newfound knowledge leads to the now-common refrain from executives for a "single version of truth" about their customers. They want to know how customers are interacting with their companies, be it by telephone, Internet, or in the brick-and-mortar store. They want to understand what customers are buying, and what they're paying. They want to distinguish between "good" customers and "valuable" ones. They want to map relationships between corporate customers and partners. They want to read and hear customer feedback. And, above all, they want to understand what accounts for the company's profits, and what can improve them.

It's a tall order, especially with the growing sophistication and impulsiveness of the customers themselves. Don Peppers and Martha Rogers bring this point home in their book *Return on Customer* when they say:

> The customer will not limit his field of view to our product lineup or brand. If we don't provide service by helping customers to learn not just about our products, but also about the whole variety of ways they can address their needs, then we are simply hiding our heads in the sand and hoping our customers will join us there, at least long enough to give us their money.[14]

Jack Garzella: "Let the data drive smarter marketing."

"E-mail drives 15 to 20 percent of Overstock's revenues, so it's a key part of our strategy. We used to send e-mails three times a week to every single customer who'd opted in. To change this, we had to get our three different lines of business to agree on our overarching policies around customer interactions. And we needed to understand what individual customers were doing across those lines of business.

"Now we're much smarter about how we communicate to our customers. We let them tell us how frequently they'd like to hear from us and give them product recommendations at their desired frequency. We've gotten a lot smarter about understanding customers' click behaviors and purchase propensities. So if you bought an iPod from us, the order confirmation used to be generic. Now we send recommendations on two or three iPod-related products, like earbuds, along with the order confirmation a day after you made the purchase. We're seeing dramatic improvements in responses and sales."

Jack Garzella, Vice President of Information Technology Operations, Overstock.com

The authors make the point that customers are a company's most valuable asset. Thus, understanding customer wants and needs at a detailed and intimate level should be the goal of every executive—indeed, of every company employee. However, neither customer nor employee goals can be met if the company lacks a consistent and up-to-date source of the truth about its customers.

Because companies don't have consolidated customer information, they can't:

- Map an individual customer back to a point of service
- Determine which consumers shop across channels
- Optimize partner and reseller referral plans
- Determine their highest-value customers
- Personalize communications with customers

- Individualize customer conversations during real-time interactions
- Understand hierarchies between and across business-to-business (B2B) relationships
- Make sense of encoded or abbreviated information
- Perform effective propensity-to-buy or propensity-to-churn analysis
- Determine "hot" prospects
- Refer customer prospects to the salespeople most likely to sell to them
- Incorporate knowledge of customer history or behaviors into the customer conversation

Success and Failure of CRM

In the early days of CRM, nobody really thought much about data, let alone consolidating disparate customer data to create an authoritative customer view. Back then, managers were much more focused on the software market leader, and on what the customer portal would look like.

The CRM vendors weren't complaining.

Nowadays, most of those vendors have acquired other vendors or developed their own technologies to facilitate the integration of customer information. They've seen their customers fail to deliver successful CRM programs due to the time and effort involved in finding, defining, designing, and consolidating the correct customer information.

> They've seen their customers fail to deliver successful CRM programs due to the time and effort involved in finding, defining, designing, and consolidating the correct customer information.

The vision of customer data flowing through operational and analytical systems has finally become a reality. So what's the problem? Well, there are at least five major ones:

1. **Data completeness.** Talk to any businessperson who uses customer data in his workaday job and he'll tell you that he doesn't have everything he needs. "What I'd really like to see . . . ," he'll confide, and then present a verbal list that is likely to include the customer's value

score, his contribution percentage, opt-in status, or other hard-to-get or unavailable data. These same users will also discuss their reluctance to make any type of important business decision with partial information, and rightly so.

2. **Data latency.** Since data is so difficult to find, capture, and deploy, it's no wonder that once we get customer data and store it in a database it might already be obsolete. Since many of the methods designed to extract data from its source and load it into a database are batch oriented, the data can be days, weeks, or months old. The frequency of the data loading itself determines how current and relevant it is. Moreover, many companies have operational systems that are unable to provide bulk data extracts in a timely way. If the database hasn't been populated since the beginning of last month, on-the-spot customer decisions or real-time business actions could be risky.

3. **Data accuracy.** In a 2001 research study, Gartner reported on the correlation between a successful CRM initiative and the quality of the customer data involved. The research firm proclaimed that "a CRM solution is only as good as the quality of the customer data that feeds it."[15] Indeed, as we'll see in Chapter 3, data quality and accuracy can make or break a range of strategic business programs, including—but not limited to—CRM.

4. **Data management.** Companies are only now realizing that data integration and propagation are not one-time-only activities. The data itself needs to be understood, defined, and managed in an ongoing way using formalized processes (see Chapter 6), and involving a range of specialized skill sets.

5. **Data ownership.** "Who owns the customer data?" is a common question. But it's a genuine one, and the answer is most of the time more than one organization or individual. The greater the number of cooks in the data kitchen, the more diluted the data stew becomes, to the point where it has no taste. It's a question worth asking, and it deserves an answer. (We answer it in Chapter 6.)

With all the gurus and pundits advocating executive sponsorship, integrated customer data is bigger than one executive in one department. It must span multiple organizations and, when done correctly, data should be integrated to support a range of functions, projects, and business needs across the company at large.

The AARP complex in Washington, D.C., could be mistaken for the headquarters of any huge commercial conglomerate. But halfway between the White House and the Capitol, the largest advocacy organization in the United States is the workplace for people with a higher purpose. That's certainly true of the organization's CIO, Tony Habash.

Talk to Habash for half an hour and you'll hear more about America's baby boomer population than you will about computer systems. Like his fellow executives, Habash is intent on strengthening AARP's relationships with its members, all 36 million of them. "Someone turns 50 every eight seconds," Habash explains. "AARP's goal is to enrich the life of every member and potential member."

That's a lot of member data, particularly when you consider that AARP has an extensive network of partners that includes health care options, technology partners, home security providers, and cruise lines, among others. "When we considered all the partners in our network, it was clear we had a gap in our understanding of our members. We want to know the entire person. But there are hundreds of different potential touch points with a member in a given year. We actually have this huge map of touch points that spans an entire wall."

Although AARP had a marketing database and could track its escalating membership—its target marketing has one of the industry's highest response rates—it nevertheless struggled to understand the breadth and depth of those relationships. For instance, the firm understood that it had three million members who had benefited from the health insurance product, but it couldn't tell whether those members had participated in AARP community events or advocacy efforts.

"Our marketing strategy has been fairly generic," confirms Sami Hassanyeh, Director of Application Development for AARP. "Although we have some segmentation capabilities, they are not specific to the individual. So it doesn't tell us how a member wants to tailor the relationship. You can be a member, a philanthropist, a volunteer, and an advocate. There are many potential characteristics about you that we'll be filling in over time."

Hassanyeh's team built a set of custom Web services that allow their other operational systems to access member details. This allows the diverse operational systems—including those in different AARP business divisions, partners, and call centers—to evolve and expand while retaining ongoing and consistent access of member detail. The goal is to have the member data de-duplicated, matched, and merged into a centralized address book and presented via a service-oriented architecture (SOA). Part of the data reconciliation involves appending additional data to member records as they're processed.

Hassanyeh points out the differences between mere personalization and CDI capabilities. "You can get a personalization engine, but if you don't have ongoing data consolidation and matching, the personalization engine won't be worth much. Getting the data as integrated as we can is a huge piece of our strategy." Indeed, the program is so strategic that Habash has secured additional funding to build out CDI functionality under the umbrella of the company's Member Relationship Management (MRM) program.

"The more the person engages with us—whether it's benefiting from the products, accessing information from our Web site, or participating in advocacy efforts—the greater the likelihood they'll remain a member," says Habash. "When we start engaging with people based on their interests and needs, that's much more powerful than simply sending out a renewal reminder. When we included relevant, personalized messages with our renewal mailing, our renewal rates rose substantially. We are building deeper long-term relationships with our members."

More relevant member interactions are only the tip of the iceberg for Habash and his team. The organization is extending its MRM strategy to its Web presence and is developing a strategy focused on recognizing members as they access the Web and finding ways to dynamically offer relevant content based on the member's lifestyle, life stage, and the issues he or she chooses to participate in with AARP. The goal is for the Web site to become the de-facto online resource for everyone over 50.

Besides its ability to help AARP know its members better, CDI also promises to help the organization's rebranding efforts. "We're redefining aging for the country and moving away from the 'old people' label and toward being an enabler of positive social change for people and their families. We've got a very trustworthy brand, so our focus on delivering quality, relevant information is consistent with that brand."

Habash maintains that AARP has already started to see significant return on investment from its member reconciliation capabilities. But, more importantly, the capabilities have become part of the corporate vocabulary. "We want to strengthen the position of the organization in the market to drive positive social change in the country with you, for you, and on your behalf. This has been one of our core philosophies since we started almost 50 years ago. The data has enormous value in helping us with this. Not a day goes by when I don't hear someone discussing MRM in the hallway."

Beyond CRM: CDI Takes Center Stage

It's remarkable how often CRM—the aim of which is to increase profitability through customer loyalty—results in the opposite: lost, disaffected, or downright angry customers. CRM should provide the processes and controls to support a company's newfound customer-focused strategy.

We've all seen companies that claim to have done CRM but that nevertheless send duplicate mailings, cannibalize their own sales, or market to customers on the Do Not Solicit list. Even as CRM has transcended the proverbial early-adopter phase and hit the mainstream, it seems it's only getting costlier and more difficult. In fact, in their efforts to deploy the heralded "quick win," many companies sacrificed a robust back-office infrastructure that could have made CRM sustainable for the long term.

While businesspeople were navigating their new CRM dashboards, the IT department was busy praying that no one would notice the customer data was wrong. Or misrepresented. Or redundant. Or not there at all. The faulty business decisions, contradictory information, overextended salespeople, and irked customers all pointed back to a single root cause: the customer data is bad.

CRM is now officially a commodity. Seventy-five percent of executives surveyed by Bain & Company claimed their companies were using CRM.[16] Most companies have—finally—challenged the prevailing folklore and delivered successful customer management capabilities. Indeed, if a CRM system applies automation to customer-focused business processes and analytics, then most companies have several CRM solutions in place.

But there's a wide gap between the rhetoric and the reality of CRM. For one thing, many managers assumed integration capabilities in their CRM solutions that never existed.

Surveys over three consecutive years by research and consulting firm CSO Insights revealed that respondents considered "Populating/ Maintaining Data" as the toughest challenge encountered in their CRM implementations. Jim Dickie, partner with CSO Insights, summarized the firm's findings, explaining that "CRM data management is often woefully under-budgeted, and so the thought of adding to the expense of a CRM initiative may seem unattractive to many. To those who balk at the idea of adequately funding this key task, I ask a question in return: If you think CRM data is an expensive investment, what's the price of ignorance?"[17]

Customer data integration is formally defined in the next chapter, but for our purposes it might be helpful to look at CRM as "vertical" and CDI as "horizontal." This means that CRM might solve one or more specific business needs, say, segmenting customers for more effective target marketing.

Exhibit 1.3 illustrates a financial institution's CRM portfolio, and the data subject areas it calls upon from its various operational systems.

There are lots of other application-to-data interactions in this portfolio— the illustration would look like spaghetti. Suffice it to say that it's a complex collection of processes and information.

CDI, however, is horizontal, meaning it's a set of tools, functions, and standards for providing integrated customer data across the application and organizational landscape—including, but not limited to, CRM. This means that CDI offers an authoritative view of the customer not just to a single system, but to the company as a whole. Authoritative customer data from CDI encompasses the myriad versions of customer information, as shown in Exhibit 1.4.

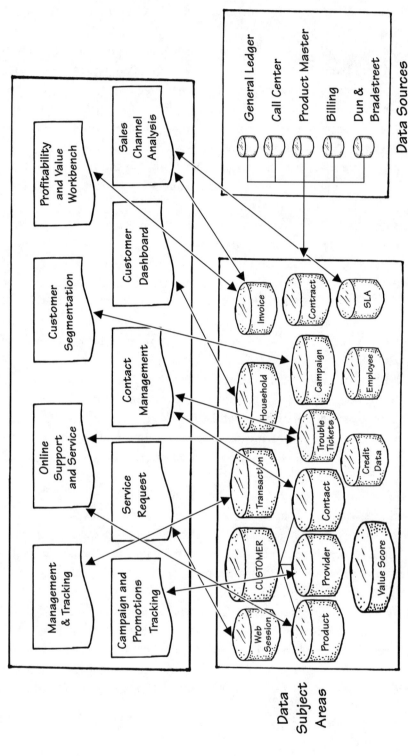

EXHIBIT I.3   A Company's CRM Portfolio and the Data It Uses

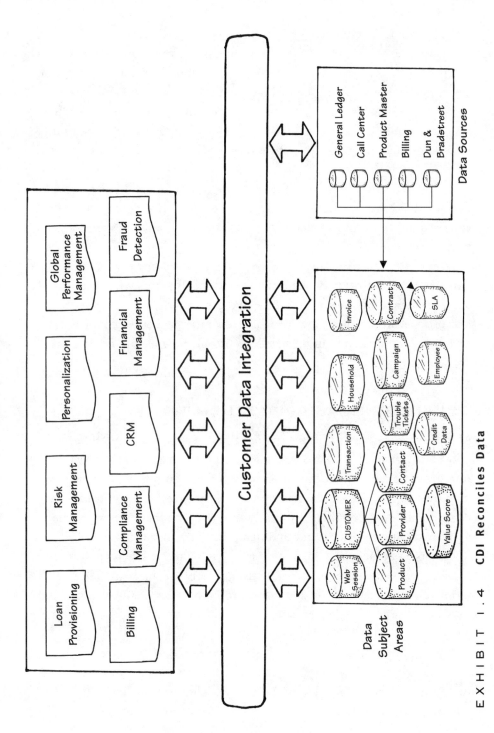

EXHIBIT 1.4   CDI Reconciles Data

27

CDI reconciles data as it travels across systems, checking the data and applying rules to prepare and avail it for a range of functions and uses. You can think of CRM as one or more of the little train cars that goes into the cave to carry the gold out. CDI is the gold mine.

Why does the distinction matter? Because many well-meaning CRM sponsors assumed that their CRM systems would take care of cleansing, matching, and merging disparate customer data from different systems. They assumed that the new CRM packages would become their companies' de-facto single version of the truth about customers. In fact, though, the new CRM applications quickly became so many new data silos, thus exacerbating the problem that there was no authoritative system for customer data.

No one foresaw that new CRM systems could become part of the problem. Many executives only realized how bad the issue was when they heard about the resulting business inertia ("We can't merge the sales territories because we don't know how to map customers to new account types") or because political infighting signaled customer ownership or data usage problems.

CDI AND CRM: A RAPPROCHEMENT

Many executives are still scratching their heads over the differences between CDI and CRM. Some imagine CDI to be a *subset* of their CRM infrastructures, in which the single view of the customer is created and managed. While this can be true, it's also rare since most companies have diverse sources of customer data, and moreover lack the necessary technological skill and rigor to create and maintain their customer hubs.

Others imagine that CDI *encompasses* CRM and other programs, and they're right, too. After all, a solid customer hub created via CDI should ultimately represent a company's de-facto customer system of record and thus be valuable to a greater landscape of applications and programs than just CRM.

Both philosophies have merit. If, at its core, CRM is the collection of methods, skills, technologies, and strategies to get a company's customers to engage and re-engage, then CDI is a vehicle for capturing and understanding who those customers are in a structured and permanent way. In our research, fewer than 20 percent of the companies that claim to have CRM also have CDI. The inverse, though, is close to 100 percent.

Either way, most companies that have implemented CDI share a common trait at the outset: they lack the necessary processes and controls. What about your company? Here's a short quiz to determine whether your company has CDI:

- Does your company agree, by and large, on a common definition for customer?

- Are customer hierarchies agreed upon and stored in a usable and accessible way?

- Can businesspeople retrieve information about specific customers when they need it, with little lag time or latency?

- Is there clarity around the availability, quality, latency, and sources of customer data between the business and IT?

- Does IT have service-level agreements in place that define the metrics for acceptable customer data and its accessibility?

- If understanding customer behaviors in real time (for instance, which of our corporate customers added a new line of business to their order today?) is a business requirement for your company, are you there yet?

In his book *Living on the Fault Line*, author and strategist Geoffrey Moore discusses the four value disciplines: operational excellence, customer intimacy, product leadership, and disruptive innovation.[18] Moore says that in order to achieve competitive differentiation, a company must "overachieve" in at least one of these areas. He even coins the term *customer relationship innovation* to convey the commoditization of off-the-shelf CRM.

Data integration has evolved from an isolated, project-based activity that was unplanned or unexpectedly complex to a strategic issue. Executives are now acknowledging that data is the lifeblood of the companies' relationships with their customers.

If your company's executive management has declared a customer-focused strategy in the last several years, as have most of the *Fortune* 1000,

CDI could mean crossing the proverbial chasm between CRM and the customer intimacy that every executive is now determined to attain.

MANAGER DO'S AND DON'TS

It's early in the book, but even so here are some do's and don'ts to remember as you begin your own education about CDI, and begin planting some political and organizational seeds in favor of its adoption:

- **Do** understand the business "need, pain, or problem." Opportunities for integrated customer data are usually revealed by some capability the business is lacking. For instance, "we can't roll up our list of financial partners fast enough to meet regulatory reporting requirements." Understanding the business's pain points and how CDI can help address them might also ensure adequate funding. (More on this in Chapter 8.)

- **Don't** assume that integrating customer data is simply about consensus building. An executive of a Web retailer recently told us that he understood there were many different silos containing customer data, but he felt he could facilitate agreement among his management team on which one was the "best" one. Not only was this decision fraught with politics, the "best" system was nevertheless still missing key customer information—and so, consequently, was the company.

- **Do** research the potential customer impact. Your company might not be interacting with key customers because it doesn't know they exist, or assumes they're part of the wrong hierarchy. Worse, your salespeople could be overcommunicating with valuable customers and driving them away. Knowing how having a single source of the customer truth will help your customers will provide you with the "mutual benefit" argument: having an authoritative system of certified customer data will help both the company and its customers.

- **Don't** think that reengineering business processes will fix the problem. Even the tightest sales process or call center script is only as good as the data available to the people putting it into practice.

- **Do** designate a single, objective person to do reconnaissance. Anecdotal examples are helpful, but no substitute for a real-life set of requirements, or a bona-fide CDI business case.

- **Don't** automatically call your CRM vendor. Although many CRM vendors have solutions or partnerships intended to solve the CDI problem, the business problems that call for integrated customer data are so diverse that a CRM vendor's answer may not be the right one for you.

- **Do** admit your ignorance. The first step many executives take is to educate themselves on the different types of CDI solutions in order to understand at a deeper level which one is the best fit at their companies. Chapter 2 should serve as an effective CDI primer.

ENDNOTES

1. *Recency, frequency, and monetary analysis, otherwise known as RFM, is a classic marketing technique that indicates how recently a customer interacted with the company, how frequently she does so, and how much money she spends. Although such analysis has been replaced at many firms with more sophisticated lifetime value scoring, RFM analysis remains a prevalent way for many companies to determine the relative value of their customers.*

2. *Survey conducted by Baseline Consulting at The Data Warehousing Institute World Conference, Orlando, Florida, in November 2005. Full survey results can be seen at www.baseline-consulting.com/resources/default.aspx?doc=Nov2005CDISurvey .htm&section=surveysresource.htm&offer=empty.htm.*

3. *For instance, a 2005 InformationWeek research survey asked 120 business technology professionals the major reason for the adoption of a new technology. Half chose the reason: "Legacy systems couldn't be cost-effectively integrated."*

4. *A 2004 study from Rochester Institute of Technology found that personalized marketing drove response rates 34 percent faster than the average rate of response; a 48 percent increase in repeat orders; and a 32 percent increase in overall revenue.*

5. *Jill wrote about cross-selling and up-selling as part of a wider marketing automation effort in* The CRM Handbook: A Business Guide to Customer Relationship Management *(Addison Wesley, 2002). See pages 31–32.*

6. *For more information on ROMI, see Sunil Gupta and Donald R. Lehmann's book* Managing Customers as Investments: The Strategic Value of Customers in the Long Run *(Philadelphia: Wharton School Publishing, 2005).*

7. *Wayne Eckerson for The Data Warehousing Institute,* In Search of a Single Version of the Truth: Strategies for Consolidating Analytic Silos, *August 2004. See www.tdwi.org.*

8. *Peter Lyman and Hal Varian, U.C. Berkeley School of Information Management and Systems. The study reported that the Internet has 17 times the data stored in the U.S. Library of Congress.*

9. *Study done as part of WinterCorp's TopTen™ Program, which monitors the ten largest production databases. The 2005 winner was Yahoo!, which has over 100 terabytes on its Oracle database.*

10. *AMR Research, "Spending in an Age of Compliance," March 2005.*

11. *2004 Accenture study of finance executives. See:* www.accenture.com/xd/xd.asp?it= enweb&xd=_dyn%5Cdynamicpressrelease_785.xml.

12. *Deloitte in cooperation with the Economist Intelligence Unit, "In the Dark: What Boards and Executives Don't Know about the Health of Their Businesses," 2004.*

13. Customer Interface, *September 2002.*

14. *Don Peppers and Martha Rogers,* Return on Customer: A Revolutionary Way to Measure and Strengthen Your Business *(New York: Currency/Doubleday, 2005), p. 31.*

15. *Gartner Research report, "Customer Data Quality and Integration: The Foundation of Successful CRM," November 2001.*

16. *A Bain & Co. survey in April 2005 of 960 executives found that CRM was more common than either balanced scorecard or supply chain management.*

17. *Jim Dickie and Barry Trailer of CSO Insights, "Sales Performance Optimization: 2006 Survey Results and Analysis." See* www.csoinsights.com/page/page/868315.htm.

18. *Geoffrey Moore,* Living on the Fault Line: Managing for Shareholder Value in Any Economy *(New York: HarperCollins, 2000). See Chapter 5.*

CHAPTER 2

Master Data Management and Customer Data Integration Defined

CDI and master data management (MDM) are getting significant buzz in both information technology (IT) and business circles. Master data management represents the data management disciplines and processes, and CDI represents the authoritative system for customer data. Indeed, the two concepts are tightly linked, but both are topics that generate a fair amount of confusion. If we've formalized our data management processes, are we practicing MDM? If we've physically centralized all our customer data in a database or have an enterprise customer information file (CIF), are we doing CDI? This chapter provides the requisite definitions and distinctions for MDM, CDI, data governance, and other related concepts with the aim of helping you to identify the gaps in your own environment and justify the need for a unified view of your customers. It provides a taxonomy that differentiates the various types of CDI and how they meet different functional and processing requirements.

Armed with this information, you'll be ready to speak the language of CDI and MDM, which will help you understand where they fit in your organization.

DELINEATING THE BOUNDARIES OF CDI

As early as it is in its life-cycle, CDI is already a subject of heated debate among industry analysts and vendors. Common criticisms are that CDI encompasses too many disciplines to be specific and that emerging CDI vendors don't have sufficient customer references under their belts. (Both of these criticisms were valid in the past, but no longer.)

The main criticism of CDI is that it's nothing new, but rather a repackaging of existing technologies and functions under a brand new rubric. It's true that in many ways CDI relates to a number of IT concepts, including:

- Business process integration
- Data integration
- Data warehousing
- Service-oriented architecture (SOA)
- Extraction, transformation, and loading (ETL)
- Data cleansing
- Householding
- Business intelligence
- Data governance

Let's start off with a formal definition of CDI:

> Customer data integration (CDI) is the collection of processes, controls, automation, and skills necessary to standardize and integrate customer data originating from different sources.

The problem is that most businesspeople are aware of their customers only within the confines of their own business processes. For instance, the marketing organization may not have a view of—or care about—a customer's service requests, just as the call center may not include order date as an important element in its customer database. At our clients, we regularly discover multiple customer databases across a company's various departments. And they're always different.

More than ever, companies need to be able to recognize their customers across diverse lines of business and touch points. CDI allows them to uniquely identify customers by reconciling data across different siloed systems. This means coalescing customer data to identify a single customer across products, purchase transactions, sales channels, salespeople, subsidiaries, and geographies. This often means the generation of the so-called golden customer record—the authoritative and reconciled profile about an individual customer, the best record possible for the requesting application. So it's apt that the processing platform that reconciles and integrates the customer data is known as a "hub."

> The problem is that most businesspeople are aware of their customers only within the confines of their own business processes.

No one ever imagined how complicated identifying the often obscure relationships among customers in disparate systems would be. As we'll see in later chapters, the different versions and definitions of customers across a company's business units can render a "single view of the customer" challenging, both technically and organizationally.

Typical Drivers for CDI

You can think of CDI as an "infrastructure"—Gartner calls it "technology, processes, and services"[1]—the whole of which is greater than the sum of its parts. In Chapter 8, we'll discuss how CDI solves problems that are particular to specific industries and market segments. For now, consider this list of business problems, all of which CDI can tackle:

- You just completed an acquisition and you can't integrate the sales teams until you have integrated the customer information.

- You are unable to determine your true credit exposure for top customers across multiple divisions.

- Your customers get inconsistent levels of service from different business units because none of them understands the aggregated value of the relationship.

- Your company's marketing department claims customer relationship management (CRM) success, but still spends hundreds of thousands of dollars a year on duplicate postage.

- Your new sales reps have a steep learning curve because they get very little information about the historical and current relationships with their inherited accounts across sales, services, and finance.

- Your sales executives can't intelligently assign territories because no one knows the difference between a "parent company" and a "billing entity."

- Your sales partners are cannibalizing each other's sales activities and their (your) customers are confused.

- Your company just acquired a competitor and someone needs to reconcile customers across accounts and addresses.

- You just received a letter thanking you for your purchase from a company you've never done business with.

- There is a dedicated staff manually correlating customer lists in Excel just to enable accurate sales rep commission payment.

These are all symptoms of a larger problem of customer data, originating from multiple "stovepipe" systems, that has not been well integrated. The bad news is that most CRM vendors didn't see it coming or, worse, overhyped their technologies to include claims of a "single version of the truth" where there wasn't one. The irony is that many of these new CRM systems have become de-facto legacy systems, thus exacerbating the stovepipe phenomenon.

The good news is that CDI is filling a market need. Many companies have realized that their initial customer-focused business initiatives were only bandages covering a much larger wound. CDI promises a sustainable remedy, and not a moment too soon.

When done right, CDI represents a company's most up-to-date source of certified customer records. This means that the data has been processed according to a series of business rules and often complex algorithms in order to ensure that it can address the demands of an array of applications and business organizations.

What CDI Isn't

There are really two separate definitions of the term *customer data integration*. On its surface, the term refers to a set of tried-and-true methods and technologies for bringing customer data together from different data sources, a classic problem for both operational and reporting applications.

But the emerging definition of CDI is more specific to the evolving technological capabilities that automate the reconciliation and synchronization of the data from disparate systems in order to offer it to the enterprise for a range of uses and processing.

As many people learn more about CDI, they compare it to their existing paradigms and often color it with long-held technology biases. In defining CDI, it's helpful to discuss how it differs from existing technology solutions. CDI is *not*:

- A CRM tool
- A solution to a technical problem
- A replacement for a data warehouse
- An "application"
- An analysis tool
- An operational data store (ODS)
- The automation of a customer data model

CDI versus CRM

By now we've established that CDI is an offshoot of the problems that plagued many CRM efforts in the early days. CDI does address what became the unfortunate assumption that the CRM solution would automatically integrate customer data from across systems. Much to the chagrin of CRM business sponsors, CRM tools were never designed to serve this purpose.

In many cases, CRM turned out to be a Trojan horse for more basic organizational issues, such as shoddy business processes; lack of alignment between different organizations (for instance, sales and marketing); poor data quality; and lack of application and data integration.

What's important to note here is that, in many ways, CDI is arguably "bigger" than many CRM projects, which can be exclusive to a single business unit. CDI's value is in reconciling heterogeneous customer reference data across a range of systems. This type of functionality offers value across an enterprise's business functions and knowledge workers. Indeed, a CDI system will not only provide data to a CRM system, it will likely source data from that system as well.

CDI versus an "Application"

Some analysts have called CDI an "application." Applications are typically focused on automating or supporting a discrete business function. CDI is really an arbiter among different applications that determines how to modify data they may have in common.

In reality, it's fairly common for different systems to contest a piece of information. For instance, a customer moves to a new area and finds an apartment while looking for a house. After six months, the customer moves into a new home and notifies her favorite housewares catalog retailer of her address change.

Behind the scenes, the catalog retailer runs a monthly change-of-address routine in order to update its customer addresses for the next mailing. (Second-class mail isn't typically forwarded by the U.S. Postal Service, which can be a costly proposition for direct-mail companies.) The change-of-address routine overwrites the customer's new home address with the old apartment address. There was no way for the company to determine which system knew the "best" address, so the monthly address routine effectively "won." But the customer—and the company—both lost.

In this example, the change-of-address routine was an automated business process—in effect, an application. It had no awareness of who else had updated the data. It was unaware of the other systems processing address data. It behaved as if it owned the customer's address.

CDI assumes there are multiple systems in need of the same data, so it's established to protect the integrity of the data, not to blindly follow the request of an individual application. In this case, it would have prevented the address overwrite by logging and tracking the "authoritative" address update. When considered holistically, CDI is more than a single business function; it's the infrastructure that supports multiple applications and how they access and process customer data.

CDI versus Business Intelligence

Many people both inside and outside of IT still relate CDI with customer analytics, particularly customer dashboards or reports. At a time when most large companies have adopted business intelligence (BI) and see it as a strategic enabler, many are looking for ways to fuel their BI capabilities in order to further differentiate their ability to make business decisions that can distinguish them in the marketplace. CDI could be the next BI killer app!

The common misassumption is that CDI is simply a faster server, designed for real-time reporting on complex, integrated customer data. It's true that CDI, when done right, becomes the single source of truth about customers, company-wide. When you think of what this means from a processing and access standpoint, CDI provides a valuable means of supporting BI. But it's not a substitute for a robust BI infrastructure, and the CDI hub itself is ill suited as an analytical platform.

People who relate CDI to customer analytics often do so with the best of intentions, since integrated customer data—in both the classic and emerging senses—is so critical for accurate information analysis. Consider the dashboard in Exhibit 2.1.

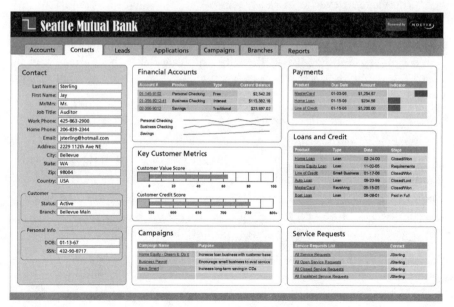

EXHIBIT 2.1   A Typical Customer Dashboard

Note that the data comes from different business domains. The customer's contact information at the left is from the sales force automation system. The service requests come from the trouble ticketing system in the call center. Marketing provides both the customer value score and the customer's campaign history. Account information can come from any number of different systems within the bank. And so on.

Yes, it's integrated data on the screen. But the good news about customer dashboards is also the bad news: when executives see dashboards, they assume that they're easy to build. The more heterogeneous the data, the more difficult the back-end work effort, where data integration is usually intensive. And this is the value of CDI to BI: the CDI hub can provision integrated data to a data warehouse or data mart in a way that's more reconciled and timely than standard data acquisition techniques.

CDI versus Data Warehousing

Data warehouses have long been the de-facto remedy for the "classic" definition of CDI—that is, consolidating the data for purposes of historical analysis and analytic reporting. But CDI has become synonymous with more real-time data provisioning. The grid in Exhibit 2.2 helps to distinguish the various levels of data access.

Unlike with data warehouses, CDI is geared less to end users and more to the provisioning of reconciled customer data to other applications and systems. CDI contextualizes the data and turns it into information. It understands the concept of "address." So when it sees a new address, the CDI hub will automatically standardize the address according to predefined rules, and that address will become meaningful information.

Conversely, with a data warehouse, all the standardization needs to occur "outside" the platform. Data integrity is optional. The data can be good or bad, depending on the surrounding data loading environment and data quality processes. And that's the key difference between CDI and data warehousing: with the CDI hub, data correction is "baked in."

In fact, we've seen CDI hubs function as a single source of customer truth to enterprise data warehouses in need of reliable customer data. CDI systems can be accessed directly by end users for data exception handling and querying, but they're broader than end-user access and are intended to be the system of record for corporate customer data across the company's various systems and applications.

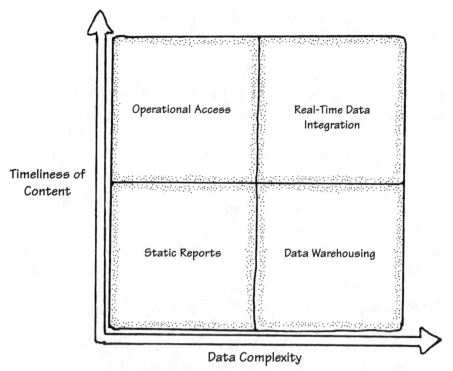

Timeliness of
Content

Data Complexity

EXHIBIT 2.2   Levels of Data Access

CDI versus the Operational Data Store

The concept of the ODS sprang from the data warehousing community frustrated with the lack of timely data availability. The definition of operational data is "data used to support the daily processing a company does."[2] Hence the ODS is a platform that processes and provisions data for timely access.

Sounds a lot like the definition of CDI. However, there are a few fundamental differences between the ODS and CDI. For one, the ODS isn't intended to perform the rigorous data matching, cleansing, and reconciliation that is at the core of CDI. Source systems populate the ODS with data in its native format; thus, it's not typically integrated. Many companies that have an ODS use it for two main purposes: (1) for more timely data access to support operational analytics and business diagnostics ("Who were our new subscribers yesterday?" or "List all the transactions for Customer X.") and (2) as a staging area for data that is likely to be transformed and then loaded onto a data warehouse. Like CDI, the ODS pulls data from source systems, but unlike CDI, the ODS is meant to be queried, not updated.

Rather than simply supporting queries, CDI can find, reconcile, and integrate data. In addition, a physical ODS system can be built relatively easily with any number of off-the-shelf technologies, including most database products. A CDI system, however, involves specialized software and logic in order to apply the reconciliation and response time rigor so often required of it.

CDI versus the Customer Data Model

You've probably figured out by now that CDI is much broader in scope than just an integrated customer data model.[3] However, many vendors use an integrated customer data model as the underpinning of their CDI solutions, so understanding how the model fits is important.

Many companies have spent years working on their enterprise customer data models. Some of these companies have proclaimed that, due to this often complex model, they are "halfway there" with CDI. Other companies assume that their CRM data models can be extended to support CDI. However, although they have customer data in common, CDI is not an inherited CRM data model.

The type of data model that supports query and analysis is going to be different than the model that supports transactional access. Most database schemas that accompany CDI products have been designed for transactional performance, and are thus very specialized. If CDI is truly intended to be the de-facto data source for all customer information, the model needs to be built to handle the quick lookup functionality and provide transactional access by other systems in need of current customer information.

For instance, a call center representative might need to know whether a customer is on the Do Not Solicit list before pitching that customer a new service. This involves a quick lookup query. Other systems might need the complete list of customers. For example, a billing system might need the most current, complete list of customers prior to launching its processing. The customer data model underlying the CDI system should be capable of fulfilling both types of requests.

Conversely, a CRM data model that supports specific functions like sales force automation might contain data that's inconsequential to CDI. Extra data within such a data model could bog down the performance of a CDI hub.

Moreover, a CDI system involves more than just how the data is designed and stored—the *raison d'etre* of most data models. CDI provides a comprehensive programming interface, enabling other systems to access reconciled customer details. CDI offers an infrastructure that can support transactional access. A data model alone is only a piece of the overall CDI puzzle, arguably a small piece. CDI offers an entire code infrastructure to support transaction volumes from heterogeneous systems.

Speaking of what CDI isn't, one of the biggest areas of confusion is the difference between CDI and MDM.

Defining Master Data Management

We'll talk about MDM again in this book, particularly in Chapters 4 and 6, but we wanted to distinguish the two definitions here to ease the way for subsequent discussion. In many ways CDI is a subset of MDM, which can be considered the overall discipline of managing information domains across an enterprise. Thus, CDI is specific to automating the management and reconciliation of customer data, while MDM involves managing the master data across domains, including product, chart of accounts, or inventory.[4] Master data spans multiple business functions and is not specific to customer data. In fact, the historical sweet spot of MDM tends to be managing so-called product catalogs or material management common in many manufacturing and retail organizations. The term *master data management* is an apt one, since the phenomenon of common data values being represented differently across business units and systems is one that both MDM and CDI seek to remedy.

Here's a good definition:

> Master data management is the set of disciplines and methods to ensure the currency, meaning, and quality of a company's reference data within and across various data subject areas.

MDM really means ensuring the consistency, accuracy, and availability of information across often global businesses. It's comprised of common work, processes, and tools necessary to administer different subject area data across an enterprise.

To go a bit further, there are four main types of data involved in a business:

1. **Transactional data.** These are usually records of individual customer interactions. A transaction represents an activity at a point in time, and is therefore static. For this reason, many companies archive their transactional data once it's been processed.

2. **Reference data.** Reference data uniquely identifies a product, customer, or other business entity. For instance, a customer's first name and last name both represent reference data. Reference data can be generated by many different systems, which often keep redundant or contradictory versions of that data. We'll discuss the reconciliation of this disparate data in Chapter 7.

3. **Relationship data.** Relationship data is data that further describes an entity to relate it to other entities. For instance, a household may represent a grouping of customers within the same family, or a "parent" company can have many subsidiaries.

4. **Metadata.** Metadata is commonly known as "data about data." It's basically descriptive data about individual data elements. For instance, metadata can define whether a "revenue amount" field calculates booked revenue or billed revenue. Metadata can include both system-level metadata, used by applications to navigate and distinguish certain data types, as well as user-defined metadata that involves persistent definitions of important data fields.

MDM usually refers to the management of reference data and the establishment of authoritative data values for that reference data across the company (although most MDM programs also include transactional and relationship data as it's needed for specific business processes). As we'll see in Chapter 6, MDM involves both enterprise-wide data management policies and practices as well as those specific to individual data domains (like customer).

CDI implies certain technological functionality like the data cleansing and reconciliation that are endemic to almost all current CDI solutions. Packaged CDI solutions include baseline data models, automated data integration and reconciliation, and data syndication (i.e., registering and sending the data) capabilities. CDI can be considered an MDM system that's "purpose built" for customer data.

The overlap between CDI and MDM can be exacerbated by vendors who recognize the advantages of labeling their solutions as MDM. However, this can confuse well-meaning managers in search of an automated customer data integration solution. (Indeed, one vendor's customer MDM server may be another's CDI hub.)

> CDI can be considered an MDM system that's "purpose built" for customer data.

Both CDI and MDM involve defining what the single, comprehensive master record should look like. MDM applies practices to enterprise data across subject areas. Exhibit 2.3 illustrates the three basic categories of MDM.

Exhibit 2.3 implies that every data subject area in the company is subject to the disciplines of MDM. CDI implies a single subject area, customer, but nevertheless multiple data sources, thus the three categories of MDM would each apply to CDI. While MDM might provide a framework for information management and sharing across various systems, CDI solutions generally provide the algorithms and infrastructure to automate it.

We would argue that many companies embarking on an MDM initiative would do well to begin with CDI. Since master data is usually physically distributed across systems, any effective MDM project involves inventorying data across various source systems, understanding the rules of uniformity around key reference data (e.g., whether product code should be comprised of alphanumeric characters, as it is on the inventory management system, or simply numeric characters, as it is in the

> While MDM might inform the infrastructure and common practices for information management and sharing across various systems, CDI solutions generally provide the algorithms and infrastructure to automate it.

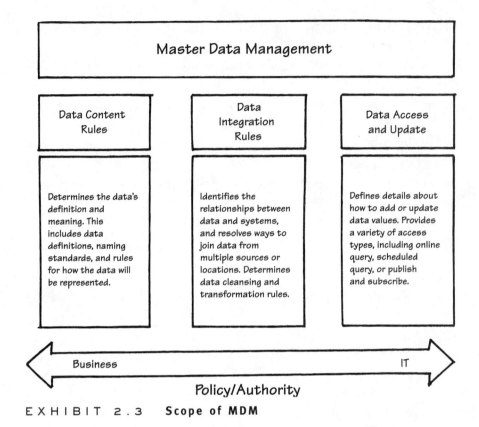

EXHIBIT 2.3 Scope of MDM

general ledger system), and agreeing on the business rules that will define and standardize it. Since customer data is so critical to a range of business functions, where better to launch an MDM program than with CDI?

A CDI TAXONOMY

Not all CDI is created equal. Whether companies write their own CDI programs or purchase CDI solutions from vendors, the way CDI processes data can vary. Although there are variations and interpretations of the different types of CDI, there are three acknowledged types: registry, persistent, and hybrid. We'll refer to them elsewhere in the book as we further explore issues around CDI functionality and architecture, but we'll introduce them briefly here.

Registry Style

With a registry style, the customer data remains on the source system and a series of pointers or data linkage details are stored physically on the CDI hub. Registry CDI acknowledges that the data "lives" on the source system(s), simply accessing and reconciling it for the purpose of creating the authoritative view or record of the customer.

The registry style (also known as the "reference" style) is arguably the most straightforward type of CDI to implement. The data remains on the source system and the CDI hub retains reference details, or pointers, to the data on the source. This minimizes the involvement of source system owners and programmers who might already be nervous about outside access of their data.

As Exhibit 2.4 shows, the CDI hub recognizes the unique customer record in each source system.

The hub assigns a unique identifier to that customer, Customer Number 1, and records the unique identifier of that record in the source system. The hub maintains a list of data elements and knows where each element resides. So when an application in need of a customer record—we'll call it the CDI client—requests a customer's account balance, the registry hub knows which source system contains the best version of balance detail.

Advocates of the registry style point to its ease of implementation and high data integrity. Detractors cite performance issues. The benefit of the registry style is that the CDI hub only propagates (or acquires) data from the source system when a CDI client requests the data. The data is "moved" only for the purposes of a request. The trade-off is that reconciliation—that is, transformation, cleansing, and integration—must occur for each new CDI client request.

Persistent Style

The persistent-style CDI hub "persists" the customer data, meaning it copies the data as a physical record, serving as a de-facto storage platform for centralized customer information. Many people first learning about CDI assume that the CDI hub is just another database since the data is copied into the hub.

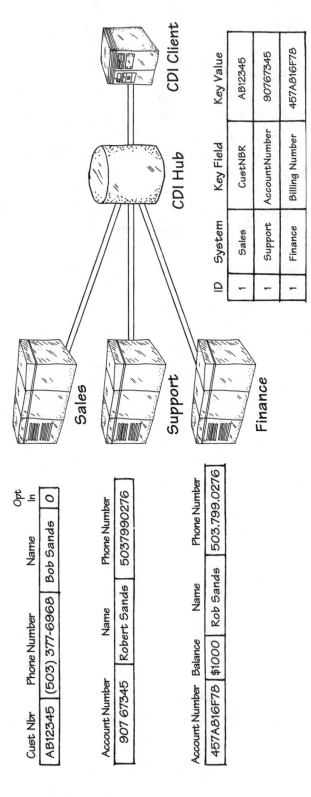

EXHIBIT 2.4 Registry CDI Reconciles Source Data

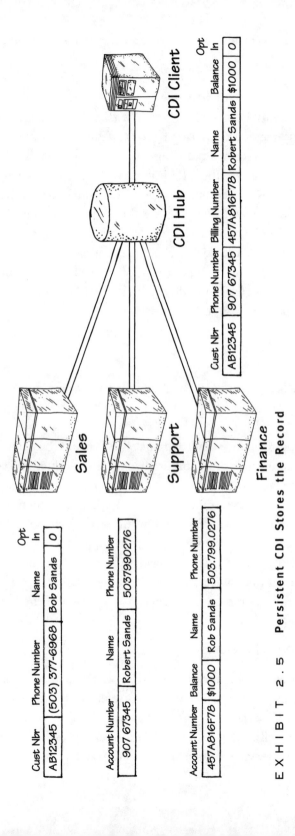

EXHIBIT 2.5   Persistent CDI Stores the Record

49

With the persistent style of CDI, all the data can be acquired and merged before the CDI client request is processed by the CDI hub. This renders persistent CDI hubs very fast. The trade-off of this approach is data latency and storage cost: the larger the CDI hub, the longer the propagation time for source data and the higher the cost of the related disk storage.

As Exhibit 2.5 shows, the CDI hub takes all relevant data elements from the source systems and combines them into a single record. Critics of the persistent style point out that because the CDI hub copies the data, poor data integrity and lower data latency can be drawbacks, requiring rigorous data synchronization and quality checking processes. Persistent hubs can be complex to implement. However, vendors that may already be incumbent in a company are increasingly offering this type of CDI functionality, often rendering it easier to adopt.

Hybrid Style

Hybrid CDI leverages aspects of the other two styles: some customer data remains on the source system while other data is housed persistently in the hub.

For high-performance environments, the hybrid CDI hub has persistent storage containing the most important customer values and a specialized logic that updates the CDI hub anytime the source system element changes. For larger environments where capacity and functionality is more important than performance, the CDI hub retains reference details to provide robust (and extensible) merge logic to support a large number of data sources. The advantage of the hybrid style is that it offers both performance and functionality for different CDI needs.

Exhibit 2.6 illustrates the differences among each of the hub styles.

External Service Providers

Some CDI taxonomies also include what Gartner analyst John Radcliffe calls the "external reference" style. This refers to third-party data service providers like Experian, Acxiom, and Dun & Bradstreet, which essentially provide the synchronization, consolidation, and provisioning of customer master data as a service to their business customers.

CDI HUB STYLES

Functional Attribute \ Style	Registry	Persistent	Hybrid
Storage Location	Source	Hub	Main elements—hub Descriptive attributes—source
Manipulation	R/W	R/W	R/W
Data Latency	Read—low Write—low	Read—high Write—high	Because storage is mixed, latency falls between others
Data Integrity	High—if supported by native sources	Lower due to synchronization delay	Typically no better than persistent
Access Performance	The slowest	The fastest	Fast for persistently stored elements, no better than registry for linked elements

EXHIBIT 2.6   Registry versus Persistent versus Hybrid

Gartner Research vice president John Radcliffe points out that these marketing and data service providers might be CDI's rightful birthplace. "CDI first arose in the marketing area with service providers who needed to bring together and reconcile customer data in order to build and maintain the best possible marketing databases. Only then did it get taken up by vendors to handle more operational requirements where master customer data had to be managed."

These companies maintain massive reference databases of consumer and business information using highly specialized programs to reconcile that data, assign unique identifiers, and provision it to their customers in a sustainable and secure way.

Many companies use these external service providers on a subscription basis, meaning that the data matching and enhancement is a regular process. This is because individual consumer behaviors are so dynamic that consumer data is constantly changing. According to Fair Isaac Corporation, there are 40 million residential moves, 4 million births, 2 million marriages, and 1 million retirements every year. Without having access to these timely changes, companies could lose touch with their customers.

Companies that use these service providers usually rely on them for the validation and enrichment of their own internal master data. Typically, a company will pull a customer list and send it to an external service provider, which will match the list against its own (usually more robust) database, augmenting it with household information, demographic or firmographic information, and other pertinent details.

These providers can be valuable CDI alternatives for a company that's lean on IT infrastructure or data-centric skill sets. Their databases contain hundreds of millions of unique records about individuals and companies, and they have institutionalized programs and processes around that data. Indeed, many are now hanging the CDI shingle and offering discrete CDI-branded services to their customers.

However, relying solely on these subscription services for customer identification and matching could be risky. The poor quality of most commercial companies' data means that the percentage of matched records can be alarmingly low.

"We sent 45,000 records to Dun & Bradstreet and got a 40% match back," says Michele Dour, Director of Order Administration for Aspect Software. "At the time our data was so bad we'd just wasted a ton of money. We didn't understand that the results were only as good as our data was. It was huge and it was stupid and it didn't get us anywhere."

Moreover, reliance on an external service provider for customer identification could represent the excuse for not institutionalizing customer data quality and reconciliation processes internally. The larger issue is the challenges inherent in outsourcing any business-critical service: it's only as good as the outsourcer's data is useful and its processes are robust. The costs are—literally and figuratively—quite high.

Since some companies have a combination of different needs, they choose to build homegrown CDI solutions. Others leverage traditional modules within their packaged CRM or enterprise resource planning (ERP) systems for CDI, using them as building blocks for any of the four categories. Many people building MDM solutions can be found on ERP development teams. This "below the radar" approach belies the heavy usage of CDI at many companies who simply consider their CDI platforms to be part of their standard enterprise system infrastructure.

When you consider the fact that *Inc.* magazine named Intellidyn one of America's fastest-growing privately held companies in 2005, it's not surprising that the company's founder and CEO, Peter Harvey, doesn't sit still. The firm, which provides consumer data, analytic, and marketing services to a range of commercial companies across industries, differentiates itself from the large consumer credit bureaus with its enriched data, marketing "combat experience," and speed of delivery. And with a three-year sales growth of 815 percent, there's no telling how much faster it can go.

"Our business is about smaller haystacks, more needles," the peripatetic Harvey explains via cell phone. "We've aggregated all the possible consumer data in the U.S. into a single repository. If you think of 210 million adults in the U.S., and 1500 attributes per person, that's not only a lot of data—it's a huge, repetitive data integration exercise."

Intellidyn acquires its data from a host of diverse companies, including consumer credit data from TransUnion and Experian, demographic information from Acxiom, and title information from First American, among others. "This data is coming at us at a faster and faster rate, and the volumes are growing exponentially," Harvey says. "Our challenge as a company is to keep pace with it all and at the same time transform data into knowledge and deliver superior service to our customers."

Harvey distinguishes his firm from its credit bureau competitors, which continue to grapple with the archived data, limited processing capabilities of their older technologies, and a narrow scope of data. Indeed, he and his management team describe the difference in one word: agility.

Intellidyn's massive consumer database has been tuned so that it not only provisions data to its corporate customers, it offers segmentation and analysis services via an outsourced model. "Our customers can navigate across all the data through us," Harvey explains, "and only pay for the records they're using. We can build them their own customized database, so we ensure that business rules and data are relevant. And we can deliver all this much faster than they can build it themselves, meaning days and weeks, versus months."

"We bring a whole new meaning to 'the 360-degree view' of customer," adds Technical Director Rajeev Kumar. "We don't just clean and store the data. It's our matching algorithms that give us the upper hand."

Kumar explains that, prior to developing its own consumer database, Intellidyn outsourced its data center to a third-party provider that was unable to provide rigorous data cleansing and reconciliation. Intellidyn acquired a data quality tool to automate the heavy-duty matching of consumer records—it creates over a billion different match keys every update, across various data sources—ultimately generating unique identifiers at the individual, household, and address levels. The intensive processing and use of "fuzzy" matching logic has given it one of the industry's highest match rates.

"The game plan is to have a full, referential database across the entire U.S.," says Sid Bhomia, a senior DBA and Unix architect. "Our differentiators are excellent match rates and superior merge-purge capabilities." Intellidyn not only acquires and cleanses heterogeneous data through their CDI hub, they know which data to keep and which data to relinquish. That complexity is compounded by the fact that the firm processes and stores consumer data at the individual, address, and household levels.

Harvey sums up the value: "The better the data hygiene, the higher the match rates; the higher the match rates, the better the model performance; the better the model performance, the more successful the campaign."

Despite Intellidyn's matching and reconciliation prowess, Harvey and his team are careful to keep the technical jargon at a minimum when selling their solutions. "When we try explaining how we do all this from a technical perspective, peoples' eyelids get heavy," Harvey says. "No one wants to hear about fuzzy matching and scaleable tiered storage. But when you explain to them what it could mean to their business performance, they stand right up."

One Intellidyn customer sends out a million pieces of mail every week. The company will often change course at the last minute—"the Friday before the campaign!" says Harvey—requesting modifications of their credit and demographic selects and counts. While this could set a normal list provider back weeks or even months, Intellidyn is able to support the change and let its customer meet its mail drop date.

"I was working in financial services companies in the 1990s when people actually thought this stuff was easy," laughs Harvey. "No one really got how complex it all was." At this point, Harvey is getting out of his car on his way to his third prospect meeting in a day. "But now people are starting to get it."

COMPONENTS OF CDI

Regardless of the type of CDI, the CDI hub is really an integrated source of customer data that incorporates automation of data quality, correction, and correlation prior to availing access of individual customer records to systems and users. The customer data hub is also known as the "master customer reference database," or even simply the "one true view."

As we saw in Chapter 1, customer data living in disparate silos across the enterprise is a serious business problem, imperiling strategic business imperatives like customer loyalty programs and target marketing. But it's also an IT problem, since it jeopardizes the deployment of new operational systems and packaged applications. CDI aims to resolve this problem by enforcing repeatable and sustainable processes for acquiring customer data.

Exhibit 2.7 illustrates a CDI ecosystem, at the center of which lies the CDI hub. The following sections briefly describe each part of the ecosystem.

Data Sources

A data source is technically any application or system in your company that generates new data. Your CDI solution will get its data from systems that are generating new customer data records. These records can originate from so-called operational systems that run the company, like the billing system, or even more focused sources like small Access databases that departments or individuals use for specific purposes. Data sources are not necessarily always monolithic legacy systems, they can also be something as simple as the spreadsheet your friend Bob uses to maintain the new price list.

Integration Services

This is the hard part of CDI. As many in the world of data warehousing have learned the hard way, the bulk of the effort isn't loading the data into the database, it's finding, designing, accessing, defining, correlating, transforming, and moving the data (usually via ETL) before it even reaches its target platform. Some estimates gauge the ETL effort to be between 60 to 70 percent of the cost of creating a new customer database.

But in the case of CDI, integration services take ETL one better, since CDI systems need to recognize, process, and reconcile incoming data and

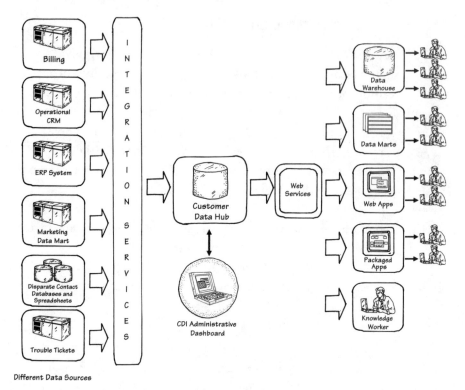

Different Data Sources

EXHIBIT 2.7 CDI Ecosystem

make it available to other systems, often in real time. Integration involves messaging, data synchronization, cross-referencing, and other tasks, rendering the functionality much more complex. When done right, integration renders the CDI platform the new, unified source of customer data. This is the crux of how CDI differs from data warehouses and CRM systems. We'll talk more about the steps in integration in Chapter 7.

CDI Hub

The CDI hub is the core of a real-time, customer data provisioning environment. The hub is basically the point of recognition and processing for assembly and storage, functioning as the central repository for both the incoming, fragmented data as well as the outgoing, authoritative records.

The hub processes data according to the rules inherent in the integration services layer. As noted in the discussion of the types of CDI, some CDI hubs physically store the customer records in a persistent state, while others leverage metadata to/from the data sources to reconcile and then distribute newly trustworthy customer records.

Many hub technologies actually take the hybrid approach and reference some data while physically storing other data. The customer data hub should also be able to flexibly support data from new sources as they are introduced. Often, the customer data hub supports connections to hubs for other master data, such as product data processed by a product information management (PIM) hub.

Administrative Dashboard

An administrative workbench or dashboard offers data stewards the ability to visually review the data across the CDI life-cycle. This is particularly useful for finding anomalies and exceptions, which certain CDI tools can "flag" for manual intervention. The data steward can examine, evaluate, and manually fix questionable data. Some CDI solutions feature continuous learning functionality, so that these "fixes" generate business rules that can automatically extend to other data.

Depending on the software tool, the administrative dashboard might also provide more advanced capabilities. Some CDI vendor dashboards allow a data steward to prioritize data based on the source system. For instance, customer addresses coming from two different source systems could be prioritized based on the administrator's general confidence level in the data, or based on which source generates the most recent address. The administrator may be able to designate a "master" source for a particular data element. Some advanced dashboards allow administrators to control settings to refine matching algorithms or control so-called matching thresholds to control the acceptability level of duplicate records.

Web Services

As we'll discuss in more detail in Chapter 7, CDI essentially functions as a service to other systems, thus SOA is a critical component of any CDI framework. Web services are the means by which data is captured, synchronized, and shared between CDI and other systems.

Applications

As we've already seen, the applications that leverage data from a CDI solution can be diverse. Often, they are industry specific: for instance, fraud prevention at a mortgage company, or claims analysis at an insurance company. In the rest of the book, we'll be referring to the applications that leverage CDI data as "client applications." We'll see some examples of CDI client applications the case studies featured.

MANAGER DO'S AND DON'TS

In many ways, CDI is less a new technology and more a new model. It can transform the way your company processes its customer information. As you begin formulating reasons why CDI might be the right answer in your company, expect to shift some paradigms. In doing so, consider the following do's and don'ts:

- **Do** take the time to scope out the immediate need for CDI. While an authoritative customer system of record is the desired outcome, where you start is more likely to determine your long-term success. For instance, sales reps for the private banking division of a financial institution didn't have a holistic understanding of all their customers' products and tried cross-selling products like mortgage insurance to banking customers who didn't have home loans. Combining and reconciling products across service and sales channels to a single customer was the on-ramp to a larger, enterprise-wide CDI effort.

- **Don't** ignore difficult people or departments when doing your CDI research. The need for an authoritative source of customer data comes from all corners of the company. People or departments that feel slighted might try their own initiative and become the saboteurs.

- **Do** articulate what you and your company mean by "customer." Sometimes "customer" is used as a catch-all for a variety of parties that may include partners, suppliers, prospects, employees, taxpayers, resellers, contractors, or anyone your company does business with and needs to track. In fact, you're likely to hear the term *party* used to earmark a broader base of constituents.

- **Don't** prematurely announce your CDI effort. Some companies applaud the "bottom up" research approach to support new technology initiatives. Others don't acknowledge the effort unless it's been preceded by a vision statement, a project kickoff meeting—ideally including a buffet lunch—and a full-blown business case. Know what type of foundation you need to lay before getting approval for the CDI project.

- **Do** begin letting vendors know that you're interested—but be honest if you haven't yet secured budget or management support. Like most vendors, the CDI players are more than happy to educate potential buyers of their products and even do a proof-of-concept in order to demonstrate their functionality. What backfires is the project manager or sponsor who doesn't manage her vendors' expectations or, worse, who masquerades as someone having more budget and authority than she has. Be honest that you're in research mode. This is the best way to transform a potential vendor into a valuable business partner.

- **Don't** hang your hat on the market-leading vendor. Just because they're the market leader doesn't mean they'll offer the functionality your company needs. Worse, you'll risk overinvesting.

- **Do** understand whether there's a "registry" system in-house that already performs some of the functions represented in the taxonomy categories listed in this chapter. Many companies needed to reconcile customers from across various systems before the CDI vendors brought their products to market. Make sure you're not trying to reinvent the wheel.

ENDNOTES

1. John Radcliffe, "Create a Single Customer View with Customer Data Integration," a Gartner report, October 7, 2004.

2. *W.H. Inmon, Claudia Imhoff, and Ryan Sousa,* Corporate Information Factory *(New York: John Wiley & Sons, 2001).*

3. *Note here that the common use of the term* data model *in CDI circles really refers to the underlying physical database schema that accompanies most CDI products, not a logical or conceptual data model in its true sense.*

4. *MDM is sometimes known as reference data management, alluding to the "reference" data that is distinguished from transactional data, which represents business activities.*

CHAPTER 3

Challenges of Data Integration

■ Data is keeping executives awake at night. In fact, almost everyone in your organization has, at some point, wondered what information they were missing, what knowledge was being lost, and how the bottom line might be impacted. With their burgeoning focus on customers, companies need information more than ever. But with new-found customer-focused programs driving the need for integrated information, we're all confronting the challenges of defining, locating, gathering, reconciling, deploying, and maintaining customer data. A company burdened by data silos has unwittingly established built-in barriers between its business units, discouraged its knowledge workers from fact-based decision making, and put itself at a competitive disadvantage.

Once executives had declared their customer-focused strategies and formulated the requisite visions, they had to acknowledge what they didn't know. They didn't know the scope of the data integration effort necessary to deliver key strategies. They didn't know what data was available, and what was missing. They didn't know the steps to provide meaningful information to an increasingly diverse business audience clamoring for it. These problems are turning out to be universal, irrespective of geography, industry, size, or growth rate. This chapter discusses the difficult data ordeals that many companies are still wrestling with, and others are in the process of conquering. ■

DATA—ALWAYS THE BRIDESMAID

In May 2002, an anonymous reader gave *The CRM Handbook* two stars on Amazon.com. He or she commented that it was "probably useful if your background is data warehousing." The reader went on to expound on the importance of process redesign for customer relationship management (CRM) projects (clearly having skipped Chapter 7) in an effort to stress the importance of business processes to CRM success.

No sour grapes here. In fact, we find this comment a helpful illustration of what CRM practitioners were going through at the time. Most were focusing on surveying customers and refining customer-facing processes like order management and sales. While a bona fide component of a CRM project, process redesign was arguably the low-hanging fruit of customer management projects. Most companies already had process design skills and tools in house, and were able to readily leverage those resources for their CRM initiatives.

Data integration skills were another story. The rationale went something like this: "Let's redesign our processes first and once we're finished, we'll go get the data and then automate those processes."

Studies have shown data integration to be the number one headache of most customer-focused projects. The truth is that most project leads tackling customer management initiatives knew deep down that data integration was hard, so they saved it for last. In fact, for most enterprise-wide technology initiatives, data was an afterthought. The state of most companies' information was downright perilous, with data waiting in the tall grass of the corporate infrastructure, and no one wanting to get close enough to it to see what it really looked like because they knew it would bite.

> Studies have shown data integration to be the number one headache of most customer focused projects.

Back in the days of individual systems development projects, data was viewed by both businesspeople and practitioners alike as unidirectional. In other words, when someone needed data, they would call someone else— usually someone they knew in information technology (IT)—and request a subset of data from a system. Once they got that data, they did whatever they needed to do with it—end of story. This so-called point-to-point

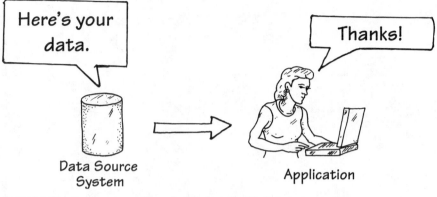

EXHIBIT 3.1   Simple Point-to-Point Interaction

approach to data usage, which still exists in even the most technologically advanced companies, treated data as ephemeral, necessary only for a point in time. Exhibit 3.1 illustrates the simple exchange.

The problem with this scenario is that it represents one of hundreds or even thousands of similar interactions between a company's systems. People get data and manipulate it and send it on to another person or system. Not only does this jeopardize the quality and accuracy of the data (more on this in Chapter 4), it duplicates labor, as many of the requests are simply versions of similar requests made by other people in different organizations.

Creating New Legacy Systems

You'd think that the customer-focused initiatives listed in Chapter 1 would be part of a company's universal shift toward customer. But changing executive vocabularies notwithstanding, the unfortunate truth was that these and other new concepts spawned a collection of unrelated projects across different organizations, with no unifying vision. These projects were usually isolated, enlisting separate business sponsors, repeating requirements activities, and often replicating the functionality of existing applications.

And each spawned a new set of technology requirements. Rather than unifying around a single source of the truth about customers, the projects begat their own, brand new legacy systems, exacerbating the already painful

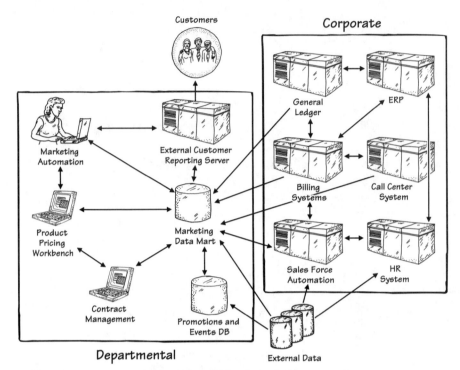

EXHIBIT 3.2   Systems Sharing Corporate Data

syndrome of stovepipe systems run rampant. Much of the logic went like this: "We already have some of the data on System X, so let's replicate that data on our Project Y server!" The resulting system interactions can become downright scary, as shown in Exhibit 3.2.

What happened next now seems inevitable. Someone in IT decided to install an enterprise database in the middle of everything to integrate customer data and provide the proverbial single version of the truth. Often, this database was introduced as an enterprise data warehouse and was pitched as the new data provisioning system for cross-functional data, with customer data as its fulcrum. Exhibit 3.3 illustrates how the new database was positioned.

Well-meaning managers imagine that connecting all the components is simply a matter of getting into IT's development pipeline. ("It's just a middleware issue, right?" one optimistic business user recently asked.) Connecting disparate systems together is fraught with challenge and risk.

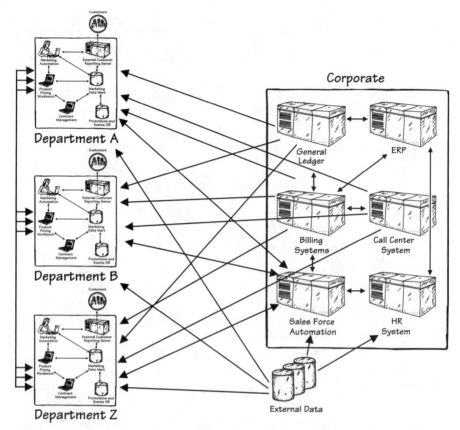

E X H I B I T   3 . 3   **Introducing an Enterprise Data Warehouse**

For instance, simply slapping in an enterprise data warehouse doesn't solve the data latency issues that are inevitable when trying to integrate the same data from disparate systems. The billing system would know that a bill was paid sooner than the sales force automation system would. Applying the correct rules to ensure that the billing system's data took precedence involves a complex set of tasks that was—and still is—frequently overlooked.

And, to make matters worse, multiple departments across the company were building their own silos. For every marketing department acquiring its own marketing automation and pricing workbench and other technology packages requiring data, there might be dozens of other organizations across the company buying their own tools and using their own versions of

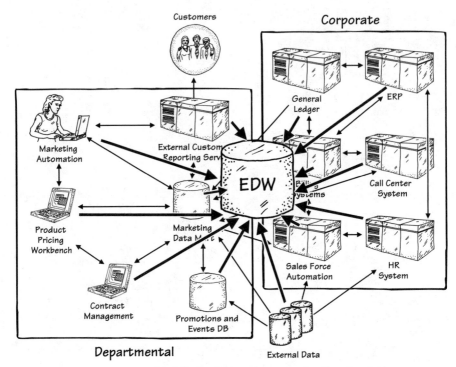

EXHIBIT 3.4   **Multiple Departments in Need of the Same Data**

company data, vastly exacerbating the spider web of data exchange, as illustrated in Exhibit 3.4.

Along with exchanging data with corporate systems, various departments would exchange data with one another. The Byzantine request methods and indecipherable formats that characterized a large portion of the data required to run critical business processes made many project managers throw up their hands and forgo the provisioning of critical information.

One project manager at a wholesale retailer, after examining his company's labyrinthine scheme of databases, couldn't make data about product returns available to other systems. Since the company had no information about returns, businesspeople were unable to determine which customers were truly profitable.

The rampant data movement across divisions, departments, and systems not only exacerbated the already poor quality of the data, it wasted time and money. Companies overinvested in software. They tapped out developers' time and morale due to the constant yet often inconsequential updates of dozens or hundreds of point-to-point system interfaces. They lost customers to whom they over- or undercommunicated. They lost money, shareholders, and even executives unable to meet the market's expectations.

Why the Data Model Matters

Many IT practitioners argue that it's not their databases but their data models that represent their companies' single version of the truth. Many companies, frustrated with not knowing what customer data they need to run their businesses, have developed rigorous data models to provide a springboard for data integration. Since data models are a source of argument and convention debates at many companies—even those that haven't yet considered customer data integration (CDI)—they merit some discussion here.

We should distinguish between the "logical data model"—which defines the relationships of the data elements in business terms and reflects actual data requirements—and the "physical schema"—which defines the database tables as they are reflected in and processed by the actual CDI software. When CDI vendors refer to their data models, they are most often referring to their physical database schemas.

The CDI environment should accommodate a diverse set of requests while at the same time supporting the loading and maintenance of potentially large data volumes. This is known as a "mixed workload" environment. It's important that the CDI hub support scalable growth of both customer and transaction volumes. When we say "transaction," we mean the application's interaction with the CDI hub to either update or delete data as well as requesting a search for specific customer details. The CDI hub should support functions as straightforward as "get customer," and as complex as "tell me all the aliases and record matches for Josephine Smith in New York City," where there may be many direct and indirect matches.

"The CDI data model has to be capable of modeling complex relationships and responding to operational needs," says Gartner's John Radcliffe. "In contrast to a data warehouse, the CDI hub does not have a data model designed specifically for analytical access, it does not have layer upon layer of aggregate data, and it does not contain enormous amounts of detailed transaction data. It's designed for operational access, not analytical queries."

Radcliffe adds that an effective CDI hub can complement a data warehouse by ensuring provisioning of accurate data.

There are two fundamental ways of loading data into the hub: either as a bulk data load or as a transactional data load (effectively loading one customer at a time). A CDI hub should inherently support a mixed-workload environment that supports a diverse set of requests, including both the transaction and load processing described here.

CDI systems are constant environments that need to support individual transactions that contain customer data. Some operational systems will be able to provide their data to the hub via a single, large file. Others will provide their data continuously throughout the day and will need to interact with the hub in a transactional manner. The CDI hub will need to conform to the way the operational systems communicate, since those systems aren't easily modified. The CDI hub's underlying schema should support different types of processing.

Some CDI vendor products include both a logical data model and a physical database schema. The benefit of this "packaged" approach is that these tools be set up and configured quickly if your company's detailed data conforms to the predefined database schema. The approach of providing predefined database schemas is common with packaged software solutions like enterprise resource planning (ERP) systems. The trade-off inevitably occurs when a company's unique customer identification and relationship details mandate the modification of the underlying schema.

The required model modifications usually involve changes to customer hierarchies or relationships, as well as detailed relationships with other subject area content. Every modification to the data model usually calls for a change to the physical schema that affects processing or workload issues. Upon reviewing their CDI data models, some companies modify the model to reflect the hierarchy and subject area details specific to their customers. For instance, a wireless carrier allows an account to have multiple phone numbers, and a bill can have multiple accounts. Understanding whether customer details need to be addressed by individual, account holder, household, or address can all mean modifications to the CDI data model.

The reason that CDI vendors emphasize their data models is so they can illustrate the breadth of descriptive and relationship details they can support. Predefined data models can simplify the design and implementation work necessary to implement CDI. It's much easier than starting from scratch.

Data models and database schemas are in many ways marketing tools that vendors use to illustrate their understanding of the business and to assure their prospects that CDI is less of a new development exercise and more of a customization project. (This was the same position many ERP vendors took a few years ago.) But the customization effort could be simple or complex, depending on the breadth of detail contained in the CDI hub.

The registry style stores only a very limited amount of data (the customer ID, some identification fields—the details that help uniquely identify the customer—and pointers to the source systems) and thus requires much less space. Registry-style CDI means keeping existing databases from other systems intact, since little data is physically retained within the hub.

These issues are more apparent in the persistent and hybrid-style hub environments because of the breadth and quantity of data stored. With these styles, the CDI hub not only contains the same information as the registry-style hub, it also contains all the descriptive details about the customer in order to support query processing. This could include anything—household income, the number of cars the customer has, the customer's purchase details, and potentially hundreds of additional attributes. As the contents of the hub grow in breadth and quantity, the performance and flexibility of the underlying database schema becomes more challenging.

As we've seen with traditional applications, as data volumes and application processing grow, the underlying technology architecture needs to change to support that growth. We've found that, because companies are unique, a one-size-fits-all data model is usually impractical. This is especially true for companies that are adding and incorporating new customer data at an increasingly rapid rate of speed.

CASE STUDY: INTRAWEST

Intrawest might not be a household name, but its products are. Best known for its ski resorts, including British Columbia's Whistler-Blackcomb and the Village at Squaw Valley, Intrawest is nevertheless a leader in adventure travel, real estate, and destination resorts. The company offers African safaris, golf vacations, and even condominium

sales to a worldwide customer list. From Lake Las Vegas to Zihua-
tanejo, Intrawest is a diversified brand.

It's that diversity that drove the company's decision to adopt CDI.
"We have a tremendous opportunity to move our customers from one
Intrawest experience to another, and we're constantly in the process of
broadening those experiences," says Jignesh Shah, Solutions Architect
for Intrawest. "We have over a dozen destination resorts with vibrant
villages, offer a variety of vacation experiences, and we also sell real
estate at our resorts. There are over 90 different entry points for customers. We wouldn't know who they were without a CDI solution."

Calling Shah a CRM veteran is an understatement. Prior to joining
Intrawest in 2003, Shah served as a customer prospecting specialist at
a range of companies. Though he works in the company's IT organization, Shah is in constant touch with the marketing organization and
speaks their language. The company maintains a robust customer data
mart and employs sophisticated campaign management software to
help it target customers and manage mailings. However, the business
challenges were bigger than the company's existing technologies.

"If you're a bank," Shah explains, "you can identify your customers
with their Social Security number they have to provide. But our customers don't have much incentive to provide their address or any
other information. If you're in a lift line at a ski resort, you're not
going to sit and give us all your contact details. And you might give
us different information than you provided when you checked into
your condo or rented your snowboard. For us, capturing customer
data at each point of interaction is really difficult and then to integrate that information to create a single view is equally difficult."

Moreover, as Intrawest steadily acquires additional properties and
travel providers, it's constantly introducing additional data sources.
"Our resorts were all acquired at different points in time," says Shah,
"and most had a diverse set of systems and technologies. We knew
we needed to build something that could support them all."

Intrawest created a custom CDI solution that leveraged a vendor
data quality tool as an engine to match and merge the data and generate cross-referenced persistent keys to each of the source systems.
"Every transaction that comes in has some sort of customer information attached," Shah explains. "The customer master data goes
through the CDI engine, and we time-stamp the most recent data.
When we merge all the data together, we overwrite data based on the
transaction date, so we're always capturing the most recent data about

the customer." The resulting unique customer identifier can be used by the operational systems across the company's different divisions.

The consolidated customer data gets loaded into the company's data mart using the ETL tool so that Intrawest marketing analysts can track customer behaviors and deliver more accurate lists to its campaign management system. Since the CDI data is already cleansed and reconciled, end users consider it accurate and trustworthy.

In an industry where customer loyalty cards are rampant, Intrawest can leverage its CDI solution for CRM-enabling its business applications.

"Before we implemented CDI," says Shah, "we had between 40 and 50 percent duplication in our marketing database. We had no intelligent matching. Our applications couldn't recognize if a customer already existed on another system."

And now? "Now we have a robust customer data mart that gives us a real 'single version of the truth' about our customers across all our lines of business. I mean, we have lots of systems out there. But they can't recognize if a customer already existed in their system or on another system. CDI's ability to generate an authoritative customer record and a cross reference from business system customer to a centralized customer will help identify the duplicates—and assist in the integration of business applications."

In an industry where customer loyalty cards are rampant, Intrawest can leverage its CDI solution for CRM-enabling its business applications. "I used to call myself a database marketing expert," says Shah. "But now I see that with CDI it's about supporting the entire enterprise. Now even our executives talk about these capabilities. To have a truly holistic view of your customers across different business domains and systems—that's a strategic advantage."

FIVE MAINSTAY CHALLENGES OF DATA INTEGRATION

It's harder than it looks. In fact, whether it's CRM, ERP, supply-chain management, or another enterprise system that touches multiple organizations and affects enterprise business processes, nonintegrated data is frequently the cause of cost overruns, poor time frame estimations, and scrap and rework. We've found this to be true across industries, market segments, companies, and projects.

In fact, we've found that, rather than lumping the challenges into a big bucket called "We forgot about the data!," there are five specific data-related issues that are the typical challenges when it comes to integrating customer data for the business.

Challenge 1: The Need for a Different Development Framework

One of the biggest problems with master data management (MDM) efforts is that the teams charged with tackling them use standard implementation methods without understanding the discrete steps involved.

Since, by its very definition, the goal of CDI is to integrate data, many companies assume that they can overlay their standard system development life-cycle or, more commonly, their data warehouse development methods onto a CDI effort. However, as we've discussed, data warehouses are intended to address a range of often strategic business requirements, whereas CDI systems are functionally oriented. Thus, the well-worn, requirements-driven business intelligence and data warehouse development methods won't work for CDI. Indeed, too much emphasis on business requirements can jeopardize a CDI initiative. In many ways CDI development is more straightforward, because the business more clearly understands the end game.

But that doesn't mean there isn't rigor. If anything, CDI is an infrastructure solution and requires not only careful development, but rigorous and often painstaking policy-making and executive-level involvement. We would argue that formal data policies and governance are wonderful activities for data warehouse, business intelligence, CRM, and ERP projects, but they are absolutely critical to the success of CDI. Because a CDI hub eventually serves as the system of record for all customer data corporate-wide, data policies and practices cannot be compromised.

We'll talk more about an actual framework for a CDI project in Chapter 5, and we'll paint a more detailed picture of data governance and organizational involvement in Chapter 6.

Challenge 2: Difficulty with Stakeholder Enlistment

This book's first several chapters aim to distinguish CDI and other customer initiatives within a company that are also likely to involve technology. It's a challenge, not just here but for CDI sponsors and project leaders who face the overwhelming task of not only pitching the value of customer data integration, but explaining how their CDI project differs from other customer-focused IT projects that have gone before it.

Enlisting businesspeople from across various departments to spend their time, and often their budget money, on a CDI project usually involves:

- **Education.** People need to know what CDI means and how the company will benefit from a CDI effort. They also need to understand CDI from its definitional and implementation aspects. The CDI project sponsor should be able to explain why CDI is different from past "integration" and "customer-focused" projects and why the company needs it.

- **Scenario building.** A good CDI business sponsor will be able to paint a picture of the "desired outcome" of the effort. Walking through a broken business process is often a good place to start explaining how CDI can help. Ending with a clear explanation of the "to be" vision once CDI is implemented, and outlining the major steps that need to take place, is time well spent for a project manager seeking stakeholder support. We'll talk more about making the CDI pitch in Chapter 8.

- **Politics.** Often, questions of ownership around data and projects will arise. A common refrain from potential CDI saboteurs is: "We're already doing that!" or "We tried that already and it didn't work!" It's best to deal with these issues early and at the individual level and come armed with a set of existing business problems, like the ones listed in Chapter 1, that will continue unchecked without CDI.

Enlisting vendors to provide you with "ammunition" for stakeholder education is a good idea, providing that you're honest with your vendor representative about the fact that you're still in the justification cycle. An effective business sponsor will do the necessary research, then—as we'll discuss in Chapter 8—do the necessary internal public relations to pitch CDI.

> *Management rarely measures operational systems on their ability to provide data to the business in a timely manner.*

Challenge 3: Operational Data Isn't Available

Your billing system and human resources systems aren't expected to distribute their data. No one is responsible for sharing extracts from these operational systems. Owners of operational systems aren't accountable for making their data available. Operational systems aren't meant to share data with others; they're only chartered with using data within the boundaries of their own functionality.

The owners of operational systems are first and foremost responsible for the operational integrity of the systems they're paid to oversee. This means ensuring that the system is always up and available, that it's delivering on its intended functionality (e.g., invoices are generated and bills are paid), and that bugs are fixed, backups occur, and code errors are fixed.

Operational system owners don't have time to support other application systems, provide additional data feeds, or correct nonoperational data. They are staffed and budgeted to keep their systems running. It's not their fault. IT management rarely measures operational systems on their ability to provide data to the business in a timely manner.

One of two things usually happens as a result of operational systems not availing their data to the outside world. People who need data build their own programs, usually from scratch. They usually do this in "skunkworks" mode with little or no access to experts and without the right utilities. They rely on guesswork. One poor developer we know got his data by reading through dumps to reconstruct the data he needed. This is inefficient, error prone, and may be relying on the wrong data altogether.

Or project teams wait for source system experts to get around to providing them with the data. This usually ends up at the end of the source system owner's to do list. One project team we know is waiting to get access to customer incident details from the company's trouble ticket system. Until then, the system is operating with partial data.

WHAT WORKS: TIPS FROM THE EXPERTS

Jeff Monica: "Don't mess with the data sources."

"We have over 60 data sources, from SAP to Clarify to overseas call center systems to spreadsheets on accountants' PCs. I learned very quickly not to try to change the way those systems do things. It's not our job to try and affect the processing of operational systems, or even to try to improve them. The advantage of our CDI strategy is that we don't have to. We get the data from those systems and take it from there. We need to get the highest number of matches possible and generate the best customer record for the business. If we've done that, we've done our job."

JEFF MONICA, Manager, Corporate Information Factory, Sun Microsystems

---

Challenge 4: Nonexistent Metadata

Much has been written about the topic of metadata. But, despite the best efforts of forward-thinking consultants and software vendors, little progress has been made.

The technical meaning of the term *metadata* is "data about data." Unfortunately, many businesspeople read this and immediately go to the *reductio ad absurdum* and start recording data definitions in a spreadsheet. Lacking the knowledge of metadata's complexity and reach and unarmed with the necessary tools, that's exactly what they do.

Metadata often involves storing information about objects, including database tables, systems, projects, and individual staff members and their departments, in a metadata "repository." This way, all cross-functional metadata is stored in a single place. Metadata expert Joyce Norris-Montanari compares such a repository to a store directory at the mall: It displays the object (in this case the store), the navigation path to the object (how to get there), and the category of the object (women's sportswear). It is depicted graphically, as well as textually, to make sure it makes sense to the reader.

As described in the book *e-Data,*[1] there are three general types of metadata: business metadata that specifies definitions for specific data attributes; database metadata that annotates the objects in a database (including tables, rows, and columns); and application metadata that explains the components of an end-user application, such as explaining which states comprise the term *territory* on a month-end sales report.

There are lots of challenges in deploying metadata, but it's essential that CDI implementations consider metadata an implementation priority. It allows data stewards to establish and control for data definitions and rules for consistency and accuracy, and can provide a baseline for data validation and certification. Moreover, it helps data stewards and application developers understand the lineage of a record or data element. But, historically, metadata has been a hard row to hoe, mainly because:

- Management doesn't really get it and doesn't really want to. Managers tend to steer clear of supporting or funding metadata efforts. For one thing, the very term implies IT infrastructure; thus, its business benefits aren't intuitive. For another thing, it's hard to explain.

- Practitioners often struggle to justify metadata. Talk about metadata to a group of business users for more than five minutes (especially right after lunch) and their eyes start rolling backward. Rather than showing examples of how metadata can help the business (picture hovering your mouse over the term *Revenue* on a month-end customer profitability report and right-clicking to see whether the term refers to "billed revenue" or "booked revenue"), IT practitioners are wont to cite statistics on the business impact of loose data definitions and discuss why industry analysts recommend metadata. They don't discuss metadata in the context of how it can help solve business problems and save the company money.

- Implementing metadata is difficult and continuous. Not to pick on IT here, but many experienced IT practitioners oversimplify metadata management, considering metadata as a tier above a persistent dictionary, storing definitions of data in an Excel spreadsheet and occasionally e-mailing the spreadsheet to flummoxed end users. Done correctly, metadata management should serve multiple business functions and applications in a sustained and rigorous way.

Like data, metadata should be beholden to a requirements process that elucidates its meaning and usage.

Challenge 5: Poor Data Quality

The issue of data quality for CDI and MDM deserves its own discussion, so we'll cover the specifics of data quality in Chapter 4. However, it's important to call out the data quality challenge early, since it's a big one. The following example illustrates an all-too-typical scenario:

A big company rolls out a multimillion-dollar system, and business users start seeing new reports. They disagree with the information presented in the reports and consequently question the value of the new system. The resulting deployment is descoped or, worse, scrapped. We once heard a user of a new customer dashboard say, "I heard that most of the data shown in the dashboard comes from the billing system. Our billing system is bad, so this dashboard is bad and I'm not going to use it." Back to the well-worn Excel spreadsheet and hours of data gathering and consolidation.

The simple fact is that poor data is a reflection of faulty business processes, misrepresenting what's really occurring in the business. It can result in bad decision making, which can in turn imperil a company's customer-focused strategy. A study done by The Data Warehousing Institute estimated that companies lose more than $611 billion every year due to bad data.[2] The study found that fewer than half of the companies surveyed had a plan for addressing data quality. The result was time and money spent reconciling the data on project after project. Such findings can get the attention of even the most IT-hardened executive.

"We learned that it's not enough to have data about the customer—

it has to be the right data," explains Art Hall, vice president of sales and customer care operations at NetBank, the leading online provider of consumer financial services. "You have to do a 'deep dive' to ensure that the data has integrity and the right rules are enforced before it's given to businesspeople. We'd be way off base if we were working with bad data. It could compromise our entire company strategy!"

But the data quality message belies its underlying complexity. Consider automobile manufacturers. Most have assembly lines with significant productivity goals. Indeed, many auto production lines award employees for getting closer to the goal of "zero defects." Auto companies are continuously looking for ways to increase productivity while maintaining or increasing product quality. But existing products change. New parts and options are introduced. Shipping details and line staff are in constant flux. So the success of the production line depends not on perfection, but on a system that is flexible enough to support change as a standard. Manufacturers need the ability to continually adjust to new specifications.

Data quality operates under the same set of circumstances. Business needs change. Products change. Data quality cannot be static since over time not only does the data itself change, but the way people use it changes, too. Therefore, measuring data quality improvements is critical. Moreover, understanding the evolving needs of the data moving across the data supply chain is paramount.

Indeed, while an admirable goal, it's a bit naïve for managers to expect zero-defect data. Rather, it's important to measure the ongoing improvements in data quality over time, record what's worked in the monitoring and fixing of that data, and institutionalize those processes and tactics to a broader set of data over time. This is why master data management should be considered less a technology solution and more of a corporate process. Companies need to begin treating their data as if it's future-proof.

MANAGER DO'S AND DON'TS

It might add time, but it's better to identify potential roadblocks to CDI before you begin talking to vendors or eyeing potential project resources. Here are some tips to ensure success:

- **Do** investigate the existence of a customer data model within your company. Check with a data warehouse, data mart, or ERP development team to find out whether a data model has already been created. If it has, leverage it for your CDI project since it can help establish what the relevant customer details will be for the CDI hub.

- **Don't** assume that the customer definition is consistent across different business areas or IT systems. If your goal is to support different applications with CDI, your company needs to establish customer data definitions that don't conflict with individual system interpretations. As we'll see in Chapter 5, this might involve a "top down" approach to CDI development.

ENDNOTES

1. Jill Dyché, e-Data: Turning Data into Information with Data Warehousing (Reading, MA: Addison Wesley, 2000).

2. Wayne Eckerson, "Data Quality and the Bottom Line: Achieving Business Success through a Commitment to Data Quality," The Data Warehousing Institute, 2002.

CHAPTER 4

"Our Data Sucks!": The (Not So Little) Secret about Bad Data

The term *bad data* has lots of implications. It can mean inaccurate data, like the wrong account number. It can mean data that's simply missing in a record, was never entered, or is unknown. It can represent data that was made up or derived, by either a system or a human being. It can imply data that's inconsistent across systems. It can even mean meaningless data that serves no valid business purpose.

Since the goal of customer data integration (CDI) is to generate authoritative customer data, the implications of bad data can be staggering. From regulatory compliance to reconciliation of company hierarchies to "person of interest" recognition, the business need for CDI implies the need for accurate data. Fixing bad data is not just a technological challenge. It requires rigor around requirements, clear organizational responsibilities, and a cultural awareness that continuous improvement begets data refinement over time.

When data quality hits the business's radar, it's usually at the business's expense. The customer notices a billing error on an invoice—for the third month in a row. Or a finance executive knows that the top-line financial reports are wrong but can't put his finger on why. Or the regulatory agencies come calling, and there's contradictory data. The business implications of lost customers, miscommunications to prospects and to Wall Street, and inability to comply with new regulatory legislation, are high impact enough at the local level.

But for CDI, data quality is a global concern. In Chapter 9, we'll discuss what that means organizationally. Here, we'll cover what that means from process and functionality perspectives.[1] ■

DATA QUALITY: THE MOVIE

The title of this chapter represents a veritable refrain from business users worldwide. Indeed, it's part of a larger scenario playing out in businesses across the world on a daily basis. (This is a "blended" story, meaning the names have been changed to protect the guilty.)

FADE IN:

INTERIOR: CORNER OFFICE OF A CORPORATE EXECU-
TIVE—DAY.

    Reclining in a black mesh office chair behind a glass desk, hands clasped expectantly is Ray, the vice president of customer service for a home décor company. Luis, the company's vice president of merchandising, walks in and takes a seat.

RAY: Hey, Luis.

LUIS: Hey. Listen, Ray . . .

RAY: Luis, I know what the problem is.

LUIS: Ray, you have no idea. My guys . . .

RAY: No, Luis, listen. We figured it out. Our customers thought they were ordering individual floor tiles, but the system thought they were ordering boxes of tiles.

LUIS: Ray, the catalogs have gone out. They say "units." Our customers think a "unit" is a "tile."

RAY: No. It's a box of tiles. That's a dozen tiles per box.

LUIS: So here's what's happening. When my customer orders 50 units, he thinks he's getting 50 tiles, but he gets 50 *boxes*. That's 600 tiles, Ray. My phone is ringing off the hook!

RAY (agitated): *Your* phone? Do you know how many more inbound calls we're getting? We've got a ticket backlog and my CSRs are swamped!

LUIS: *Your* CSRs? Our distribution center is getting 12 times the volume that it should be handling! And guess who has to eat the shipping cost for the extra boxes of tile we're sending out? My merchandisers are already complaining that the inventories are running low.

RAY: Well, we can't very well change all the catalogs! We've just mailed out another 250,000 of them.

LUIS: Well, we gotta nip this thing in the bud. You need to give your reps special instructions on how to take an order for those tiles.

RAY: Special instructions? Oh yeah, right, we just start giving people special instructions on how to take an order for every product! Luis, there are over 4500 items in that catalog!

LUIS: We need to put a hold on all new orders until we contact these customers. And we should probably think about sending out an e-mail . . .

RAY: What? We're already swamped! I can't ask my guys to stop taking orders and start demanding merchandise back from customers! Plus, it'll take time to get that list . . . how many more orders will there be between now and then???

LUIS: . . . and give them a shipping number for the return, right? I'd better call our carrier . . . We can't expect the customers to eat the delivery cost for the returns. It was our mistake. Plus, they've got to inspect and repackage the tiles.

RAY (head in hands): Jeez, we're gonna lose a fortune. We've got to fix this.

LUIS and RAY (simultaneously): I'll call IT!

FADE OUT . . .

BAD DATA'S HIGH COST

At her retirement party in 1983, Grace Hopper predicted that information itself would one day be carried on the books of companies, having become more valuable than the machinery that processed it. The time has come to manage data as a corporate asset. Managers must agree on the value of information to their businesses, and data quality is a key lever in realizing this value.

Answering the question "What does dirty data cost us?" is easier said than done. A more realistic test is to begin with the end in mind, addressing instead critical business issues that may be decomposed into the root cause of bad data.

At a simple level, "What is a lost customer worth to us?" can be reduced to "Why are we losing customers?" and again to "What percentage of customers are frustrated with billing mistakes?" to "How many billing mistakes do we make in a given month?" to finally, "What are the mistakes and where do they originate?" This last question can magnify specific data problems and their sources.

> Managers must agree on the value of information to their businesses, and data quality is a key lever in realizing this value.

In a study of 413 manufacturers who shared data with their retailing customers,[2] there were 2784 data errors that included bad data about products, quantities, and brands. Such data mistakes not only represent a barrier to efficiencies—in this case 44 suppliers were cited as having data so poor that it could sabotage the supply chain—it can result in millions of lost dollars in revenue due to poor merchandising decisions. And with the razor-thin margins already plaguing the retailing industry, these are millions neither the manufacturer nor the retailer can afford to lose.

In another oft-cited study, AT Kearney discovered that 30 percent of item data reported by grocers was erroneous and that the consumer packaged goods industry is losing $40 billion in annual sales because of bad product data. The same study found that 43 percent of invoices include errors leading to unnecessary price reductions.[3]

And retailers aren't alone. A study done by the Automotive Aftermarket Industry Association (AAIA)[4] found that trading partners sharing product data were forced to manually enter or synchronize purchase orders. The AAIA estimated that the costs of such manual rework combined and the resulting lost sales cost the automotive industry $1.7 billion a year. The study also cited excess inventory, invoice payment deductions, and delays in new product launches as other costly by-products of dirty data.

In an extreme example of the impact of bad data, the National Aeronautical and Space Administration (NASA) lost the Mars Climate Orbiter in 1998. NASA blamed miscalculations on the use thruster data measured in English units instead of metric units. "A single error should not bring down a $125 million mission," a NASA official said before admitting that NASA had used metric units "for a long time."[5]

The irony is that the high percentage of bad data across industries hasn't stemmed the tide of purchases for analytical and business intelligence products. Companies are investing millions of dollars on tools that generate canned reports, help power users drill down, and generate predictive models on customer behavior. Tools from companies like Business Objects, Cognos, SAS, and Microsoft are only as valuable as the data they use is accurate.

Executives who spend millions on analytical software and database platforms have been known to nevertheless disallow relatively small investments in formal data audits or profiling activities. Data quality doesn't emerge as a bona-fide business issue until data is at the fingertips of the end user, when it's often too late.

In early 2004, Baseline Consulting did a survey of the effects of bad data.[6] Over 170 respondents, largely comprised of information technology (IT) practitioners, project managers, and knowledge workers using business intelligence tools for a range of business initiatives, cited "Delay or rework of IT projects" as the biggest impact of poor data quality, as shown in Exhibit 4.1.

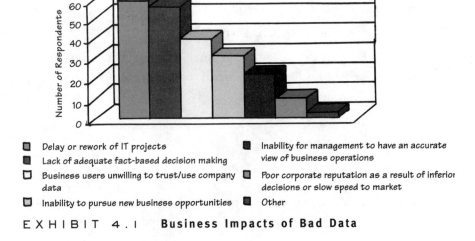

- ■ Delay or rework of IT projects
- ■ Lack of adequate fact-based decision making
- ☐ Business users unwilling to trust/use company data
- ☐ Inability to pursue new business opportunities
- ■ Inability for management to have an accurate view of business operations
- ■ Poor corporate reputation as a result of inferior decisions or slow speed to market
- ■ Other

EXHIBIT 4 . I   Business Impacts of Bad Data

In the same survey, respondents estimated that bad data was costing their companies "at least a million dollars a year" and that most executives were unaware of the role bad data played in their companies' business troubles. The fact that the survey respondents were data professionals, ostensibly intimate with the daily business dramas caused by bad data, was most interesting. Evidently, even the people who understood the business value of accurate data were still struggling to deliver it to their companies.

DATA QUALITY: JOB NUMBER TWO

The problem with data quality used to be that no one knew it was a problem. Those days are long gone. The new problem with data quality is that everyone now wants to roll up their sleeves and start fixing the data. Usually, this means writing code or talking to vendors.

Not so fast. Though we're big fans of data quality automation, we often see companies rush toward automation without first recognizing the flaws in their data. After all, data quality is a business problem and it's not enough to know that data is missing, contradictory, or doesn't make sense. Businesses need to understand the "desired outcome" of good data. They should ask themselves the following questions:

- What can't we do as a business because our data is bad?
- Does the lack of standards for customer data impede our ability to sell additional products and services?
- How will improving our customer data improve revenues?
- What are our data acceptance criteria?
- How will improving our customer data increase operational efficiencies?
- Who's responsible for fixing the data?
- How "good" does the data have to be? What are the metrics of good data?

This last point is an important one. Since operational systems are rarely responsible for their data quality, understanding how data is used will inform its quality metrics. Typically, operational data is "good enough" to support operational processing. However, data used for strategic purposes—like analyzing customer behaviors—requires a higher degree of quality. Questions like "Are invoices being delivered on time?" have a different impact than "How profitable are our top ten business customers?"

Understanding that the data is bad is a great first step, but it's the tip of the proverbial iceberg. Understanding what the data should look like, how it should be represented, and who should be the tiebreaker in the case of disagreements are the really hairy issues. But you've got to address them before automating any sort of data cleansing.

CASE STUDY: PITT OHIO EXPRESS

Pitt Ohio Express was in the throes of a major enterprise resource planning (ERP) implementation project when Scott Sullivan joined the company as vice president of information technology and services. Sullivan had joined Pitt Ohio Express from Kellogg's, the famed Battle Creek, Michigan, institution that had product distribution down to a science, so he was no stranger to complex IT projects. His new position at the leading "less-than-truckload" delivery company presented a host of new challenges.

Like any seasoned executive, Sullivan asked questions before he began prescribing answers. The ERP development effort was ambitious, and Sullivan immediately recognized its potential impact. "The ERP system was going to tie some major legacy systems together," he remembers. "When I asked the CEO about the project's mission, he said that his primary objective was to get a better understanding of our customers. And he couldn't get that understanding with the current systems we had in place."

But the project required heavy customizations, performance was suboptimal, and the vendor didn't have all the answers. During testing of the first release, Sullivan made the difficult decision to pull the plug.

But the team's efforts weren't wasted. Sullivan saw the value of some of the in-process data quality and migration work. "I figured we could use the data cleansing process as the first step to building a customer database without replacing our core systems. I went back to the CEO and explained that there was great customer data available—it was just buried in the legacy system. That was the real beginning of our customer data project."

Sullivan and his team set about the work of identifying individual customers. They found that, from a systems standpoint, Pitt Ohio Express had over 650,000 customers. However, upon closer data profiling, they found that only 8000 to 10,000 of those could be considered active customers. They had to decide on new business rules and data standards to support true customer knowledge.

"We were calling suppliers 'customers' and vendors 'customers.' We had a lot of duplicate records. And we had customer hierarchies we needed to link—many of our customers have more than one location or have multiple subsidiaries. Sometimes they're all on different contracts or they go by different names. At the end of the day, we decided that whoever generated revenue was a customer."

The technical challenges notwithstanding, Sullivan and his team were savvy enough to secure high-level business sponsorship. Although the sales organization was the initial target for the newly integrated customer data, Sullivan found an ally in Ray Johnson, the company's chief financial officer.

"It's a bit counterintuitive," Sullivan admits. "Usually, you'd go over to the sales management and get their buy-in. But our CFO is a really analytical guy who believes in the need for good customer data, but isn't afraid to get his hands dirty. He'd actually work with my development team, then go over to the sales organization and convince them of the value. It had a ripple effect."

The company rolled out customer data in incremental steps. Sullivan used a version of rapid prototyping, delivering data in three-month windows and soliciting feedback from the business.

The results have generated payback. Pitt Ohio Express can now distinguish its valuable customers and give them value in return. For instance, the company would traditionally impose an across-the-board rate increase. Now rate increases are contingent on the customer's value. In an industry where capacity is king, the company can spend more time with its best customers. "Now we can interact with our customers on a one-to-one basis," says Sullivan. "It's no longer one size fits all."

As Pitt Ohio Express realizes its new strategy to become a full-service transportation provider, its customer data will serve it well. "We are really an entrepreneurial organization," he says. "Our customer data lets us think outside the box and do things differently." From a business standpoint, Sullivan and Pitt Ohio Express are both delivering the goods.

DATA QUALITY AND MASTER DATA MANAGEMENT

Most companies that have taken on the data quality challenge have done so in a reactive and fragmented way. It's easy to proclaim that "every customer must have an address." But what if the customer record doesn't include an address? Which address should be represented? We routinely meet finance executives who expect to see the customer's billing address, call center reps who need the service address, and salespeople interested in the headquarters location. What constitutes a "bad" address can be relative. Few businesspeople have visibility into how their peers in different organizations need data delivered.

A casino we worked with decided to send out a campaign to frequent slot players. Reviewing the list of targeted customers, an observant marketing manager couldn't help but notice that a large percentage of the customers on the list were 104 years old. Upon further inspection, the data team discovered that each time the date of birth field was marked as "Null," the system inserted a "dummy" value to represent "Null." The value was 1/1/0, or January 1, 1900. While there was one slot player who was indeed in her 80s, the other birthdates were invalid and had to be fixed. (And they've yet to meet the "high-value" 104-year-old craps player.)

Many people confuse data quality, data governance, and master data management (MDM). Given the definition of MDM in Chapter 2, we consider data quality to be a subset of MDM, which should support the policies and standards for data, including its quality policies. We see both data quality and MDM as parts of a larger practice called data governance, which we discuss at length in Chapter 6. The implicit hierarchy is represented in Exhibit 4.2.

Most large companies today have some sort of IT governance process that is the locus for approving and funding IT projects and managing their delivery, and establishing the metrics for that approval. Data governance is a subset of IT governance that focuses on establishing processes and policies around managing data as a corporate asset. As we discussed in Chapter 2, MDM is the set of disciplines and processes involved in defining and maintaining core data subject areas such as customer and product.

At this time we want to distinguish the differences between data quality at the "global" and "local" levels. Global data quality is an enterprise func-

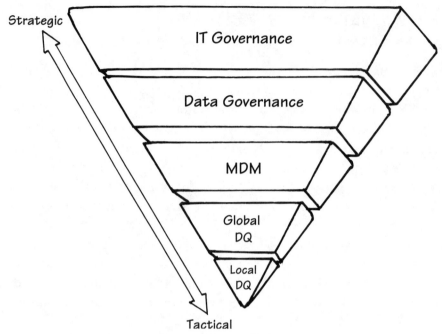

Strategic

IT Governance

Data Governance

MDM

Global
DQ

Local
DQ

Tactical

EXHIBIT 4.2   Data Management Hierarchy

tion that serves to consolidate corporate-wide data quality standards. It focuses on the corporate-level definitions of customers and customer hierarchies. These standards apply to master data (like customer and product data), but should also apply to transactional data and analytical data. At large companies, global data quality organizations are strategic and often represented as centers of excellence with discrete processes and tool sets to manage enterprise data quality.

Depending on the breadth of the company, individual lines of businesses might also have their own local data quality functions. These efforts apply specific business unit subject matter expertise, but leverage the standards and technologies established by the global data quality group. Typically, local data quality responsibilities are departmental and owned by individuals who are chartered with tactical data error detection, and (depending on the global data quality group's goals) data correction.

McDonald's is an apt analogy. The fast food chain has a "global" menu that includes hamburgers, soft drinks, and fries. However, at certain times of the year in certain areas of the country, franchises in certain geographies offer special menus. For instance, in the summer, some McDonald's franchises in Massachusetts serve lobster rolls. Such offerings depend on local tastes. Local data quality is similar, as it depends on the product set within the line of business. However, the global data quality area should be aware of the unique data requirements and should provide support via standards and tool sets, yet at the same time encourage local autonomy and flexibility.

WHAT WORKS: TIPS FROM THE EXPERTS

Michele Dour: "Formalize a data quality management council."

"Initially customer data integration meant finishing our data cleansing and interfacing the systems. But people are passionate about customer data, so they need to participate in its management. We formed a Customer Master DQM Council. It governs policies around customer data, approves architectural changes, oversees line-of-business communications, and ensures the alignment of our customer master data to our strategic master customer road map. Members of the council meet every month. They understand that changing our data—for instance, splitting an account into two—affects our systems and business processes. We've had some pretty painful discussions. But the council participants are engaged and committed to fixing the company's customer data. They understand what the benefits are. In fact, they're change agents."

MICHELE DOUR, Director of Order Administration, Aspect Software

To further distinguish data quality and MDM is to understand how data quality fits as a subset of the categories of MDM. Exhibit 4.3 shows a variation of the MDM categories we introduced in Chapter 2, and illustrates where data quality fits.

As we'll see in later chapters, MDM also encompasses other tasks such as data administration and data security oversight. As a practice, data management represents the day-to-day work necessary to maintain a company's data.

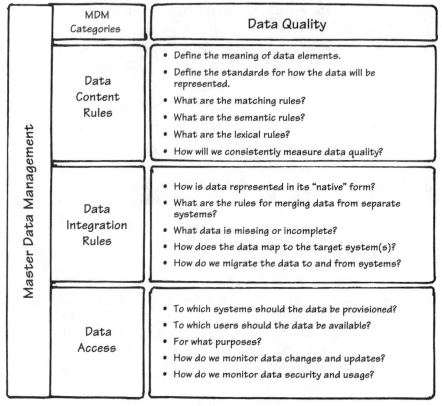

	MDM Categories	Data Quality
Master Data Management	Data Content Rules	• Define the meaning of data elements. • Define the standards for how the data will be represented. • What are the matching rules? • What are the semantic rules? • What are the lexical rules? • How will we consistently measure data quality?
	Data Integration Rules	• How is data represented in its "native" form? • What are the rules for merging data from separate systems? • What data is missing or incomplete? • How does the data map to the target system(s)? • How do we migrate the data to and from systems?
	Data Access	• To which systems should the data be provisioned? • To which users should the data be available? • For what purposes? • How do we monitor data changes and updates? • How do we monitor data security and usage?

EXHIBIT 4.3   Data Quality's Role in MDM

Data Quality in Customer Data Integration

Data quality is a combination of processes, job responsibilities, technology, and cultural change. As the well-worn aphorism goes, it should be considered an ongoing "program," with the accompanying executive commitment, funding, and organizational socialization that ensure it's incorporated into every new IT project that involves data.

From a CDI perspective, data quality is a make-or-break proposition. A core tenet of CDI, after all, is to identify the individual customer who can be represented by many different attributes. These attributes can originate from dozens or even hundreds of different heterogeneous systems within a company. They must all be combined and weighed in order to comprise a complete customer record. Data quality functions are thus embedded in all of the current CDI technologies offered by vendors.

"It's a never-ending battle to reconcile and match your data," says Dave Frieder, vice president of IT at XO Communications. "Your data might be clean today, but your company is always introducing bad data into its systems. CDI isn't a one-time thing."

For CDI, data quality involves six primary steps: (1) define, (2) locate, (3) profile, (4) standardize, (5) match and merge, and (6) deploy. Each individual process functions as input into the next process, ensuring that data is not only captured but transformed and provisioned based on the requirements of the customer data. This process is illustrated in Exhibit 4.4.

> Companies have learned the hard way that they should start with a subset of customer data and run that subset through a data correction process.

Like all good data quality processes, the one in Exhibit 4.4 is circular. This suggests that not only is the data quality process continuous, it is iterative. Companies have learned the hard way that they should start with a subset of customer data and run that subset through a data correction process.[7] Once that data has been cleansed and merged, other data can be added. This "slice at a time" approach ensures that the process can be proven and tuned on small sets of data at one time, and subsequently refined and improved for the next set.

Let's take a look at each of these steps in more detail and examine its role in customer data integration.

Define

The "define" step refers as much to identifying requirements as it does to defining data. It enforces deliberate thought about what the business is trying to achieve and what data applies to these goals. We have traditionally called this process "requirements definition," but in this case it focuses on data requirements, including deciding on content requirements, representation formats, and its relationship to other content.

In Chapter 5, we'll discuss why the requirements gathering process is different for CDI efforts than it is for transactional or data warehouse

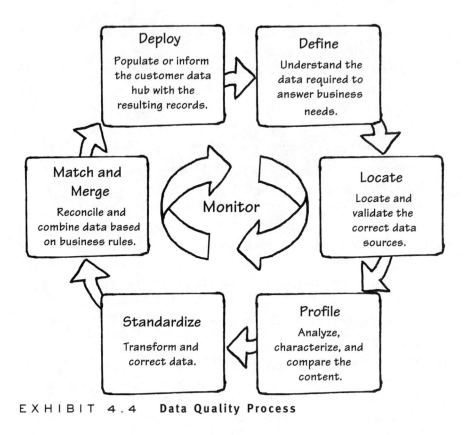

EXHIBIT 4.4   Data Quality Process

development projects. As far as data quality in CDI is concerned, it's imperative to designate which data is in scope.

Locate

Understanding "what" data is involved is a good first step, but understanding where that data currently resides is deceptively complex. Many companies make the mistake of assuming they know the de-facto systems of record for key customer data, only to discover that certain "outlier" systems contain critical data attributes. Data sourcing can be prolonged and difficult. Companies that have never developed an inventory of their data sources for customer data can find themselves conducting a protracted research project to locate customer data across multiple systems.

Some vendors offer tools to help automate the sourcing process. These tools reach out to the various operational systems, read their metadata, and determine whether there is data of interest on each system. The tools may then automatically profile the data to see if it's relevant.

Profile

Data profiling is the act of examining granular, structured data and characterizing it prior to using it. Many companies still do data profiling manually, using queries to return the data for an expert to visually scrutinize, and have developed custom-written data profiling programs that extract the data based on certain predetermined rules. However, since data profiling should be an ongoing activity within a larger data quality program, repeatability is key. The emergence of sophisticated data profiling tools that inspect the data and then statistically characterize it has facilitated the institutionalization of data profiling as a standard step in IT development projects.

Data profiling allows business and data experts to determine how closely data adheres to defined standards in its native source. It can save a company untold time and money by telling the truth about data in a system. Often, development teams extract data from one system and load it into another system only to discover—sometimes after deployment—that the data is poor, missing, or inaccurate. The iterations of fixing the data result in delay and wasted work. The results of data profiling helps data stewards determine whether the data in question is fixable or not worth the effort, before it winds up in the CDI hub. It can offer a significant productivity gain.

Several CDI vendors have embedded data profiling into their solutions, offering reports of source data to data stewards or subject matter experts. This allows data experts to "green light" the subsequent standardization of the data.

Standardize

Data standardization ensures that there is a standard for every data value. For instance, standardization includes reconciling various abbreviations for labels (e.g., "Rd." for "Road") or content (e.g., "UK" for "United Kingdom").

This usually involves several different steps, some of which entail the application of detailed business rules or complex algorithmic reconciliation of the data. It's largely contingent on the rules associated with the requirements for data usage.

Data standardization can include the following steps:

Step 1: Parsing. Determines the granular data elements that should be deconstructed or combined. For example, "157 Wisteria Lane" is deconstructed into its components: street number, street name, apartment number, city, zip code, and so forth. This type of standardization (also called tokenization) deconstructs the values in a string. This ensures that data elements are uniquely identified and maintained at a granular level, so that if data needs to be captured at its most detailed form it can be stored. Part of lexical analysis contextualizes the order relationship of the data elements themselves (so that city precedes state, but follows address text). A common example of parsing is deconstructing the passenger name in an airline record to identify an itinerary, seating, connections, and class of service.

Step 2: Semantic reconciliation. Compares the semantic meaning of two or more heterogeneous data elements. For instance, a global automobile manufacturer might spell the word *tire* as *tyre* in certain regions. Semantic reconciliation applies the same definition to both terms. Semantic technologies allow the data to be maintained in different ways by applying rules to determine their relative meanings.

Step 3: Address standardization. Most of the data quality tools on the market, and many CDI solutions, include capabilities to match addresses according to (usually predefined) U.S. Postal Service or other international postal standards. This means automatically correcting bad addresses or assigning correct street addresses or zip codes.

Data standardization will reengineer the data values themselves in order to create logically consistent keys that uniquely identify customer records,

Legacy App

Cust. Id	First Name	Middle	Last Name	DOB	SSN	Address
30391-244	William	James	Sosulski	04/12/39	563-49-1234	123 Oak St., Eves, IL 30319

CRM

Cust. Id	First Name	Middle	Last Name	DOB	SSN	Address
30391244	William	J.	Sosulski	4-12 -39	563491234	123 Oak St., Eves, IL

Online Chat

Cust. Id	First Name	Middle	Last Name	DOB	SSN	Address
14239	Bubba	J.		April 12		BubbaJ@bubbagroup.com

ERP

Cust. Id	First Name	Middle	Last Name	DOB	SSN	Address
3721B	William	James	Corp.	April 12	56349123	3224 Pkwy G, Los Osos

Data Warehouse

Cust. Id	First Name	Middle	Last Name	DOB	SSN	Address
30391-244	William	James	Sosulski	04/12/1939	563-49-1234	123 Oak St., Eves, IL 30319

EXHIBIT 4.5 Different Systems, Different Records, Same Customer

and, by extension, individual customers. Its goal is to harmonize individual records for accuracy. For instance, a company that captures a customer's online chat stream might register that customer by his nickname. However, as shown in Exhibit 4.5, that nickname is not the standard by which the company will recognize that individual customer.

The problems with the variances in this data are typical of those at many companies:

- Name anomalies, including the use of nicknames.
- Missing data fields.
- Misinterpreted data; for instance, the online chat program considers the "address" field to be the customer's e-mail address, and the customer's business address is included in one record.
- Misspellings of names and addresses.
- Lack of standard conventions, including use of the middle initial versus middle name, and address standards.

In addition, the lack of structure in "string" fields like address renders address matching more difficult. The increasing need for unstructured data such as customer e-mail and chat text makes data quality an even bigger challenge.

Data standardization can change how the value is represented, meaning that data standardization implies updating records. This may mean filling in certain missing data according to the data found in other records, or changing existing data to conform to business rules (e.g., changing "Bill" to "William"). Once the records are changed to reflect the "best" version of each record, they can be matched and merged together to establish the authoritative version of the customer record.

Match and Merge

Matching is the heart of most data quality and CDI solutions, whose aim is to arrive at the best record for the individual customer. The goal of matching is to identify all the data in the enterprise for a particular customer. It's used as a catch-all term to compare like records, eliminate

Cust. Id	First Name	Middle	Last Name	DOB	SSN	Address
30391-244	William	James	Sosulski	04/12/39	563-49-1234	123 Oak St., Eves, CA 91403

Cust. Id	First Name	Middle	Last Name	DOB	SSN	Street Address
30391244	Willaim	J.	Sosulski	4-12 -39	563491234	123 Oak Street

Cust. Id	First Name	Middle	Last Name	DOB	SSN	Address
14239	Bubba		James	April 12		BubbaJ@bubbagroup.com

Cust. Id	First Name	Middle	Last Name	DOB	SSN	Address
3721B	Willaim	James	Corp.	April 12	563491123	3224 Pkwy G, Los Osos, CA

Cust. Id	First Name	Middle	Last Name	DOB	SSN	Address
30391-244	William	James	Sosulski	04/12/1939	563-49-1234	123 Oak St.

1001	30391-244	William	James	Sosulski	04/12/1939	563491234	123 Oak Street	Eves	CA	91403

EXHIBIT 4.6 Generating the Golden Record

duplicates, and combine them into the "best" version of the record, as shown in Exhibit 4.6. Depending on the software being used (matching is best done as an automated process), this usually involves assigning a "match key" to individual customer records.

The process of householding falls into the match-and-merge category. A household is a nest of individuals. Recognizing that different customers or account holders are members of the same household can save a company a fortune in reduced mailing costs. Moreover, it allows more accurate demographic and psychographic profiling of individual customers, enabling more traction in target marketing campaigns and personalized interactions.

Since they're challenged with applying often complex logic to heterogeneous data, matching software can be highly complex. There are generally two types of matching:

1. Deterministic matching, which compares and matches records against business rules according to their precision. For instance, the system can be told, via a rule, that William Sosulski and "Bubba" are in fact the same person if their address and Social Security numbers are identical. These rule sets can be complex depending on the attributes considered in the matching logic. To be effective they should be exhaustive and describe what action to take for each of the possible outcomes on each attribute (e.g., match, partial match, or mismatch). Each time a deterministic matching record recognizes the two records, it will merge the best fields into the ultimate customer record. Deterministic matching works best when comparing records where an "exact match" is anticipated.

2. Probabilistic matching uses statistical algorithms in order to deduce the most reliable match. They typically produce a continuous statistic, which reflects the statistical confidence that the records refer to the same customer. This statistic is compared against a threshold to determine the appropriate action (e.g., link, don't link, or review). A CDI tool using probabilistic matching could recognize a "slash" in an account number rather than a

dash; it would deduce the character as unnecessary and remove it. Probabilistic matching applies more "fuzzy logic," such as applying typographical distance measures to record matches, often achieving a higher degree of matching, while the program "learns" patterns in the data to incorporate in future matching functions. This approach is usually preferred for large data sets or when many attributes are involved in matching.

Sometimes data is so poor that manual intervention is necessary. With some CDI products, as the matching process runs, the system captures data errors and earmarks them for review by a data steward or administrator. The bad data records, often referred to as "survivors," are flagged and the data steward can determine how to remedy the errors. With some CDI systems, these records are sent to the CDI administrative dashboard we introduced in Chapter 2.

Understanding the data errors that filter out of CDI processing can result in a data steward's changing or adding new business rules in order to satisfy previously unarticulated data requirements, thereby fostering the continuous improvement of data quality over time.

Golden Record versus Best Record

Like any emerging technology area, CDI is replete with semantic differences that can be confusing. One person's "single version of the truth" might be someone else's "unified view" of the data. Two terms that you'll hear are *golden record* and *best record* (alternatively, the "best version of the truth").

The golden record implies a single, authoritative record that has usually been generated with data from multiple source systems. The CDI hub recognizes, matches, and consolidates the data into a master record for that customer. The CDI hub will pull the most accurate value from each source system so that the golden record may contain the customer's first and last name from one system, the phone number from another system, and home address from another system. CDI hubs are distinguished from other technology solutions in their ability to identify the optimal values that comprise the golden record for a customer.

The CDI hub has the ability to "tie-break" between data sources and individual elements and decide on the best combination of elements to comprise the golden record. Ultimately, the golden record becomes the enterprise view of an individual customer's information.

The best record also reflects the most accurate view of a customer's information and contains the best data elements based on the optimal data from various data sources. However, the best record provides individual data elements based on the specific needs of the individual user or application.

Consider the need to retrieve a business customer's contact name and street address.

- Finance requests the contact details for Company A and receives John Smith on Spring Street.
- Meanwhile, customer support requests the contact details for Company A and gets Amy Brown on Fourth Street.
- Sales requests the contact details from Company A and gets Sally Wright on Highland.

Which answer is the correct answer for Customer A? Surprisingly, each record is correct. There are three different versions, none of which is the most accurate. The reason is simple: the answer is different based on the needs of the requesting user or application. The best record for finance is Company A's comptroller, John Smith. Customer support considers Amy Brown, a programmer at Company A, as their primary contact, while sales communicates with Sally Wright, who works in Company A's purchasing department. Indeed, John, Amy, and Sally all work for Company A. But the best contact for Company A depends on the context of the request.

This suggests that there can be multiple versions of the truth about a customer. The beauty of CDI is that it enables the application to access the best version of truth based on its specific needs. In some cases, a single golden record might not be sufficient. In the case of the best record, the answer depends on the usage context.

Hierarchy Matching

The examples in Exhibits 4.5 and 4.6 suggest how complex reconciling customer records can be in a business-to-consumer (B2C) environment. But in a business-to-business (B2B) environment, matching can become even more complex—and more critical. For companies like high-tech firms where an individual customer can represent millions of dollars in revenues, understanding linkages between various companies can be mission critical.

Companies can also represent millions of dollars of credit risk. When MCI went bankrupt, many of the company's suppliers were unable to quantify how many MCI affiliates were represented in their receivables. Parent-child-subsidiary hierarchies are not only complex, but in these days of merger mania they are constantly in flux. Consider, for instance, a partial list of companies affiliated with the JPMorgan Chase & Company family of companies:

- JPMorgan Chase Bank, N.A.
- JPMorgan Insurance Agency, Inc.
- JPMorgan Trust Company, N.A.
- JPMorgan Chase Card Services
- Chase Bank USA, N.A.
- Chase Auto Finance Corporation
- Chase Home Finance, LLC
- Chase Investment Services Corporation
- Chase Insurance Agency, Inc.
- Bank One Trust Company, N.A.
- Banc One Securities Corporation
- Bank One Acceptance Corporation
- Bank One Education Finance Corporation

Obviously, some of these relationships are more intuitive than others. It might not be readily apparent to your new sales guy in Columbus that

Bank One Acceptance Corporation is part of your firm's JPMorgan Chase Bank account, and thus owned by the firm's major accounts team in New York. A salesperson unaware of these relationships could mean your company's cannibalizing its sales to an important client, or worse.

However, a CDI solution would have built in the necessary account linkages to the sales force automation system, enforcing the recording of company hierarchies and an understanding of account ownership. Even within single companies, organizations merge and spin off, and there are different charts of accounts that must be reconciled across their lines of business.

Deploy

Deploying the data involves the formatting and delivery of that data to the customer data hub. Deployment also has a timeliness component, since the business requirements often dictate that customer data be migrated to the customer data hub at the time of its change or addition in the source system.

When discussing data quality at the "global" level, we're implying that data quality should be delivered on behalf of the enterprise. In this sense, it can be a superset of CDI, since it will ostensibly touch other cross-functional enterprise data such as product and supplier.

However, data quality is also a subset of CDI, itself often set up as a series of different services to detect errors and correct them. Data quality is an embedded function, and—as part of an overall service-oriented architecture—can be capitalized on by new systems and users as the business evolves. Indeed, many of today's CDI vendor solutions embed third-party data quality vendor software functionality into their tool sets.

Of course, the backbone of any data quality effort is the ongoing monitoring and measurement of the data as it changes and improves. One publishing company client we've worked with distributes a monthly data quality update report to key businesspeople, allowing them to track ongoing anomalies, data fixes, and accuracy improvements over time. The businesspeople can then assess whether or how business programs may have been impacted by data fixes, and can circle back to source system owners or their own internal systems to ensure the accuracy of business rules applied to the data.

Why would Dave Frieder go to work for a telco start-up? After all, he'd been in management positions at communication industry pioneers like Bell Labs and Bell Atlantic, not to mention holding partner roles at heavy-hitter consulting firms like KPMG and Accenture. "I like a challenge," Frieder says modestly. And he got one.

When Frieder joined XO Communications as vice president of IT, the young company was in the midst of some classic problems not confined to just start-ups. As Frieder explains it, the firm was facing the challenges associated with duplicate manual efforts, siloed systems, and human error.

"Back then, when we got a new service order it had to be entered into our order system. Then someone rekeyed it into our provisioning system. Then we manually entered it again into our billing system. You can imagine all the mistakes that were made in data entry—and when we tried to correlate all the data, well, we couldn't."

Frieder was lucky. His fellow executives already suspected that there were problems, they just didn't know the details. Frieder's team was able to pinpoint two major root causes, and they presented their findings to management in business terms, focusing on the potential productivity improvements promised by being able to streamline and automate the data flow.

"First, we had to address the flow-through problem," Frieder explains. The flow of data across the company's three core systems needed to be managed so that systems could intercommunicate across the data supply chain. "Then we needed to clean up the data on those systems, since it didn't match."

Frieder's team was circumspect about their data and where they needed to start. "We looked at how our data was really structured. We knew we had to start at the account level. Sometimes there were many-to-many relationships with the same account. We needed to look at accounts and figure out how many really matched. Eventually, this would let us see the different service locations each customer had."

Frieder's team researched vendors, which led to their purchase of Purisma, a customer identity management tool that would help them with their data reconciliation and matching. "We did a quick prototype and presented our findings in one of the COO's operations review meetings. One of the executives in customer care caught me afterwards and asked how he could support us. That's when I knew we were getting traction."

Automating the data reconciliation was not only fast, it had significant business impact. Customer care reps accustomed to manually navigating disparate silos were now able to do a single customer lookup—a substantial productivity gain. The sales and marketing groups are now also able to view individual customer profiles easily, and the data is current.

And XO also increased the speed of its business. "Improving our match rate increased the flow-through of orders across our core systems. We did benchmarks along the way and watched how we tuned our business rules and the effect it had. It's iterative: you write your business rules as loose or as tight as you want. The looser the business rules, the worse the match rate."

Frieder considers data reconciliation and matching an ongoing process. "We didn't really know how bad the problem was when we started," he says, "but it's gotten so much better. This year our priority is to tackle even more legacy data. We're continuing to work with customer care, and now we're working with our customer retention people, using the output of the tool to give them a much more complete and accurate view of our customers. We're right where we need to be."

Preparing for Data Quality: Some Advice from the Trenches

> *There are no limits. There are only plateaus, and you must not stay there. You must go beyond them.*
>
> —BRUCE LEE

Here are some important and valuable tips that we have given to clients in the past as they prepare to fix their data and formalize rigor around data cleansing. They apply equally well to CDI initiatives that will inevitably involve data reconciliation.

1. **Decide on data ownership.** We'll talk more about data ownership and data-specific roles in Chapter 6. For these purposes, it's important to identify an individual on the business side who is intimate with the meaning and the usage of customer data. This person can determine whether a "supplier" who is also a "customer" should be listed as the former or the latter, or by a new term. He or she can also explain how the data will be used downstream, describing scenarios and decisions that can inform how the data will be represented in the CDI hub. (We've been known to take a heavy hand with some business stakeholders, admonishing them that "If you complain about it, you own it." Otherwise, you'll be beholden to someone else's rules.)

2. **Focus on data quality measurement to help operations people improve it.** This is an unpopular one, but we've seen more than one data quality initiative fail because managers were unwilling to enforce data improvement at the level of the source system. This doesn't mean that all source systems should have identical data. (Indeed, CDI allows source systems to continue representing the same data in different ways.) It does, however, mean that source system owners should be made aware of data errors and be allowed to take the appropriate steps to address the root cause.

3. **Know what applications are dependent on the data.** This means understanding the downstream dependencies of other systems. If your company embarks on a data quality effort but doesn't understand which systems are beholden to that data, it's like fixing a bicycle blindfolded. You can get the right tools and feel your way around, but it will take a lot longer, and the outcomes will be uncertain. Only when you understand how the data is used can you truly determine what it should look like.

4. **Establish metrics for data acceptance.** Application owners should establish what their data acceptance criteria are, and the CDI

system should adhere to those metrics. If indeed "all customers should be assigned a billing address, and that customer record should not enter the system until the address is attached," someone should discretely define this—and examine a few customer records to ensure that the address fields are correct.

One of our retailing clients does a weekly Webcast with its global service directors called "Here's What Happened With Your Data This Month." The Webcast shows examples of new data records and annotates them, soliciting feedback from the Webcast attendees about accuracy and definitions. The Webcast attendance averages 80 percent of the invited managers.

5.   **If you agree that "sometimes the data should be left alone," define what those times are.** There are circumstances in which some applications or users expect to see data as naked as the day it was born. Regardless of the data standardization processes occurring in the CDI hub, there could be risk in changing the data and not providing lineage back to data in its "raw" form. The data might need to be in the format it came from, regardless of its accuracy, so that it's traceable.

For instance, a risk management system at a bank we work with wanted to see data as it was entered in a loan application, regardless of its correctness. This allowed the risk management system to determine the likelihood of fraudulent data. However, most of the errors on mortgage applications turn out to be data-entry typos, which ultimately need to be fixed in order to provide the business with accurate customer data.

6.   **Understand the concept of "point in time."** Recall the data supply chain we showed in Exhibit 1.2. It illustrates a customer's life-cycle with the company, from initial contact through order fulfillment and support. And, as we discussed, the data changes or evolves at each point in the life-cycle.

For instance, when the customer initially calls the company (or vice versa) to make a purchase, he provides his name and contact details. When he actually purchases the product or service, he may also provide credit card, billing, and shipping information. The company is then likely to track when the product is picked from inventory, when it is shipped, and when it arrived at the customer's location. The company may then analyze the turnaround time and provide support to that customer. At any of these touch points, information about the customer may be introduced or existing information may change.

Business stakeholders must be clear about not only what data they need, but at what point in time they need to see or process the data about the customer. A company striving to increase a customer's value must understand that there is an innate workflow that affects customer information at each stage.

> The number of times a piece of data is manipulated is inversely proportional to that data's quality.

It's a fact that manual data entry exacerbates data quality. The number of times a piece of data is manipulated is inversely proportional to that data's quality. However, data entry is still a fact of life at most companies. Because of point-in-time issues, the propensity to corrupt or overwrite data is high.

At a telephone company we work with, a large business customer moved its headquarters from the northeastern United States to the Southeast. Hearing the news during a customer service call, a customer service representative entered the new information in the company's call center system as the customer's new service address. The customer's sales rep filed a new address with the company's billing system. Meanwhile, the customer contact went online and entered a different address as "headquarters." Hence, three separate addresses for the same customer were introduced to three different operational systems.

Even before the customer had actually moved, the operational systems updates were recorded by the data warehouse, which replaced the customer's current address with the most recently updated address, in this case from the sales rep. The rules differentiating the three different addresses were never well defined. Moreover, there was no rigor at the time of data entry to ensure that the new addresses complied with existing business definitions. As a result, salespeople analyzing customer purchases were misled, since new revenue fell into the wrong geography.

If a CDI system were in place, it would have applied centralized rules to ensure that the correct address was provided to the individual applications that needed it, no matter who updated the address or when.

For enterprise-level data quality initiatives, it's important to build routines into all data creation processes to reduce the likelihood of bad data coming in. This is especially important when the data has been manually generated via human data entry. The U.S. Census Bureau applies "edits" against all completed questionnaires to ensure that all fields are complete, that responses are reasonable, and that the data is accurate and consistent.[8] Not coincidentally, the U.S. Census Bureau estimates that one in seven consumers changes addresses within a given year, a statistic with major implications to any B2C company.

On a larger scale, it's been proven that there is a steady rate at which data—volatile or not—decays within a business. For this reason alone, rigor around customer data quality is imperative.

Questions to Answer before CDI

There are some cursory but worthwhile questions you can use to evaluate your customer data before embarking on a CDI project. The questions aren't scientific. In fact, it's not even about knowing the answers to the questions as much as it is being certain you could find the answers if you needed them. In many cases, these questions draw blank stares from data stewards—we'll formally define the role in Chapter 6—who are responsible for defining and maintaining customer data. Your ability to answer them will provide an interesting lens through which to view the accuracy of the data across various source systems or in your favorite customer database:

- Are there more than 50 values for "state" in your database? Okay, 51 including the District of Columbia, 52 if you count Puerto Rico, and 53 if you count Guam. (See where this is going? It's all about rules.) But if you have 137 states, that's bad data.
- How many accounts don't have an associated account holder name?
- Are there transactions not associated with a valid account?

- How many customer last names are NULL?

- How many of your customers are less than ten years old, because call center reps or tellers often enter a "default" birth date of 01–01–01? How many are over 100 years old?

- Are there Social Security numbers where the "dashes" count as one of the nine characters and the result is a truncated number?

- How many business customers didn't get a bill every month last year? (One of our communications clients had over 20,000 customers who hadn't received their monthly bill.)

- How many closed accounts have a negative balance?

- How many rebate checks were sent that were worth less than 37 cents, the cost of first-class postage?

- How many duplicate customer records do you have in each source system?

- Is the same customer spread across systems inconsistently?

Remember that data anomalies may not be data quality problems, but instead represent bad business practices. A customer who has returned more items than they've purchased may indicate a pattern of refunding activity, not bad data. There's a great story of a man whose car license plate read "NO TAG." Funny, huh? But police reports for abandoned vehicles reported them with "No Tag," and the guy was nailed for over $50,000 worth of parking citations. Not bad data, simply incorrect usage.

MANAGER DO'S AND DON'TS

Here are some final tips for managers who might be embarking on CDI and need to get their arms around data quality issues in advance:

- **Do** be willing to see requirements through the eyes of applications owners. CDI data is less about how people use the data than it is how systems use it. Ensuring that your CDI developers understand how applications use the data is an important step toward ensuring that CDI data is correctly provisioned.

- **Don't** get sucked into invention mode. Yes, your team is smarter than everyone else. And no, the users don't really care how the data is cleansed. You can build your own CDI solution from scratch. However, if you're finding that a key business system needs new data and you can't cleanse the data for a week and a half, maybe a vendor tool could speed up the process. If something breaks, is it easy to fix? If something changes, does someone have to write code? Are the people who know the homegrown tool consistently available? Consider costs of building and maintaining a homegrown CDI solution.

- **Do** talk to vendors to understand the functions and features available in "off-the-shelf" tools before committing to an internal development activity. This could save a lot of time and effort, and moreover prevents the trial and error that new development paradigms like CDI can introduce. For data quality, this can also help you understand common methods and practices used by companies with comparable business objectives.

- **Don't** rely solely on the IT liaison or business analysts. Many IT organizations have designated IT business liaison or business analyst roles. These individuals communicate with business users and monitor their needs. However, they don't necessarily know how the systems need to access customer data and thus shouldn't be the only conduits of CDI data requirements. Be sure your development team has direct access to developers of the CDI client applications.

ENDNOTES

1. *This chapter aims to discuss data quality issues from the perspective of customer data integration and master data management. For a more thorough look at data quality as an enterprise practice, see: David Loshin,* Enterprise Knowledge Management: The Data Quality Approach *(San Francisco: Morgan Kauffman, 2001).*

2. *Study reported in* InformationWeek, *June 7, 2004.*

3. *Study reported in* Internet Retailer, *November 2002.*

4. *Study reported in* Frontline Solutions, *October 2003.*

5. *Daniel Sorid, "Unit's Blunder Sent Craft into Martian Atmosphere," www.space.com, September 30, 1999.*

6. *Surveys were distributed to attendees of two Data Warehousing Institute conferences in February and May, 2004; 171 responses were tabulated.*

7. *How to define which subset of data to begin with should be dictated by your business requirements. For instance, you might start with a subset of data sources such as data from the marketing automation system, then move to the Web server, and so on. Another approach might be defining a subset of data elements, for instance, customer contact information, and adding new attributes like privacy preference, account, and purchase information over time.*

8. *Malcolm Wheatley, "Operation Clean Data," CIO, July 1, 2004.*

CHAPTER 5

Customer Data Integration Is Different: A CDI Development Framework

One of the biggest barriers to customer data integration (CDI) success is the assumption that a CDI hub can be delivered like any other database. CDI development differs from the implementation frameworks that have been sanctioned for other types of systems, be they operational systems or analytic platforms.

Indeed, CDI represents a combination of different IT development best practices, encompassing the source system analysis and data profiling so important to business intelligence implementations with complex functional specifications common to operational system construction. Thus, a CDI-specific development method ensures that the processing needs and data complexity are supported during construction. A specialized approach to CDI development reduces risk, ensuring that specific steps are followed and thereby preventing the "we didn't think about . . ." discoveries so common to other enterprise-level development efforts. Companies new to CDI might fall into the trap of using their standard development life-cycles for CDI. But CDI implementation involves some unique considerations that should inform project planning, staffing, and time frames.

Nevertheless, some of the tasks described in this chapter will be very familiar to project managers and developers. As we'll see, the steps in CDI implementation can leverage the tools and skill sets your organization already has. It's a matter of making sure that all the steps occur and that existing data is well understood. ■

NOT YOUR FATHER'S DEVELOPMENT METHODOLOGY

One of the great Yogi Berra stories describes how, during the 1957 World Series, Berra noticed that hitter Hank Aaron was holding the bat the wrong way. Berra told Aaron to turn the bat so that he could see the trademark. Aaron looked at his bat, then at Berra. "Didn't come up here to read," he replied. "Came up here to hit." Aaron went on to break Babe Ruth's home-run record.

Aaron's remark reminds us of many of the best executives we work with. Most are smart people who do their research and aim for results. They've gotten over "the vision thing" and are ready to do the hard work. From chief executive officers (CEOs) to chief financial officers (CFOs) to marketing execs, management has finally come to understand the "whys." That customer loyalty is important because it drives profit. That automation drives cost savings through efficiencies. That understanding customers means differentiating them as individuals, and tailoring corporate behaviors around them, and that's a competitive advantage. What executives need help with now is the "hows."

As managers and practitioners alike embrace the idea of a true single version of the truth about customers, they face the fact that their data warehouse and customer relationship management (CRM) systems, however successful, haven't reached this goal. As they turn their collective heads toward CDI, they are learning some valuable lessons, including that:

- CDI systems represent the single "certified" list of customers for the company at large.
- CDI incorporates business rules to ensure data accuracy.

- Operational systems that contain customer information are constantly changing and there should be an authoritative system for this data.

- The greater the number of departments in a company, the lower the likelihood that there will be total consensus around data definitions and meaning.

- The work tasks involved in customer identity matching and data cleansing are much more difficult than they sound. (Indeed, they are more complex than many standalone applications.)

- Despite the numerous business applications and systems that lay claim to centralizing customer data, their companies still have hard work ahead of them when it comes to an authoritative source of customers.

Although many of the most senior executives can articulate the business problems associated with not having a single version of the customer truth, few understand where to best begin tackling a problem that continues to vex even the smartest information technology (IT) executives. The major question for CDI projects is really, "Where do we begin?"

TOP-DOWN VERSUS BOTTOM-UP

One of the most important decisions a CDI team can make is whether the development approach will be top-down or bottom-up. The term *top-down* connotes a requirements-driven approach to development, usually involving careful planning, requirements gathering, and group consensus-building activities in an effort to understand a superset of business needs that call for a new technology. Top-down development often includes a discussion of aligning individual projects to corporate strategic or business goals.

However, *bottom-up* development is more tactical and aims to deliver software functionality in a quick and incremental way to satisfy specific and more immediate business needs. It's light on up-front analysis and group consent, involving a heavy focus on important functions and features that will be initially delivered and then built upon.

The distinction between top-down and bottom-up is an important one for CDI, and should be determined by a number of factors:

- The purpose or goal of CDI
- Who's driving the CDI initiative
- Who will own the CDI project
- The scope of the business issues that call for CDI functionality
- The level of organizational agreement about the need for CDI
- Whether there's a business sponsor for CDI
- Whether CDI is the result of executive edict
- Whether CDI is intended to solve a near-term tactical problem or a larger, more strategic set of issues
- The scope of the initial project

A top-down approach is often the assumption when there is a high-level business sponsor calling for integrated customer data. A top-down approach is often used when data is being sourced from multiple systems. Top-down implies rigorous methods around reaching agreement on the best data sources and the right definitions for data elements.

We recommend top-down development for CDI when strategic alignment is a priority. Many companies require acknowledgment of company strategy in the business cases for key IT programs; thus, a more structured strategy mapping and requirements facilitation process is probably in order.

Conversely, bottom-up CDI is appropriate when IT has identified a functional need for automated data reconciliation, or for when CDI represents a solution to different technological problems. Since the majority of new CDI implementations begin with a small prototype, the bottom-up development is often more straightforward, since it can leverage incremental development principles, and be more palatable to experienced IT developers and impatient business people.

Exhibit 5.1 illustrates the issues common to the top-down, bottom-up decision.

Also, bottom-up CDI development is useful for any type of proof-of-

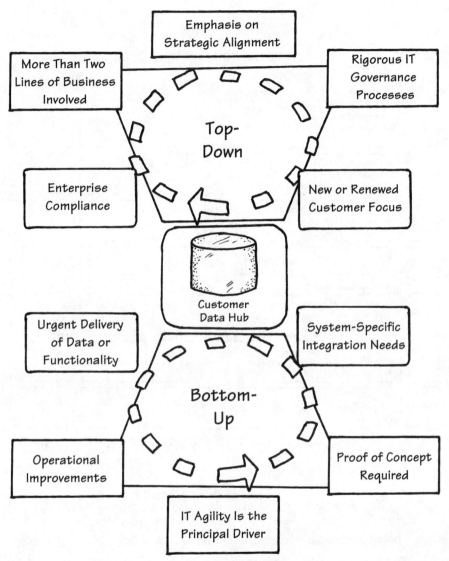

EXHIBIT 5.1   Top-Down versus Bottom-Up Development

concept effort, for which a functional prototype will be the unit of management buy-in and funding. However, integrating CDI technology into an existing IT infrastructure isn't trivial work, so developers should be careful about positioning CDI delivery as "rapid" if they're advocating the bottom-up approach.

True or False?	True	False
1 There are still arguments over the difference between a "customer" and an "account." CDI can address these differences and give everyone the data they need.		
2 Every quarter there's another "mad scramble" to generate the customer list.		
3 The company's M&A work has resulted in significant staff changes. We're losing a lot of institutional knowledge about our customers.		
4 We have multiple groups of people across departments and lines of business generating their own individual lists of customers.		
5 The IT group wants to implement a CDI solution, but not everyone's sure that we need it—or how we'll use it.		
6 The definition of customer or the rules around household aren't consistent across our ERP, SFA, and order systems.		
7 Sure, the data warehouse gives us customer details— but it's usually at least 30 days out of sync with the data we need.		
8 Our enterprise CRM system should do this!		

EXHIBIT 5.2   Top-Down or Bottom-Up? Take the Test

Exhibit 5.2 offers a short test that can help you determine whether you're better served by starting top-down or bottom-up.

Give yourself 1 point for every "true" answer to questions 1, 3, 4, 6, 7, and 8. If your score is "5" or above, the top-down approach might be better for your first CDI effort.

The key here is to understand the perceived scope of need. When a client asks a question like: "How can we align our business actions with executive priorities for corporate growth?" or "How do we achieve organizational agreement around customer data definitions?," we realize that these are big issues that might call for some facilitated requirements definition and scoping decisions. In instances like this, vendor conversations and architecture blueprints are probably premature.

However, if a client tells us, as a mortgage company recently did, that they thought CDI was the right answer but weren't sure it could meet the response time requirements of the CRM system, we suggest doing a CDI proof of concept.

Of course, there are some gray areas. For instance, CDI is often a boon to companies that undergo frequent merger-and-acquisition activity. In some cases, this might call for a bottom-up approach to avail the newly acquired company's data to the parent company as soon as possible. In other cases, particularly when the acquired company is of a similar size or scope to the parent, a more consensus-driven and facilitated top-down effort might be in order.

Many CDI early adopters launched their CDI efforts as an initial top-down project in order to gather cross-functional requirements, unify definitions for key reference data, and establish corporate-wide data standards. But subsequent projects have been bottom-up, focusing on incremental delivery of additional functionality and data. Simply put, if you choose the top-down route, get ready for a lot of questions, a lot of analysis, frequent question and answer sessions, and yes, meetings.

CDI from the Top Down

Many of the CDI projects we've helped implement have obtained approval and funding based, at least in part, on the ability of data to help the company in question achieve its strategic objectives. Aligning a CDI effort to the company's existing or new strategic objectives is an effective way of selling the effort to management. It's especially recommended for political environments where data ownership might be problematic, or where there may be more than one opportunity for CDI.

In fact, we believe in a proven truism: a company's ability to achieve its strategic objectives is directly proportional to the degree to which that data is integrated.

"Having a corporate culture of fact-based decision making is not only a competitive advantage—*not* being a fact-based organization is a competitive *dis*advantage," explains David Snyder, vice president of data warehouse and business information groups at Charles Schwab & Company, Inc. "When we have meetings with the business about our data integration initiative, the conversations are about millions of dollars. Integrated data helps us to be customer focused and to help our business partners."

Snyder advocates the business value of the company's data. "Our best measurement is whether our customers feel that they're getting value from us. My boss, the CFO, has told us that failure is not an option. The entire range of our business—including central marketing, operations risk, legal, trading, and HR—need help. This initiative is a key strategic differentiator for the firm. Not just for finance. Not just for our MIS organizations. But for the firm."

There are risks involved with a top-down approach to CDI development. The main one is that it invites protracted discussions and drawn-out mapping and documentation activities as everyone tries to model existing data flows, or schedules protracted meetings to reach compromises on data definitions and transformation rules. Many companies overdo the rigor. Consensus building around customer definitions and business roles can often take months, and many companies simply can't overcome the deeply held biases and ownership wars that often plague cross-functional data integration efforts.

The launch phase of a CDI project is often the most fraught, since expectations management is job one for the project leaders trying to get the effort off the ground. We've seen many CDI projects flail after a "mission statement" is printed out and pasted on the office wall of the CDI business sponsor as the project team struggles to define tactics. After all, a strategy statement doesn't:

- Establish the scope and boundaries of the initial CDI effort
- Explain to management what the costs and benefits are
- List the stakeholders and their responsibilities
- Imply a rigorous set of business requirements
- Identify the necessary data
- Delineate success metrics

- Offer candidate software tools
- Optimize customer-facing business processes
- Determine whether teaming and organizational effectiveness are metrics for CDI project success

In their book *Strategy Maps*, Robert Kaplan and David Norton define strategy as the way a company "intends to create value for its shareholders, customers, and citizens."[1] This is a tall order and one that transcends CDI. Most companies have strategic objectives that were painstakingly crafted and approved at the board level, to encompass a veritable value framework that includes financial and internal process performance as well as customer value.

Sometimes our executives make it easy on us. An executive vice president of retail banking in one of our financial services clients recently proclaimed that no proposed project would get funding unless it could fulfill at least one of the following four strategic goals:

1. Increase revenue from existing customers
2. Improve customer retention
3. Increase customer satisfaction scores
4. Increase revenue per transaction

True to his word, the executive flung any business case that didn't address one of the four criteria—irrespective of the robustness of its cost-benefit analysis—in the wastebasket.

In *The Strategy-Focused Organization*, Kaplan and Norton asserted that many strategies failed not because the strategies themselves were poor, but because of "bad execution."[2] The same can be said of CDI projects. The CRM failure rates bandied about so freely a few years back weren't due to the lack of a lucid and consensus-driven CRM strategy statement. Rather, they were because of the lack of a set of defining principles—"We need to stem customer attrition." "We have proven that higher customer satisfaction scores mean higher profits, so let's work to raise scores."—that implied the tactics necessary to achieve them.

**Art Hall: "Link your project and your budget
back to corporate strategy."**

"Customer care recently evolved from being a cost center to a revenue center at NetBank. So our agents who are making decisions about customer treatment need data at the time of the interaction. When the customer is on the phone, we need relevant, actionable information.

In order for customer care to be a differentiator, we needed to understand the strategic 'themes' that are enabled by customer data. We have regulatory, privacy, and personalization goals at NetBank, and they're all data enabled. I recently facilitated a strategy-linkage meeting with some key stakeholders. We're not going to tamper with the company's mission, vision, or values—but we should understand how they're impacted by our information. One of our big lessons we've learned is that linking our budgeting to corporate strategy can help us really achieve what we want to in customer care."

ART HALL, Vice President of Sales and Customer Care Operations, NetBank

So where does this leave CDI and strategy? In a word: alignment. If you work at a company that has defined a new set of customer-focused strategies but isn't sure how to implement any of them, it could be a savvy move to identify which strategies can be fulfilled, in part or in full, with integrated customer data. Consider developing a strategy map that links high-level corporate strategies—for instance, "increase revenue of existing mid-size business customer segment"—with CDI capabilities like reconciling individual customer reference data and tying it to products for more effective cross-selling.

This, of course, means that your company's current strategic direction has been well articulated by executives—often the major hurdle involved in any type of strategy mapping effort. Typically, your company will emphasize a set of individual strategic objectives annually. These strategic objectives usually map back to the company's strategic vision, which communicates the company's overall direction. Exhibit 5.3 shows the individ-

Strategy	Objectives	Key Initiatives	Master Data
Financial Growth	• Create new revenue sources • Increase revenue per customer	• Develop new products and services targeted to individual customer segments • Develop specific product programs for top resellers • Understand current customer revenue breakdown	Customer Product
Reseller Loyalty	• Provide resellers with more sales support • Reward "above the line" resellers	• Develop reseller segments to profile performance • Develop specific product programs for top resellers • Understand current customer revenue breakdown	Reseller Product Customer
Customer Retention	• Increase current customer retention rates • Increase cross-selling capabilities	• Introduce Rewards program • Anticipate customer need based on behavior trending • Optimize interaction channels around customers' preferred channel	Reseller Product Customer
Customer Satisfaction	• Increase service excellence scores • Create new metrics for customer satisfaction	• Deploy segment- and product-based satisfaction surveys • Optimize customer conversations around preferred touch points • Develop customer communities of interest	Customer Product Research
Attract and Retain Top Talent	• Provide incentives to peak performers • Use new channels to recruit new talent	• Launch automated employee measurement tool to department managers • Distribute quarterly employee satisfaction surveys • Create Best of the Best club for top performers	Employee

EXHIBIT 5.3 Deconstructing Strategies into Data

ual strategies being deconstructed into objectives, which define specific goals, then key initiatives, which represent programs the company will undertake in the coming year to achieve those objectives.

Assuming your company's strategies have been well defined and are truly customer-focused, you can create a simple strategy map that deconstructs individual strategies into their need for integrated data, as shown in Exhibit 5.3. This exhibit also suggests that you can go further in deconstructing strategy by going all the way to the data element or source system level. By using individual strategic objectives to understand the major projects the company expects to launch, it's possible to map those projects back to master data, and put the projects on the radar of the data management organization, as we'll discuss in Chapter 6.

The advantage to this top-down approach is that it provides a clear answer to the "why?" question of managing master data and integrating it. It also offers a way to measure the results: did the newly integrated customer data help us achieve our objective of increasing revenue for mid-size business customers? This in turn provides firmer metrics for success.

CASE STUDY: ASPECT SOFTWARE

As director of order administration for Aspect Software, Michele Dour's title belies the scope of her responsibilities. And that's putting it lightly. Although she technically works on the business side, Dour is as comfortable discussing data quality automation and customer master data as she is the mechanics of order management and contracts administration. Good thing, too. As the leader of Aspect Communications' customer master data initiative, she's been able to bring executives and IT to the table and gain corporate-level buy-in for CDI.

Providing contact center software and services to thousands of global companies demands an understanding of who those companies are and the hierarchies and ownership issues across and among them. It also means being able to distinguish individual accounts and roll up various business relationships. Dour recognized that Aspect's growth would be contingent on the company's ability to understand those relationships in order to develop them. And she knew that it wouldn't be easy.

"We needed to establish a culture within the company that wasn't only customer focused, but customer *data* focused," Dour explains. "This meant that the management, quality, and stewardship of customer data could no longer remain in the realm of the back office."

Dour's first priority was to educate executives and secure their support. She enlisted the CIO and CFO, describing the issues and challenges of managing customer master data across Aspect's lines of business, and what the payback would be. (It didn't hurt that leveraging existing customers had already been articulated as a corporate strategy.) She then got their support to take the issue to the executive management committee.

Not only did the executives buy in, each hand-picked a representative from his or her department to participate on the company's customer master council. "There were so many different places in our company where—if we didn't fix our customer master data—we simply couldn't move forward as a business," Dour says.

The council's participants represent marketing, IT, sales, support sales, order management, and credit and collections, among other departments. The group is comprised of executive-sanctioned data owners. "The council makes decisions about what's in the data integration and correction pipeline," explains Dour, "because each of the council members knows where we're trying to go as a company. Most of them also own departmental systems. They get why this is important."

In late 2005, Aspect Communications was acquired by Concerto Software, a producer of tools that automate customer telemarketing and contact centers. Initially concerned about the momentum of her customer master project, Dour visited Concerto executives in Boston and laid out her plan. "They were in the middle of their own discussions about customer data," she laughs. "With their history of acquisitions, they understand how critical this is."

For the combined company, now called Aspect Software, Dour doesn't expect the effort to end anytime soon. "The challenge still lies with how we educate the entire company and influence the culture. There are people in departments who simply aren't as intimate with the overall view of the customer. Our call center people really only see the data as it exists in the Clarify system. We have to make sure we don't bury them in the details, but nevertheless help them understand the business value this has to the company."

Dour rejects the notion that CDI and data correction are technology issues. "You need to ask what the root cause is—are the problems really technology problems, or is it the data? We asked ourselves this question and realized that no matter what packaged application we implemented next, we wouldn't get to where we needed to be unless we fixed our data. A new tool just delivers bad data faster."

Her advice to others just starting out with CDI efforts? "Divorce yourself from preconceived notions of what a customer is. It's no longer about 'who you bill to, who you ship to'—you have to understand your customer from multiple perspectives. It's hard for some people to get there, but the customer relationship shouldn't be based on an invoice. You need to understand the customer's role in the business at the highest levels, and peel back the layers from there."

Bottom-Up CDI

One of the biggest problems with CDI projects is that the teams charged with tackling them use standard implementation methods without understanding the discrete steps involved. Top-down projects often get bogged down in analysis paralysis: everyone understands the business goals for CDI, but no one knows how to actually begin development.

To illustrate this point, consider the case of a major insurance carrier. The carrier needed a patient "matching and linking" process to ensure that the same patient—entering the network through multiple channels, including his doctor's office, the pharmacy, and the lab—was immediately recognized, thus ensuring that his complete medical history was available at the point of care. This "requirement" was so universal and well understood across the company's various organizations that it didn't mandate lengthy deconstruction of business requirements, just fail-safe identity matching. The carrier's need for such identity matching was so pervasive and urgent—a pharmacist should have electronic information about a patient's care history and existing allergic reactions before filling a prescription—that management funded the project without a business case.

CDI projects aren't implemented according to business requirements as much as they are by functionality, which is why a tactical, bottom-up approach is viable. CDI projects should be bound by the functional requirements of complex and work-intensive processing such as data con-sistency checking, householding, identity matching, and other processes necessary to corroborate incoming customer data from different sources and enrich it for use by other systems. Hence, the bottom-up approach of quick, incremental delivery—often connoted by rapid prototyping—is an ideal way to deliver tangible results.

The advantage of the bottom-up approach is not only speed of delivery, but the ability to modify and supplement CDI functionality as its benefits become recognized and new learning occurs. Indeed, an incremental proto-typing approach is the development method recommended by CDI tech-nology vendors. And many IT organizations have standardized on "agile development"—which maintains that traditional, top-down processes are too rigid and artificially segregate users and developers—for some of the implementation projects. Thus, the aphorism "start small, think big," is an apt one for CDI.

The challenge with the bottom-up approach is that it eliminates the consensus building that is often important in securing stakeholder support. Such consensus building is particularly important when those stakeholders work across various lines of business or have different business goals. Thus, having a plan for CDI beyond the initial project or prototype is critical when pursuing the bottom-up approach. Failure to have a story for "what's next" risks that the resulting CDI project won't meet everyone's needs and might fail to get the wider support that it needs to process addi-tional data and provide more functionality.

As we'll discuss in Chapter 8, CDI delivers functional and processing benefits that address economies of scale issues and can thus drive down costs. Ultimately, though, CDI allows for the efficient execution of strate-gic business programs that rely on integrated customer data. Bottom-up CDI development delivers incremental value but doesn't mandate a thor-ough understanding of management's vision or even specific business strategies, as with the top-down approach. Planning for how business processes will become institutionalized via corporate policies, procedures, job roles, and training may be overkill for many organizations that never-theless require the nimble delivery of customer master data.

Whether you've chosen the top-down or bottom-up approach for your CDI implementation, the development steps themselves are constant, and likely to differ from your company's standard system development life-cycle.

A CDI IMPLEMENTATION FRAMEWORK

Since by its very definition the goal of CDI is to integrate data, many companies assume that they can overlay their standard system development lifecycle or their data warehouse implementation process onto a CDI effort. However, data warehouses are primarily geared toward analytics whereas CDI systems are functionally oriented. Thus the well-worn, requirements-driven business intelligence (BI) and data warehouse development methods won't work for CDI. Indeed, too much emphasis on business requirements can jeopardize a CDI initiative. In many ways CDI development is more straightforward, because the business more clearly understands the end game: to deliver an authoritative customer record to other systems.

Hence, with more of a focus on functionality, CDI implementation steps reflect operational systems. Exhibit 5.4 illustrates a simple CDI implementation framework.

It's critical that CDI, like all enterprise-class IT efforts, be done incrementally. This prevents the "big bang" approach that dooms large IT projects, and ensures a well-scoped effort. Incremental development also means that data security and privacy requirements can be considered in a more deliberate and well-bounded way.

Many companies have an overarching business need that warrants quick delivery of CDI. The two most common needs are compliance—"We need to recognize the account holder as an individual so we can accurately report his deposit activities"; and mergers and acquisitions—"We need to combine the two sales forces around common customers so that we're not over- or underselling our products." For cases like these, the scope of the

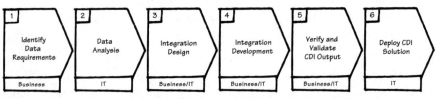

EXHIBIT   5.4   A CDI Implementation Framework

first release of CDI is relatively straightforward and should be to provide a baseline of functionality to support the business problem.

The assumption that the CDI system will have multiple releases is nevertheless a safe one to make. Like any operational system, CDI will involve maintenance and upgrades. Enhancements to a CDI solution could be more complex as they involve both data and functionality, not just data, as with data warehouses, or functionality, as with many operational systems.

Most of our clients don't have a single, pressing need for CDI, but rather see many benefits for an authoritative system of record for customer master data. For companies that have a multitude of applications that can benefit from CDI, we advise choosing a single existing application as the CDI "client"—the first system that will be accessing the new customer data. This ensures an incremental approach, since CDI is developed according to each successive application that needs data. More than one firm we've worked with has launched a new CDI effort with their operational CRM system as the initial CDI client.

This CDI method also provides what we call "context for usage," meaning that you can frame the needs and the scope of the necessary data attributes. Make sure that data usage is well defined. For instance, your call center application might need customer list details to begin recognizing individual customers. The needs of this call center system will define the initial set of data and functional requirements. It's about planting a few special trees rather than trying to seed the entire forest.

The following sections briefly describe each step in the CDI implementation process illustrated in Exhibit 5.4.

Step 1: Identify Data Requirements

Requirements are fundamental to the success of any IT project. But start down the wrong path, and you'll arrive at the wrong destination. Not all requirements are created equal.

Once you've targeted the initial CDI client application or identified a general business goal like compliance, it's time to address the question: What data does this application need in order to perform effectively? Step 1 involves determining how the data will be accessed and used by applications.

For instance, if you've chosen your company's call center system as the initial CDI client, developers of the call center system should be able to provide a list of their required customer data elements. These elements might include customer ID, name, account number, trouble ticket number, and product ID.

Determining data requirements includes defining:

- The data elements associated with the customer, specific to the particular application need (as well as the definition and description of each element)
- The definition and description of each element
- Application-level business rules (e.g., "high-value customer" is someone who spends more than $100,000 a year in support fees)
- The data usage and formatting needs of the client application
- Application value representation for each element (e.g., is customer ID "account number" or a seven-digit numerical value?)
- Cleansing and standardization details to ensure the data is represented as the application wants to see it
- An explanation of whether the data will be query-only or whether updates are allowed
- The application access method: transactional, batch, publish/subscribe, and so forth
- An explanation of CDI system availability needs, and impacts if the data is unavailable
- Operational metrics, including expectations for concurrent usage, transaction rates, and throughput response time
- Certification and acceptance criteria, to ensure data accuracy (you'll use these criteria in step 6 for data validation)

In the process of data requirements gathering, the data needs to be accurately defined. For instance, if the call center application owner identifies "customer number" as a data requirement, the CDI data steward needs to understand that the customer number refers to the customer's support ID from the customer support system, not the customer ID from the sales force automation system. The complexity of this work is determined largely by the number and complexity of the data sources and the data within them. Since the data sources aren't likely to represent similar data in the exact same way, it's critical that domain standards be defined (in other words, how will the hub represent Social Security number—with or without dashes?). Thus, it's important to establish standard data value representations for all customer data elements, since the goal of CDI is to provide customer details in a consistent way.

As we'll discuss in later chapters, it's the role of the data steward or data administrator to understand the differences in meaning and establish data standards. The challenge here is ensuring that the element identification and naming details coincide with current enterprise data management standards.

Note that some CDI solutions are application specific, meaning that the CDI hub serves only one critical system, like the call center system we've used as an example so far in this chapter. However, most companies adopt CDI with an aim of making it the single source of the customer truth for the enterprise. In this case, CDI data needs to be aligned with existing corporate data standards.

In other cases, CDI standards become the company's de-facto corporate data standard for the customer, thereby circumscribing a data infrastructure for a larger master data management (MDM) effort. This means data standards need to be thoroughly documented in a centralized, accessible way. It also means that the CDI standards should become the acknowledged authority for customer master data.

Step 2: Data Analysis

Part of functional requirements means understanding when data should be "pulled" from its sources. For instance: Do we need new customer details when someone signs up as a new customer? Or when they order their first product? Or when we receive that customer's first payment?

Data requirements are prerequisites for data sourcing since we not only need to understand data requirements, but the usage of the data also determines its source. For instance, the customer service rep needs the current service address when a customer requests service, not the customer's headquarters address. Step 2 includes:

- Identifying the best data source(s)
- Determining domain standards—how the data element should be represented from an enterprise perspective, to be as flexible as possible
- Mapping data sources—developing a specification that maps source data elements to their targets on the CDI hub

Step 2 doesn't target all a company's data sources, just the ones most likely to contribute to the ultimate authoritative customer record, establishing their specific outputs. This means identifying where the data values that support the functional requirements defined in step 1 actually reside.

Many people think data sourcing for CDI happens magically, particularly for the registry or hybrid solutions that can access the data "on the fly." However, the CDI hub cannot simply recognize data based on its source system naming conventions. This involves a developer's determining the best elements from the source systems and the rules for accessing and transforming that data. Depending on the type of CDI solution, this might involve copying the data—as in the persistent style of CDI—or simply mapping to it, as with the registry style. In any case, step 2 should be considered a design activity for the development that occurs in steps 3 and 4.

Step 3: Integration Design

Integration is the whole ball of wax—it's not just data retrieval. It's not just matching and merging the data in the hub. It's not just identifying the best record. It's all those things and more. Step 3 is when you determine the approach to perform all this work now that the data requirements are well understood.

For instance, decisions about how to pull data off the various data sources will be informed by the sources themselves. The extraction process depends on whether the data source is a flat file, an application system, or a database. Decisions about registry or persistent hub styles are also timely during the integration design step, since this will determine how the data is processed and has data access, usage, and performance implications.

Data matching methods should also be decided on here. We discussed probabilistic versus deterministic matching in Chapter 4. There are pros and cons for each type.

There are choices to make about how the system interfaces to the applications, and what the application interface will be. The most common method is a Web services interface, which we'll discuss more in Chapter 7. There are other decisions to make during the integration design step, some of which will tie to the existing technology infrastructure and decisions about data conversion so that it can be matched and merged to arrive at a harmonized customer record.

Step 4: Integration Development

Step 4 dictates how to change the data representation to match the CDI standards. It also applies the rules defined in step 1 to know how to get and match data from multiple locations, and how to evaluate the best source in the case of multiple data sources. Defining data integration rules can be broken down into defining business rules and data conversion methods to identify and transform the appropriate source data. The functional requirements may have pointed out the different variations of "new customer." For instance, the authoritative customer address might come from the company's billing system once the customer has paid, not the CRM system. In step 4 a CDI developer defines, often through a scripting language, the transformation, cleansing, and deduplication rules that will be applied during CDI processing.

Step 5: Verify and Validate the CDI Output

Once the rules have been established—or, depending on the CDI tool, the appropriate statistical algorithms have been chosen—the data should be subjected to metrics in order to certify that the incoming data is accurate. Measurement usually includes determining if the data adheres to the data acceptance and certification criteria. This ensures that the new CDI data will be useful to the client application.

Step 5 ensures that the data is an accurate reflection of the context for usage defined during functional requirements. This involves a formal data acceptance process with a data steward responsible for defining the rules of acceptance. This is an initially challenging job that gets easier with time.

Step 6: Deploy the CDI Solution

Step 5 ensures that business users agree to the record content before the CDI system is enabled in step 6. Your initial CDI client application should be able to link to the CDI system and pull its customer data.

WHAT WORKS: TIPS FROM THE EXPERTS

Scott Sullivan: Deliver Value Quickly

"We did a lot of work quickly, which meant not soliciting a lot of business input up front. We followed more of an iterative prototyping approach to data deployment. We delivered some information, then got feedback, and then did it again. This helped our salespeople figure out what they really wanted—they'd come back to us and ask for additional data or summary-level information—and we'd give them what they needed."

SCOTT SULLIVAN, Vice President of Information Technology and Services, Pitt Ohio Express

---

Mantra of Measurement

You never know who you're going to meet at a conference luncheon, but in our case it was an attendee who, tray in hand, joined us at a large communal table. As we dined, Joe—a former consultant who was now working at an insurance firm—told us about his recent success with a CRM project. "We started with 15 seats," he said, "and now we're up to 250!"

Joe clearly knew about the struggle for CRM adoption. But as we chatted it became clear that—despite its widespread deployment—Joe's CRM project was in trouble. We coaxed him into describing what made his company adopt CRM in the first place, listening to his lamentations about implementation speed and the number of users clamoring for the tool.

Joe's company had failed to establish what "success" meant. And the ability to articulate and measure success is one of the pillars of any development best practice.

CDI success measurement can be fairly complex and time consuming, two truths that tempt managers to skip the step. It often begins as a formal activity in which the company's customer-focused strategies are deconstructed into a set of initiatives, each of which has its own list of quantifiable success criteria. The basic rule of thumb is the ability to finish the sentence:

"We'll know this CDI project is a success when it . . ."

The answers will vary with the type of project and the company's objectives.

"We do extensive testing and measurement," says Jack Garzella, vice president of IT operations for Overstock.com. To the extent that one can be an Internet marketing veteran, Garzella is right up there, having worked at marketing giant Matchlogic, as well as database vendors Teradata and Oracle. In using integrated customer data for customer segmentation and target marketing for Overstock, Garzella's team discovered that improvements couldn't be measured in a vacuum. "With some of our online personalization efforts, we discovered we were improving revenues but we were also increasing opt-out rates. We realized we had to be really specific about what we were measuring—we couldn't just focus on 'opens and clicks.'"

Sample CDI success metrics might be:

- "Eliminates homegrown extract files that support operational reporting."
- "Allows us to support newly introduced customer records obtained via recent mergers."
- "Decreases the rate of product sales cannibalization across our sales teams."

We remind clients to continue soliciting the "desired business outcome." While our new friend Joe's outcome—the number of CRM software installations—was indeed quantifiable, it wasn't desirable: it didn't translate into business success. In fact, there are five common mistakes companies make when establishing project success measures:

1. **Creating measures without defining requirements.** Establishing what business problem needs to be solved, then outlining the measurements that will ensure the solution is effective, is the right order of things.

2. **One-time-only measurement.** CDI success measurement should be continuous. Indeed, it should be operationalized. Metrics such as up time, response time, and concurrent usage should be measured and reported, ideally every day. Each individual CDI deployment—and there will be iterations—should be subject to regular and rigorous measurements around functionality, data quality, and timeliness.

3. **Measuring at 35,000 feet.** General improvement goals such as "happier customers" are too high level and subjective to be meaningful. CDI success measurement should be performed at the level of the project, not the strategy.

4. **Overemphasis on cost cutting.** Saving money may be a great incentive to start CDI—the metric of recouping costs is a common one—but there should be accompanying business improvements. Ultimately, development costs for CDI will be reduced as more applications leverage the hub, but those savings won't be visible with the first or second release of CDI. For CDI, cost savings should be seen as a perk, not an incentive.

5. **Failing to drive postmeasurement improvement.** Companies should acknowledge the results of their measurement efforts—for instance, manual data quality error fixes decreased by an additional 2 percent—and aim for bigger improvements.

Failure to establish and continually measure CDI results risks lack of discernable business improvements, overinvestment in CDI development, or—as we suspect will be the case for our new friend Joe—growing disaffection of business sponsors. Our advice to Joe is our advice to everyone: measure now, and measure often!

"One thing I'll say is this has definitely strengthened our relationship with the business," says Sun's Jeff Monica by way of explaining the success of the company's entry into CDI. Monica and his team at Sun have undertaken a project to not only cleanse and standardize customer data, but to provide the "best record" of the customer to the company's business functions, including marketing.

"Our marketing group had some clear requirements," Monica explains. "They were basically leading the charge for North America when it came to sending out customer mailings and Sun collateral. By cleaning up customer data and generating the 'best record,' we were able to help marketing get better match rates and assign accurate Dun & Bradstreet numbers. This has helped them target their mailings and messages. They've had a much higher hit rate."

Monica and his team began their CDI effort as part of StorageTek, which Sun acquired in 2005. They have not only delivered important best-record functionality, they convinced the business side to take ownership of its data. "It wasn't easy, but we've helped incorporate data quality into daily line of business job roles," he says. "It's counterintuitive. Our businesspeople don't understand what CDI is and really don't care. They just want their information, and they want it to be accurate. And they're willing to participate in that."

Like many CDI early adopters, Monica knew enough to encourage measurement not only from a business perspective—the initial CDI effort delivered a 30 percent reduction in returned mail—but also in development. In order for them to measure their workload and ensure positive results, they measure five key areas:

1. The number of new business rules that have been established. This ensures the continuous refinement of data over time.

2. Quality improvements in the data.

3. How many customer records were successfully consolidated. ("There are lots of different 'IBM's," Monica explains.)

4. The number of records for which a Dun & Bradstreet number was successfully assigned.

5. The percentage of revenue represented. "Marketing really doesn't care about the number of records we've processed. It's about the overall revenue those customers represent."

Even so, the rate of record consolidation has gone from 52 percent to 76 percent, and the Dun & Bradstreet match rate has increased from 22 percent to an astounding 77 percent. The resulting revenue increase from matched records has reached 91 percent.

The goal of delivering the best customer record to an organization as far-reaching as StorageTek was ambitious enough. The Sun acquisition has driven a new priority: full global integration between the companies.

And other organizations within Sun are noticing. The company's customer service organization would like to understand the correlation between customer satisfaction and other data attributes. And the global accounts group, which handles the care and feeding of Sun's top 25 "gold" accounts, has also engaged Monica and his team. But Monica has his sights set on improving customer relationships on a broader scale.

"Sun is a $12 billion company," he says. "There are real opportunities to leverage what we built at StorageTek and take this forward to real-time cleansing and standardization on a more global scale. If you're going to generate the best record for the customer, you might as well do that for the company at large. It could have a huge business impact."

When asked what he's learned at the helm of such a strategic effort, Jeff Monica is modest. "I have to keep reminding myself and my team that this is new. The companies that have pioneered CDI have gotten a lot done really quickly. Getting data standards agreed to across the company has been a challenge. We'll make mistakes, but we've made amazing progress."

CHANGE MANAGEMENT FOR CDI

Mark Twain once said, "I'm all for progress. It's change I don't like."

It's important to understand that CDI involves a continuous set of practices to refine and maintain the data. It also involves rigorous steps for changes that can occur at one of three different levels:

1. The application might need new data that's not currently in the CDI hub. This usually occurs when a new business requirement is introduced.

2. The CDI hub might change the way it identifies a particular data element, forcing the client application to change.

3. The source system might change, leading to a change in incoming data.

Change management is a critical practice for CDI. Successful CDI projects incorporate the knowledge that systems and their data are constantly in flux; hence, plans to support these changes are critical. CDI development teams need to constantly communicate with source system data stewards to understand the changes that may be affecting the data in advance. The following list exemplifies the most common types of data changes:

-   The source system might add new data fields.
-   The source system may repurpose existing data fields.
-   The source system application processing logic might change.
-   There could be new transaction types.

Change management for CDI needs to be both reactive and proactive. The CDI development team members should ideally attend the source system team's change control meetings to understand upcoming source system changes. (They need to communicate their data changes as well.) The CDI developers should coordinate scheduled enhancements to the CDI hub via release management so that existing applications are ready for the changes. CDI developers thus should be prepared for changes as well as communicate them to other development teams.

Since every element in the CDI hub needs to be managed, understanding which data isn't being used or accessed can lead to decisions about which data should stay in the hub. Data should also be consistently profiled so that the data steward can monitor data quality and prevent the root causes of data decay.

In achieving a true unified customer view, a company is essentially developing a new operational system—one that offers the most current, updated customer content for a moment in time. This means low-latency, highly available data open to any number of other systems across the firm.

If this sounds like an operational system, it is. CDI isn't a reporting engine as much as it is a data provisioning system. How customer data is used by other systems is determined by the CDI client application or the overarching business need.

MANAGER DO'S AND DON'TS

Before you embark on project planning for CDI or begin talking to vendors about their CDI solutions, consider these do's and don'ts:

- **Do** identify a single candidate application. This approach enforces scope of effort and renders requirements more straightforward, since the necessary functionality is already well understood. Take a look at your company's IT development pipeline for the next 6 to 12 months. Perhaps there's an opportunity to use the CDI hub as the de-facto customer data source for an upcoming application. By choosing an application that's been scheduled for development, CDI functions can be "baked in" to the necessary data provisioning. If no new applications look like good candidates, choose an existing application that's having trouble getting or providing integrated customer data. By identifying a single application for CDI to support, you're delimiting requirements and avoiding scope creep.

- **Don't** take on a business-critical system. Enabling a call center system to hit the CDI hub on the first try might risk existing customer relationships. We recently recommended that one client begin its CDI prototype by providing integrated customer data to a monthly revenue report that relied on specialized extracts from the operational order system. By getting the data from the CDI hub instead, the company could eliminate the custom extract programs that required support and ongoing maintenance. This also mitigated the risk involved, since if there were problems with the CDI system, the report users could go back to the existing extract program.

- **Do** leverage your IT department's existing skills. It's likely that your IT folks already have expertise with enterprise application integration (EAI); publish-and-subscribe; and extraction, transformation, and loading (ETL) development techniques, to name a few. As we'll see in the next several chapters, these skills can come in handy when it comes to the knowledge necessary to implement CDI.

- **Don't** take your eye off the data timeliness issue. CDI isn't about copying data; it's about the transactional movement of that data. Hence, other development methods might not emphasize the functional or workflow requirements inherent in CDI implementations. Part of functional requirements is understanding the flow of data and its processing within and across operational systems so that the "whens" of access are as important as the "hows."

ENDNOTES

1. Robert S. Kaplan and David P. Norton, Strategy Maps (Boston: Harvard Business School Press, 2004).
2. Robert S. Kaplan and David P. Norton, The Strategy-Focused Organization (Boston: Harvard Business School Press, 2001).

CHAPTER 6

Who Owns the Data Anyway?: Data Governance, Data Management, and Data Stewardship

In Chapter 4 we discussed how data governance was bigger than customer data integration (CDI). Data governance is the organizing framework for establishing strategy, objectives, and policies for corporate data. It pervades the enterprise, crossing lines of business, data subject areas, and individual skill sets—but so does CDI. The difference is that while you can—and should—have data governance without CDI, the inverse isn't sustainable. We've written this chapter because we have clients for whom establishing a clear data governance framework is a meaningful and necessary step toward CDI implementation.

Ironically, we're asked regularly by CDI vendors if we would mind calling their prospects and introducing ourselves and our data management services. It seems that many companies recognize the need for CDI, and yet they postpone CDI adoption because their data is such a mess, no one knows where the expertise lies, or data ownership issues are fuzzy. This chapter presents a workable framework that you can adopt and use in your own organization as a foundation for a more formalized and sustained data management effort. Practicing some of the tenets we discuss here eliminates some of the well-worn excuses for not delivering integrated data. ■

STURM UND DRANG OF DATA OWNERSHIP

It's the single most prevalent question we hear from our clients, prospects, and conference audiences: "Who in the company should own the data?" Moreover, when we ask people about who owns the data in their companies, the answers are tentative, as if the respondent had never considered the question. However, the lack of a clear, concise answer to the question of corporate data ownership has daily consequences. Consider these three scenarios:

1. The marketing organization at an automobile company won't share its data. With anyone. Ever. The data mart contains important strategic information like the customer segments who responded most frequently to high-profile campaigns and what the return on marketing costs were. The product design organization would like to see the data as they target certain demographics for new model features. But marketing won't budge.

2. An international bank we work with recently assembled a compliance SWAT team to examine the various operational systems that could provide loan data for support of Basel II. (Basel II regulation dictates that financial services companies must understand and communicate their corporate exposure when they make loans to certain parties.) The company's loan origination was homegrown and had been in place for almost 20 years. It contained proprietary codes without supplementary definitions, requiring a team of highly specialized programmers to routinely maintain it. Unfortunately, this group of specialists didn't have the time or extra resources to help the SWAT team decipher the proprietary codes.

3. The sales team at a semiconductor development company has a rich database of customer contact information. But the salespeople

are stonewalling. They don't want to share their contacts with any-one, especially customer service, which was recently transformed from a cost center to a revenue center. "Once a CSR gets the names at my accounts and starts dialin' for dollars," a sales manager told us, "there go all my commissions." Consequently, he and his colleagues are uploading their contacts less frequently to the cor-porate server as their laptop spreadsheets become richer with cus-tomer detail.

The phenomenon of data hoarding is pervasive at most companies. People won't avail their data to a larger audience for fear that they will have to be ac-countable for fixing it or, by extension, be account-able for the decisions they've made based on data that's essentially inaccurate. Business organizations,

> *The phenomenon of data hoarding is pervasive at most companies.*

already overwhelmed by their data volumes, see sharing data as a hindrance to getting important work done. It slows them down. More insidiously, some embrace the philosophy that "knowledge is power" and consider their data as political capital.

And some organizations haven't been staffed sufficiently to maintain the data. They don't have the resources to support the sharing, management, and correction of the data. As we'll discuss again in this chapter, data stew-ardship costs money.

This is certainly a barrier to CDI and master data management (MDM) projects, since you can truly manage only data you can access. However, underneath the "we can't get the data" issues is a cultural awareness of the impact of information on the business's bottom line.

The challenge is to stop thinking about data in the way we've been thinking about it. The flow of data is not linear—out of one system and into another—as we explained in our discussion of the corporate data sup-ply chain in Chapter 1. Data flows across systems, often multiple times. And the administration of data is not an isolated function, confined to applications or individuals within various departments who are responsible for looking at a small but redundant subset of a company's data through a tiny colored lens. The challenge is to start thinking about and treating data as a corporate asset.

THE TRUTH ABOUT MANAGING
DATA AS AN ASSET

Nowhere is this truer than with customer data. Indeed, our esteemed Foreword writers, Don Peppers and Martha Rogers, have advocated that customers themselves should be considered assets to a company.[1]

It's helpful to consider the definition of the word *asset* here. Webster's defines an asset as "a valuable item that is owned," but in general an asset has four qualities:

1. It has value.
2. Its value can be quantified.
3. It helps a company achieve one or more of its strategies.
4. There is an awareness of the asset's importance among company management and employees.

For example, a retailer's inventory is usually considered an asset. A bottle of shampoo on the shelf has value—the retailer has paid for it and a customer will hopefully buy it. The shampoo's value can be quantified, since it has a cost and a purchase price. And the shampoo can definitely help the retailer fulfill its strategy of generating revenue. Other examples of corporate assets include a company's stock, its fleet, its cash, its knowledge, and its real estate.

If a company believes its customers are indeed assets, information about them should likewise have value. And it does. Many companies have quantified the value of their data in different terms, but most often:

- The data's contribution to revenues and profits
- The data's role in enabling efficiencies and cutting costs
- The opportunity cost of not having the data

It's not hard convincing executives that data is an asset. In fact, many already use that vocabulary when describing success factors of critical projects. But it's a bit more challenging to get executives to step up to the plate and invest in their data asset. Sometimes if we're friendly enough with a chief information officer (CIO), we try the following test. We ask her if she considers her data to be a corporate asset. Most of the time she'll agree that data is indeed a corporate asset because "it's very important to our business."

We then ask, "Does that mean that you're investing in data proportional to your other corporate assets?" You can usually cut the silence with a knife.

Here is a sobering exercise to share with your executives, preferably your CIO. Give the CIO 2 points for every "Yes" answer, 0 points for every "No" answer, and −1 point for every "I don't know."

Is the company giving data the resources comparable to your
   other corporate assets?   _____

Are you dedicating technology to data comparable to your other
   corporate assets?   _____

Relatively speaking, is the funding you're allocating to data equal
   to the funding of your other corporate assets?   _____

Do you measure the cost of poor, missing, and inaccurate
   data?   _____

Do you understand (or have you quantified) the opportunity
   cost(s) of not delivering data to the business when it's needed?   _____

The issue of investing in data is an interesting one, since many executives immediately go to their comfort zones and begin discussing head count. The assumption is that the company is already investing in data since it employs some data modelers and database administrators. However, as important as the people issues are, there are organizational and cultural changes likely if management is serious about sustaining data governance.

The fifth point on the list is one that gets executives to stop and take note, since many companies have made serious investments in strategic projects only to see them scrapped for lack of good or available data. This was the case a few years ago with customer relationship management (CRM). At one time, most executives and CRM project managers considered data as an implementation afterthought only to discover that delivering key CRM functionality would be impossible without customer data that was clean, consistent, and useable. The resulting botched cross-selling campaigns, overcommunicated marketing messages, customer churn, and abandoned shopping carts cost companies tens of millions of dollars. The opportunity cost of nonintegrated or dirty data can be staggering.

By way of scoring the above test, any score below 6 usually indicates trouble with information, and that trouble is likely due more to issues of poor data-enabling processes or political and ownership issues than it is due to the lack of technology. In fact, these problems are so rampant that we recommend avoiding a foolhardy career move and taking the test yourself before giving it to your CIO.

A CASE FOR DATA GOVERNANCE

If data were just an information technology (IT) concern it would be simpler to manage. But data is inextricably linked to the business, and thus needs to be defined, cleansed, integrated, and deployed. The hard part is carving out the processes and policies to ensure that all critical data is managed correctly and consistently.

Recall in Chapter 4 that we introduced data governance as a subset of IT governance. This is because data governance is frequently launched under the auspices of a larger, IT governance structure. IT governance is a more overarching set of processes that administer the use of IT assets to maximize business benefits. In their book *IT Governance*, Weil and Ross define IT governance as "specifying the decision rights and accountability framework to encourage desirable behavior in using IT" and pair it with the governance of information.[2] IT governance is, of course, broader and more complex than data governance. But they share principles of formulating policies and convening cross-functional teams from both business and IT. Both focus on resolving conflicts around the sharing and usage of their respective assets, and both aim to leverage the asset in the best way possible. The IT governance body usually deals with overarching issues such as the approval of business cases for strategic IT projects, prioritization of new projects, decisions about capital expenditures, and general funding issues.

However, data governance can exist apart from IT governance or can exist independently where no IT governance structure exists. We've seen several circumstances where an effective data governance process serves as the basis for a broader IT governance effort. Both IT and data governance ultimately scale to the size and complexity of their respective assets.

The Boston Consulting Group has defined *good governance* as "making optimal decisions about what to pursue and how to pursue it."[3] In its general definition, governance occurs at the highest level of the organization to ensure oversight, compliance, and risk management of a company's key assets—namely, money, people, and data. The goal of data governance is to establish and maintain a corporate-wide agenda for data, one of joint decision making and collaboration for the good of the corporation rather than individuals or departments, and one of balancing business innovation and flexibility with IT standards and efficiencies.

The concept of data governance has emerged to circumscribe the centralized and enterprise-level oversight of corporate data as an asset, establishing the policies and procedures necessary to direct the management of the data. Data governance ensures that the right people in the organization are involved in determining the standardization, integration, and proper usage of the data across projects, subject areas, and lines of business.

It's important to distinguish between "governance" and "management." Governance is high-level oversight—the "who" and the "why." Management is the day-to-day execution of the governance policies. Your accountant might help you manage your money but won't "govern" it. Likewise, data modelers and data stewards help manage data, but might only participate in its overall governance. Exhibit 6.1 illustrates how data governance and data management relate.

Few companies have succeeded by managing data under the radar. Those that have did so by convincing business stakeholders to participate in defining requirements for their data, and quietly incorporating data design and integration activities

> The goal of data governance is to establish and maintain a corporate-wide agenda for data, one of joint decision making and collaboration for the good of the corporation rather than individuals or departments, and one of balancing business innovation and flexibility with IT standards and efficiencies.

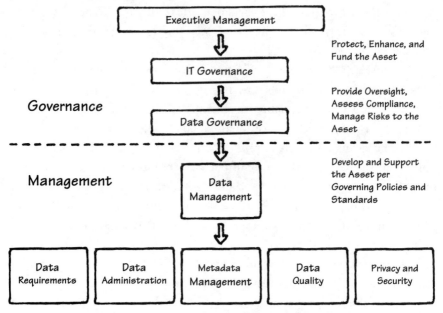

EXHIBIT 6.1   Data Governance and Data Management

into their development projects. Typically, these companies have IT and business employees whose full-time jobs have nothing to do with data, but who understand data's importance to their business strategies.

The vast majority, however, continue to struggle to understand, scope, and fund data-specific work and job roles—often redundantly. The common complaints tend to be:

- "Our executives are just tired of hearing about the data problem."
- "IT says I'm their data steward, but they won't support my requested changes."
- "IT refuses to address or acknowledge the problem."
- "We don't need data management—all our data's in our enterprise resource planning (ERP) system."
- "Isn't our data warehouse the single version of the truth?"
- "The application systems own the data and they change it to suit their needs."

- "I've been asking IT to fix our data for five years—they say they don't have the time or budget."
- "Sorry, management thinks this has been fixed."
- "Everyone's too busy."
- "Wasn't the CRM tool supposed to do that?"

Of course, heeding such excuses is fraught with risk, since it is often a smokescreen for not knowing where to begin. Companies that manage data on a reactive and ad-hoc basis spend more money and erode productivity through repeated work efforts, redundant technology platforms, duplicate data, and general overinvestment than companies that have institutionalized their data governance and management functions.

For example, in the old days, grocery stores reordered the product when

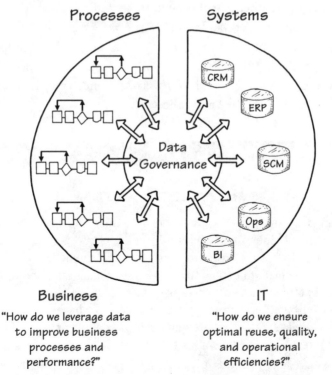

EXHIBIT 6.2   Data Governance Touches Both Business and IT

it sold out. The reorder was likely done by the store manager—every store did this independently. The problem was that the order process was guesswork. It wasn't uncommon for some stores to overorder some goods while others ran out. To solve this problem, grocers centralized the management of store inventory using technology to track asset depletion and movement.

Likewise, part of the charter of the data governance body, which we'll call the data governance council, is to ensure the reuse of the data asset across diverse lines of business, divisions, systems, and business processes. This means that the data governance council should be comprised of businesspeople—ideally owners or experts of specific business processes—and IT managers, who are also given authority to make decisions about data. Exhibit 6.2 illustrates the way data governance touches both business and IT functions, and vice versa.

Data governance begins with the organization. Although we argue that data is a corporate asset, we also need to be realistic about the viability of that from a management standpoint. Corporate executives will usually give more time and attention to the governance of financial and property assets than to IT or data. Although data should be treated as an asset, it's actually even more important to establish governance mechanisms to ensure that data policies are established and followed.

WHAT WORKS: TIPS FROM THE EXPERTS

John Walker: "Get close to the business."

"I would tell developers who are close to their data to get close to the business. Spend time with business users and get a good understanding of what they want to do so that you can deliver quick wins. We started small, targeting our right party contact rate, and drove incremental revenue from there. It's easier to make the CDI business case like that. If you go to an exec and say, 'We have bad data,' his eyes will glaze over. If you tell him you can deliver $500K in incremental revenue, you'll have his full attention."

JOHN WALKER, Associate Director, Customer Insights and Analysis, Bell Mobility

Evolution and Justification of Data Management

Executives recognized that isolated technology platforms were inefficient as far back as the 1970s, as IT was becoming a business function in its own right. They learned that when they allowed different business areas to own and manage their own systems, costs became exorbitant. The result was redundant systems, duplicate storage, and inconsistent support strategies. Every group invented their own policies to deal with business continuity, IT purchases, security, and standards. The costs of managing disparate IT assets became expensive and the work efforts were cumbersome.

The decision to standardize and consolidate these assets soon followed. IT executives realized that by forming a discrete organization to manage the technology platforms for the company—usually via the creation of a separate operations group—they could maintain their assets as a shared resource. Moreover, they could enforce a set of platform standards and make them available to a range of different development efforts.

The key to the success of these centralized standards was that any changes or modifications couldn't affect the usage of that asset. For instance, when IBM introduced a newer, higher-powered Unix platform, many IBM customers consolidated their myriad small servers onto one large platform, thereby saving money on software licenses while ensuring that business usage was unaffected.

Centralizing the management of IT assets alleviated application developers from having to manage and maintain technology platforms—the asset—and allowed them to focus on their real jobs. Operations organizations dealt with capacity planning, installations, upgrades, and access. Centralized operations gave application development teams the freedom to focus on their core responsibilities.

The analogy of consolidated IT platform management is an apt one for data management. Without integrated customer detail, each individual system or application must manage and integrate data independently from different sources. This means different value representations across systems, duplicated or conflicting data hygiene methods and rules, and overlapping data integration processes. This is why reports coming from different systems never match: because standard data processes aren't formalized and consistent. Data management comprises the day-to-day operational tasks involved in defining, creating, designing, maintaining, and deploying the data. Data management can also be an organizational function that enforces the policies and procedures established in data governance.

ORGANIZING AROUND DATA

Once we've established that data is an asset that needs to be managed and maintained, the natural question most of our clients have next is: "Who?" We recommend establishing a separate organization to manage data. This will ensure that data is shared across the enterprise, with stakeholdership from both IT and the business, undistorted by specific, functional perspectives. Data management as an organizational function participates in the prescriptions of data governance while incorporating the tactical job roles around day-to-day data issues.

> As they say in Texas, if you're drilling for oil, it's better to dig a 100-foot well than to dig 100 one-foot wells.

As they say in Texas, if you're drilling for oil, it's better to dig a 100-foot well than to dig 100 one-foot wells. Establishing a centralized data management organization and putting formal processes is master data management writ corporate-wide, and enforces data administration, requirements definition, standardization, cleansing, and maintenance across all data, not individual applications multiple times.

Launching the Data Governance Council

It's important to note that data governance can work regardless of whether there's a formal IT governance infrastructure in place. The features of an effective data governance council are:

- **Its members come from multiple organizations from both IT and business areas.** This is often the most difficult to enforce, since potential council members need to be convinced that participating on the council is worth their time.
- **It meets on a regular basis.** The data governance council is an ongoing function because the business is constantly changing, and so

is its need for data. As such, the governance council should meet to discuss new and emerging business programs, as well as current IT activities and their effect on data. How regularly the council meets depends on the size of the company, the breadth of the IT organization, and the number of departments involved. Many data governance councils meet quarterly and maintain procedures for convening more frequently when an issue can't wait.

- **Key lines of business are represented.** This ensures economies of scale. For instance, if a new customer loyalty program has been announced and management has approved and funded a new technology, it's imperative that representatives from sales, customer service, marketing, and product management participate in the data governance council since the data will be shared across these, and potentially other, functions.

- **There is a list of sanctioned standards that serve as operating principles.** These standards represent mechanisms for tie-breaking in cases where there are competing projects or different agendas, and may include investment approval metrics, new hire versus consultant considerations, project status reporting guidelines, and exception policies.

- **The council communicates upward.** The data governance council should have regular interaction with executive management as well as exposure to corporate governance when appropriate. The data governance council at an insurance company recently attended the IT governance board meeting en masse in order to deliver a presentation outlining the company's data management and integration challenges and make a pitch for CDI. The data governance council representatives wanted a show of force to cement the point that data quality was a cross-functional issue.

- **The council manages downward.** Data stewards, project managers, businesspeople not typically on the council, and other such ancillary stakeholders should be invited to attend council meetings, particularly if they need to present new business requirements or provide status updates for critical, data-enabled projects. Application development teams are responsible for adhering to the data gover-

Data Governance Council Charter

The data governance council has seven objectives:

1. To provide common processes and policies for information on behalf of the company.
2. To enforce the adoption of data standards on every IT project.
3. To guide the management of master data across subject areas.
4. To reduce scrap and rework associated with poor, missing, inaccurate, unavailable, or hard-to-find data, and to measure that reduction.
5. To be accountable for the ongoing improvement of the quality and value of the corporate data asset.
6. To support individual project teams in the access and use of common corporate data.
7. To establish a common vacabulary and culture around the deployment of company data.

EXHIBIT 6.3   Data Governance Council Charter

nance council's policies. The council should have an effective means of communicating its decisions to development teams across the enterprise.

Of course, with such an ambitious list of responsibilities, the data governance council should have a charter that communicates its focus and goals. The data governance council is, after all, a decision-making body and, as such, should circumscribe its boundaries and authority.

Exhibit 6.3 shows the charter for one data governance council we helped form at a high-technology firm. A data governance charter is the umbrella under which policies are developed, delineating the data governance council's role relative to daily functional project oversight or tactical data management activities. It decides meeting agendas and discussion topics, ensuring that the data governance council meetings are structured, with a well-defined set of topics and discussions. The data governance council meeting is often a company's only means of building understanding and a level of consensus on important data-related issues, and should thus be run efficiently and scoped appropriately.

Indeed, as author Patrick Lencioni contends in his best-selling book *Death by Meeting*, meetings are unpopular with most people because they lack contextual structure. Lencioni advocates the idea of having "multiple types of meetings,"—for instance, the IT governance board and the data governance council meet separately, and have different agendas—to avoid the all-too-common problem of participants not knowing "whether they're supposed to be debating, voting, brainstorming, weighing in, or just listening."[4] Having a council charter, along with crisp and well-planned meeting agendas, helps alleviate this problem, thus discouraging the randomness and grandstanding common to meetings focused on enterprise-wide ownership and standards issues.

The charter in Exhibit 6.3 implies that someone is in charge of the data governance council. It's difficult to assign a specific role or job title, since so much depends on the authority and specific expertise of individuals within a company. However, in general, the data governance council should have an assigned chairperson who:

- Is also a member of the IT governance board or participates in high-level IT planning and direction setting
- Understands why data issues involve discrete processes and skills
- Has the authority and clout to represent data issues to the IT governance board and to senior management, if necessary
- Understands data's impact and value to business users and their organizations
- Has deep expertise in an enterprise-wide business process, ideally as a subject matter expert on the business side
- Is willing to advocate the importance of data—particularly the formalization of data definition and implementation processes—across the enterprise

The data governance council chairperson is ideally more than just an advocate—he or she is an activist on behalf of corporate data.

The scope and reporting structure of the chairperson depends on the size of the organization. At a small catalog retailer we work with, it's the CIO. At a large insurance firm, it's the director of claims. The claims director has worked at the company for 13 years and has an intimate knowledge of the company's key data sources, the data subject areas, problem data, and the history of data usage throughout his tenure at the firm. He also has bulletproof credibility with executives. Ideally, this person will be the company's appointed data czar, a position we'll describe later in this chapter.

One of the data governance council's main responsibilities is to track the data necessary to enable business processes. While one could argue that *every* business process in a company needs data, the data governance council should focus on those processes that:

- Are creating new data needed by more than one function or application
- Are integrating disparate data for the first time
- Track back to the company's major strategic programs
- Involve data infrastructure

No wonder the data governance council and CDI are so symbiotic!

CASE STUDY: CHECKFREE

When CheckFree Corporation won The Data Warehousing Institute's Best Practice Leadership award in 2005—beating out over 80 other companies across industries and market segments—Kevin McDearis and Bedeke Cresci took the victory in stride. After all, as part of a financial electronic commerce company that owns the lion's share of the rapidly growing online bill payment market, they still had much to do to support ongoing innovation and process enhancements.

Since joining the company in 1994, McDearis, CIO of CheckFree's software division, has helped create a framework that defines how the firm's various business divisions interoperate. Known as CheckFree's enterprise model, the framework circumscribes the company's high-level business processes, from strategic planning through CRM, serving as a touchstone for business process interrelationships across the firm. "Business processes create and consume data. They have owners," McDearis explains. "It just makes sense that business processes should drive everything. So we define the business processes first, understand the data that supports those processes, and then engineer the applications."

Such rigor isn't unusual for a company that emphasizes peak performance and has institutionalized Six Sigma as a company-wide standard. CheckFree's vocabulary of quality and metrics pervades even the most tactical IT development discussions. What was new for McDearis and his team was establishing a data governance body—the trustee council—to ensure consistent management of information across business processes, departments, and projects.

Comprised of executives at the director or vice president level across both business and IT, the trustee council provides the checks and balances for enterprise data. Bedeke Cresci, director of information services, helped develop the trustee council and serves as one of its leaders. Cresci and his team were careful to delineate the various roles and responsibilities before introducing the concept. The three core roles on the council are trustees, data stewards, and subject matter experts (SMEs).

Trustees appoint data stewards and SMEs to represent their business areas. The data stewards are responsible for managing the data created by their respective business processes, including its definition, quality, metadata, and security standards. SMEs monitor the specific data requirements and quality needs of assigned business areas, periodically measuring the business impact of new and refined data. With one or more members from each process area, the Trustee Council could be considered the corporate "owners" of CheckFree data, but Cresci sees it differently.

"We stay away from the term *owner,*" he explains. "We prefer the term *steward,* which conveys responsibility. Ultimately, our data stewards are accountable to the rest of the organization to ensure that the data meets business needs."

McDearis and Cresci acknowledge that data stewards don't just belong on the business side, and are appointing technical data stewards as well. "If you have the business agreeing on the definition of *customer* and then throwing a requirements document over the fence, it makes it really hard for developers to build an effective solution," Cresci maintains. "You still need people on the IT side to ensure business needs are consistently and accurately supported. There's a lot of behind-the-scenes data work that might not directly involve the business, but that adds value."

From its inception in 1981, CheckFree has encouraged innovation and entrepreneurship. Unlike many data governance efforts that begin with blustery executive speeches and theoretical value propositions, CheckFree's trustee council launched in the context of a real-life project.

"At CheckFree, we are encouraged to test concepts as part of new or existing projects," says Cresci. CheckFree happened to be under way with a complex operational CRM project, known as ROME: Road to Operational Maturity and Excellence. "ROME needed to support an integrated source for customer data, so we were able to test how we defined *customer* and the associated business rules within the project," says Cresci. We socialized the concept of data stewardship from the beginning. ROME gave us an initial opportunity to create formal processes around data management and governance."

McDearis continuously stresses the linkage between data stewardship and business processes. "Data steward accountability is determined by the specific business process that created the data. For example, a new customer will be enrolled by the customer acquisition process, so the owner of that business process is responsible for checking and approving that data." This process-driven approach to data governance gives CheckFree a built-in way to measure the effectiveness of data stewardship. For a company immersed in Six Sigma, it only made sense to measure data improvements over time.

"We'll be formalizing data quality into our corporate Six Sigma measurement," says Cresci. "Eventually data quality will be measured and added to the metrics to which the entire company holds itself accountable."

"We've proven time after time that people don't care about what you don't measure," McDearis adds. "We are where we are today because we've measured progress."

Both Cresci and McDearis acknowledge that the trustee council is a work in progress, but it's already paid off. "We're increasingly meeting our vision of being 'data driven, customer focused, and process-centric,'" says McDearis. "And when you're in the business of moving people's money, there's zero tolerance for error."

MDM Organization

While the data governance council is the authoritative body for data policy, your company should also have a separate data management organiza-

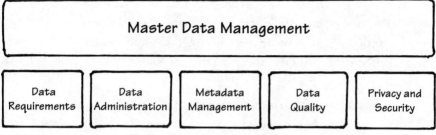

EXHIBIT 6.4   Master Data Management Functions

tion to handle the day-to-day administration of its master data. To date, most of what's been written about functional roles of managing data includes the strong and overarching recommendation to introduce the role of data steward into the organization. However, data stewardship can mean many different things. Ideally, data should be managed based on the various categories of master data. Likewise, data stewards should be assigned at the level of the master data subject area. This ensures ongoing subject matter expertise and evolving intimacy with detailed data elements.

Exhibit 6.4 illustrates the major functions involved in an MDM organization. Let's define each of these functions so we can then delineate the job roles within them.

- **Data requirements.** We discussed data requirements in Chapter 5 in terms of their importance to CDI. But at a more general corporate level, data requirements should be part of the overarching business analysis and requirements definition work that usually occurs with each individual development activity. In the case of data management, data requirements definition should be offered as a service to projects for which data is a critical component.

> *Ideally, data should be managed based on the various categories of master data.*

- **Data administration.** Data administration focuses on understanding and inventorying the data at the enterprise level and defining standard terminology and representation for that data. This includes working with source system owners or data stewards to profile and correct data, as well as develop logical models of key data subject areas. It also involves defining and maintaining the business rules and workflows that may be part of CDI software administration. For smaller organizations, metadata management may be part of this function as well.

- **Metadata management.** Metadata management is about assigning standard definitions to data and maintaining those definitions, often in a centralized dictionary or metadata repository. The team is also responsible for knowing the system origins and locations of data. This usually involves working with system owners and users to understand how the data is used and accessed in order to refine metadata in an ongoing and consistent way. In more advanced organizations that are experienced with MDM, this role can also involve managing a central dictionary of master data that is updated and synchronized via the use of specialized MDM software.

- **Data quality and delivery.** In Chapter 4 we discussed the importance of data quality and the fact that data quality can be both a "global" and a "local" concern. Ideally, your company will establish a centralized data quality function under a larger data management group that established corporate policy and metrics for data quality and enforces them. Such a centralized group can guide the local data quality efforts that may exist in individual departments or on certain projects.

- **Privacy and security.** Having a discrete function dedicated to establishing and enforcing data privacy, protection, and security ensures that there are specific, data-centric policies. While this function shouldn't establish those policies—that should be done at the corporate level—its job is to establish the rules and controls to enforce them. This often means helping to ensure how specific compliance issues are addressed, namely:

  - ○ **Regulatory compliance.** Regulatory compliance issues can be imposed by governmental or legislative bodies. Many, like the Health Insurance Portability and Accountability Act (HIPAA), are industry specific, and others touch multiple industries. For instance, adhering to federal Do Not Call legislation means that data stewards or data security managers collaborate with the data administration group to establish business rules for Do Not Call data and work with developers to ensure that those rules are enforced.

○ **Legal compliance.** Legal compliance helps ensure that a company isn't subject to libel for availing private data. This means preventing unsanctioned access to data, particularly customer records. Often, data security managers establish access and logging rules so that the company can prevent unauthorized access and monitor each time a customer record is queried, and by whom, so that it has an audit trail and can protect itself legally.

○ **Corporate compliance.** Corporate compliance involves helping enforce a company's rules around data access. For instance, employee compensation information should be subject to rules and guidelines about who can view and update it.

Of course, the effectiveness of a data management group is proportional to the clarity of corporate policies and business rules. One of the significant responsibilities of a data management organization is thus interfacing with the business to understand strategic, regulatory, and competitive objectives in order to help formulate those rules.

Like the IT operations department discussed previously, MDM should be leveraged by individual development efforts and be built into a company's standard development methodology. Clearly, a company's system development life-cycle (SDLC) needs to conform to central data management standards and guidelines. This is no different than requiring developers to adhere to coding standards. Ideally, this can be done quickly and seamlessly, becoming second nature for developers who don't themselves have the time or inclination to be data experts.

The MDM organization is responsible for more than just customer data. It should work with all key master data subject areas identified as data assets for the company. Each master data area should be subject to the same methods and techniques across the various data management functions as they're depicted in Exhibit 6.4, but have its own rules, definitions, and workflows depending on data usage, as shown in Exhibit 6.5.

In other words, the MDM function has separate groups of data stewards responsible for ensuring consistency within each data subject area (e.g.,

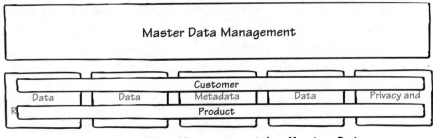

EXHIBIT 6.5   Data Management by Master Data
Subject Area

customer or product). Where CDI is concerned, CDI developers would not be the de-facto customer data stewards, but would be responsible for working with the data management group to understand and conform to steward-established data standards and guidelines prior to and during CDI development. The challenge here is in knowing who's who within the MDM framework and what their jobs are.

Roles and Responsibilities in MDM

Most of our clients start out by having the "who" discussion before the "how" discussion. Assigning staff members to new, data-centric positions would be the easiest way to launch an MDM organization, but it's not the best. We recommend understanding the functions described above, and then understanding the roles necessary to enable those functions. Only then should an MDM group be staffed with skilled individuals.

Exhibit 6.6 lays out what we have seen to be the core responsibilities for a data management group.

You can use the job descriptions in Exhibit 6.6 as a baseline for formalizing these jobs if they don't already exist, and even working with a consultant or your human resources group to build specific job descriptions, staff requisitions, and compensation structures for each one.

It's important to note here that "job role" may mean one person, several people, of even a part-time role. This decision is usually dictated by the size of the company and the number of organizations that are data stakeholders in a master data subject area. For instance, a small catalog company

Job Role	Description	Representative Responsibilities	Skills
Director of data management	Guides the design, delivery, and maintenance of data across both subject areas and projects; defines priorities and ensures that teams are intercommunicating to define both departmental and enterprise data strategies	• Schedule, convene, and lead data governance council meetings • Assign data steward to critical projects and business processes • Prioritize data management functions to leverage reuse and support business strategy • Serve as "secretary" to the data governance council, organizing meetings and providing status updates to IT governance board or other IT advisory committee • Conduct design reviews, data acceptance activities, and CDI prototype demos as necessary	• Leadership and facilitation skills • Consensus building and conflict resolution • Understanding of project management issues; ideally, has experience managing and scheduling program-level activities within IT • Background in a data delivery function such as metadata management or data administration
Business data steward	Functions as the point of accountability for a data subject area or domain on behalf of the business	• Create ongoing business rules for data • Serve as the tie-breaker for business data definitions • Support business analysts in the alignment of business requirements with data requirements	• Excellent written and verbal communication skills • Experienced using data for business decision making • Adept at explaining the need for data in business terms

EXHIBIT 6.6   Roles and Responsibilities for Managing Master Data

Job Role	Description	Representative Responsibilities	Skills
		• Support the metadata administrator in the definition of key data elements • Define data formatting and value representation • Aid the data quality manager in defining data quality, matching, and standardization rules that reflect business usage • Track and determine the need for additional and new data elements for new projects • Determine opportunities for reuse of existing data across projects and lines of business • Act as spokesperson for how business terminology is defined and used across the enterprise	
Business subject matter expert (SME)	A user or manager within a business unit who has deep expertise with a particular application or business process	• Serve as the SME for how data is used in a particular business area • Explain key business processes that use data • Approve resulting CDI data as it is furnished to the business system	• Excellent verbal communications skills • Familiarity with process and workflow concepts

EXHIBIT 6.6   *(Continued)*

Job Role	Description	Representative Responsibilities	Skills
		• Provide mentoring about business processes and requirements to members of the CDI development team and other teams as needed	
Source system data steward	Provides deep knowledge of data as it exists in the operational system or systems that will source CDI, as well as other databases and systems; ideally, there will be one source system data steward for each operational system	• Provide definitions and formats for data in its "raw" form • Deliver common extract files of source system data to various application development teams and explain them • Profile and explain source system details, and identify exceptions and outliers • Work with data quality manager to correct data at the source and instill continuous improvement principles • Explain operational systems processing and the data flows within it • Participate in data governance council meetings to represent data sourcing and transformation efforts	• Familiar with operational system platform and processing • Understanding of data processing flows within transactional systems • Knowledge of data profiling technology and its usage

EXHIBIT 6.6   (*Continued*)

Job Role	Description	Representative Responsibilities	Skills
Business analyst	Serves as the point of contact for understanding business requirements and translating them into data, functional, and technical requirements	• Schedule and facilitate requirements gathering interviews and workshops • Document business requirements for individual line of business projects • Interface with business data stewards to gauge the impact of new business requirements on data	• Excellent meeting facilitation skills • Verbal and written communication skills • An understanding of structured documentation techniques • Experience with knowledge management systems
Data analyst	Profiles data from different sources and determines whether and how data can support business and data requirements	• Determine how to convert and transform the data from the source systems to be useful for CDI • Work with business data steward to identify potential data errors and recommend methods for data correction	• Excellent written and verbal skills • Solid analysis skills to understand data's ability to reflect business requirements and metrics
Data administrator	Delivers standardized data element definitions and descriptions in order to both unify and separate departmental views of data with a goal of data integration; may also roll up and maintain enterprise data model based on individual subject area models	• Track and store data definitions across projects and platforms • May also act as data modeler, creating and maintaining enterprise data model	• Knowledge of modeling conventions for both data (data models) and process (data flow diagrams and process models)

EXHIBIT 6.6   (*Continued*)

Job Role	Description	Representative Responsibilities	Skills
		• May also act as metadata administrator in tracking and recording business definitions of data	
Metadata administrator	Supports the ongoing definition and annotation of business data, and tracks and records those definitions in a managed metadata repository	• Track all business element descriptions • Participate in data requirements gathering • Work with business data steward to ensure reuse of current metadata • Create source to target data mapping • Maintain data definitions and mappings in a metadata repository or library	• Knowledge of data modeling and metadata modeling conventions • Experience managing and tracking data with a metadata repository tool • Understanding of modeling, database, and business terminology
Data security manager	Sets and tracks regulations around data usage across the company	• Establish data security policies • Track company and legal regulations around data usage and availabilities • Formalize and communicate data security policies to application development teams • Work with individual development teams to enforce data security rules • Conduct periodic security audits to ensure compliance	• Excellent written and verbal skills • Knowledge of various data security enforcement protocols and technologies

EXHIBIT 6.6   *(Continued)*

Job Role	Description	Representative Responsibilities	Skills
Data quality manager	Institutionalizes ongoing data quality throughout the company via the standardization of data quality rules and measurements	• Work with business data stewards to establish data quality and business rules • Establish clear and agreed-to data quality metrics, as well as measurement processes and time frames • Define data cleansing and standardization processes • Work with source system data stewards to profile source system data and fix data errors at the point of origin • Represent data quality in data governance council meetings, providing status of ongoing improvements • Acquire data quality tools to automate data cleansing and matching • Direct regular and ongoing data quality audits across data subject areas and projects, measuring improvement over time	• Excellent written and verbal skills • Knowledge of process and workflow modeling • Knowledge of various data profiling and quality technologies

EXHIBIT 6.6   (Continued)

Job Role	Description	Representative Responsibilities	Skills
CDI data administrator	Provides support to application developers in need of access to the CDI hub	• Support application developers in interfacing to the CDI hub • Provide details and information to developers so that they understand the contents of the hub • Define linkages between different customer data elements • Work with source system data stewards to understand changes to operational systems that could affect the data on the CDI hub	• Familiar with system architecture issues specific to the company's IT standards • Must have prior experience in application development and support experience

Data czar	An executive position responsible for managing data as a corporate asset to support company strategy; owns data management function or center of excellence for the enterprise; ensures that regulatory, privacy, and information sharing policies are created and followed	• Manage data governance council (may also lead meetings)
		• Establish data management job roles and qualify and hire staff
		• Provide regular status reporting to executive staff on improvements to:
		  ○ Data speed of deployment
		  ○ Data quality
		  ○ Return on investment
		  ○ "Soft" benefits
		  ○ Process efficiencies
		  ○ Regulatory compliance
			• Must have leadership experience at the corporate level
			• Excellent presentation skills
			• Effective at consensus and team building

EXHIBIT 6.6   (*Continued*)

we know has one full-time data administrator whose job it is to define data requirements, model the data, and maintain the metadata. She is basically the company's single point of contact for data questions and new data deployment.

Conversely, a large automaker that supports many different subject areas has a data steward and a metadata administrator for each subject area— including customer, dealer, parts, vehicle, and warranty—and a data administrator responsible for synchronizing data requirements and models at the broader enterprise level.

Because every company is organized uniquely, with its own reporting hierarchies, job grades, and ownership domains, there is no one-size-fits-all structure for a data management organization. The key is to provide the function and enforce accountability for the data-specific work that needs to be done in order to manage data as an asset. Focus first on how the work gets done. The chart shown in Exhibit 6.7 is one that we've seen work with several of our clients, since it involves both the business and IT organizations in data management roles.

Your organization structure and job titles will probably be a bit different. The point is ensuring that the necessary functions and their interrelationships are formalized and well communicated within your company. As with CDI development, the "start small, think big" approach to establishing data management roles is the one most likely to pay off.

Reality of Data Stewardship

The answer to the question, "Who owns the data?" is ultimately the data steward.[5] The data steward should be given the authority to manage the data so that it reflects the desired business outcomes. The data steward should participate in data governance to the extent that the data governance council's policies dictate discrete data management execution priorities and tactics.

> *The answer to the question, "Who owns the data?" is ultimately the data steward.*

You might have noticed that in Exhibits 6.6 and 6.7 we distinguish "business data stewards" from "source system data stewards." Our experience has been that the term *data steward* has come to mean anyone with

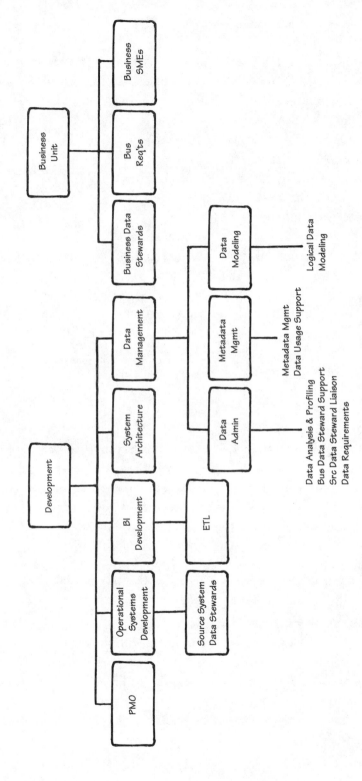

EXHIBIT 6.7 Data Management Involves Both IT and Business

ideas about how data should be used. It's a fact that many businesses already have people acting as data stewards without having the formal job roles. Assigning data stewards in an informal manner, or hoping that data stewardship organically becomes part of people's everyday jobs, encourages nebulous and subjective definitions of the role and ultimately a much more costly approach.

Though many well-intentioned companies have recently created a data steward role, the responsibilities and success definitions of the job often remain vague. Data stewards at these companies aren't accountable for delivering, since few managers understand the boundaries or tasks necessary for a data steward to succeed. Thus, many data stewards are rendered "roving linebackers" in their organizations, showing up to meetings and blessing data definitions, but either not being given or not assuming the authority of true data ownership. Some organizations have decommissioned their data stewards, sending them back to their formal roles as business users or data modelers.

> *It's rare that a data steward can adequately address the needs of data from both the source system and the business perspectives, so we recommend two discrete data stewardship roles.*

Nowadays, businesses simply expect too much from their data stewards. A nonprofit firm we worked with expected their data steward—a single guy from marketing who happened to understand customer data attributes better than anyone—to be able to explain everything from why segment codes were alphanumeric in the marketing automation system to the meaning of XML (extensible markup language) tags to the agenda items for the data model walkthrough. He was asked to choose a metadata repository tool for the company and to define a data retention strategy. Needless to say, the poor guy was exhausted—and not happy.

We designate business data stewards as experts on the business side who speak the business vocabulary and are intimate with the important business programs that mandate data. Business data stewards represent detailed data definitions, business rules, and usage scenarios to IT on behalf of the business. IT can still talk to business users, but data stewards are the arbiters for data requirements. Ideally, they report to a line-of-business function, like finance, and understand detailed data, its meanings, and its usage, at a granular level.

Conversely, the source system data steward is the authority on the data where it originates. This often requires a technical intimacy with very specialized or proprietary systems, and the skills to translate the operational environment of that system into more universal business terms. It's rare that a data steward can adequately address the needs of data from both the source system and the business perspectives, so we recommend two discrete data stewardship roles.

Moreover, you might consider initially launching the business data steward role within IT, with the aim of eventually migrating the role over to the business side. Often, business managers initially don't understand the value of the data steward until they witness the formal role in action, so IT must take a leadership role in defining the boundaries and setting the tone of the role for the company. The goal is to prove the value of the data stewardship so that the business will be willing to incorporate it into its day-to-day functions and ultimately fund it.

CHALLENGES OF ADOPTION AND CONSENSUS

It's rare that the individuals best suited to participate in data governance are the same people who welcome the change. It's important to frame the benefits of a formal data governance process—centralized oversight, tie-breaking, and results monitoring—and to continue to sell the improvements that are made to the rest of the business community. When people actually see proof of irrefutable benefits, they'll inevitably come around.

The main problem in adopting data-centric organizations and job roles is that the transparency scares people. For the first time, businesspeople or application developers are accountable for what their data looks like, how they've been using it, and what they've been doing to ensure its accuracy and integrity. And the truth hurts.

At the beginning of this chapter we identified the phenomenon of data hoarding, which essentially means that people refuse to share the data, usually on the pretext that it's sensitive or proprietary. Most of the time the data is dirtier or less complete than the current owners would like to admit, and they'll do anything possible not to come clean.

However, there's also the phenomenon of "pride of ownership." The group or individual who owns the data feels that they know the data better than anyone else. They are the de-facto experts. The problem isn't an unwillingness to share data; it's taking the time to teach others the details, rules, and derivations behind the often complex data elements that have been so painstakingly crafted. Pride of data ownership is valid, and the people who have it are usually ideal business data stewards.

Notwithstanding the cultural changes necessary to convince people to open up their data to the enterprise, we find the main barrier to formalizing data governance and stewardship is management's lagging attitude when it comes to data's critical role in business programs. The use of firefighting as an excuse for never solving data accuracy or availability issues is an example of management shirking its duty to act in the business's best interest. The challenge is not only educating management about data as a corporate asset—it's getting key executives with the authority and budget to listen to the story in the first place.

It's difficult to convince executives to invest time and budget in formalizing data management. It usually involves an initial meeting to educate them on the issues. (Such meetings are often run or facilitated by an outside expert or consultant whose objectivity ensures he can take a circumspect and structured view of data management.) The goal of such a meeting is to frame the concept of formalized data management, alert executives of the risks of failing to adequately manage data, and educate them about a sober, step-by-step approach for getting there.

WHAT WORKS: TIPS FROM THE EXPERTS

David Gutierrez: "Think creatively."

"We've done a lot of things right, but there are three factors that I think have been critical to the success our CDI program so far:

1. We've established a chief knowledge officer. She's defining all the policies and rules around data. It's a big job, but a necessary one.
2. We've implemented repeatable processes. Our data model, our development processes, and our reporting are all reuseable. That's been a big benefit.
3. And you have to think creatively. There are so many different

ways to solve the problem that sometimes you need to take a step back and realize that it's not just about technology. It might be a people or a process issue. Just because you have a hammer doesn't mean everything is a nail."

DAVID GUTIERREZ, Chief Information Officer, ING Insurance Americas

Understanding how to sell data management as a series of job roles and tasks is half the battle. The other half is knowing what success means and measuring progress.

COMING FULL CIRCLE: DATA MANAGEMENT AND CDI

Why have we spent an entire chapter on formalizing data governance and data management? Because these topics are routinely ignored in the rush to deliver CDI functionality. The risk is throwaway code, a canceled project, or the validation of organizational cowboys who are doing their own thing with data, thus perpetuating the isolation and underfunding of a critical corporate asset.

The details of data conversion, data cleansing, data standardization, and data storage are all too often one-off tasks that are done over and over again, exacerbating already dire problems of inconsistent data. If a customer data hub contains invalid or bad data, it may end up propagating that data to other enterprise systems. Regardless of whether the team is taking a top-down or a bottom-up development approach as defined in Chapter 5, the CDI team should be prepared to function within a larger MDM framework that includes both formalized job roles and data policies. This means that the CDI development team must collaborate with staff that has data governance and MDM responsibilities in order to:

- Profile the data as it comes onto the hub. (In the case of a persistent hub, the data should be profiled before it's acquired by the hub.)
- Work with the source data stewards on change management, and ensure that source system data stewards haven't changed or repurposed data elements.

- Understand the changes in the business. For instance, sales district assignments or customer groupings can change. These aren't just data element changes, they're structural changes that the CDI system will need to reflect.

- Understand data representation standards. We'll talk about this more in the next chapter, but it's critical to understand how certain data elements are represented. Should Social Security numbers contain dashes? How is data represented? How data is consistently represented to various applications should align with operational standards within the company.

> *The details of data conversion, data cleansing, data standardization, and data storage are all too often one-off tasks that are done over and over again, exacerbating already dire problems of inconsistent data.*

Ongoing CDI development is easier when data governance is institutionalized and data management processes are in place. Data migration and standardization means less invention or research by the development team. Data management also ensures that applications that will use the CDI hub know how to expect the data. The CDI system can make data reconciliation straightforward, seamless, and repeatable if the rules are agreed to by a larger, authoritative body. It's the best way to deliver a reliable version of the truth about the customer. If your company hasn't established a data governance structure or formalized data management roles, an initial CDI effort might be an effective pretext for one or both.

As MDM transcends customer data, sharing data across different hubs will become a reality. The extent to which a company can formalize its policies and coordinate workflows with CDI is the extent to which it will be ready to embrace other types of master data with open arms.

MANAGER DO'S AND DON'TS

Here are some tips to keep in mind as you consider launching more formalized data management practices within your company:

- **Do** use the scope of your initial CDI project as a testing ground for data governance. CDI and data governance go hand in glove, and targeting an initial business area or application is an ideal way to launch a data governance infrastructure.

- **Don't** succumb to "warm body syndrome." Just because someone has been with the company a long time ("She knows how our business runs") or has worked on another project that has involved customer data doesn't mean that she is qualified to participate in a data governance council. Be sure to vet data stewards as knowledgeable about data and ready to deliver. Data stewards ideally come from inside the business. However, they need to be willing to practice formal and rigorous data management tasks, and be accountable for doing them. Having a deep understanding of specialized data because of regular usage or historical exposure is the best job qualification.

- **Do** use standard terminology for data governance. Your company might use the terms defined in the chapter differently than we do. As CheckFree calls its data governance team the trustee council, the names can vary. What's important is the consistent usage of those terms throughout the organization, so that when people hear the term *data stewardship* they recognize its boundaries and understand where the responsibilities lie.

- **Don't** forget to measure the benefits. We've discussed measurement elsewhere in this book, but it's important to be able to justify the continuation of data management, and there's no better way to do that than measuring the cost of data governance to the company (in terms of resources and dollars) as well as the payback (in terms of reuse, economies of scale, and improved data quality and availability).

ENDNOTES

1. *We particularly like the chapter in their book* Return on Customer *(New York: Currency/Doubleday, 2005) called, "Violate Your Customers' Trust and Kiss Your Asset Goodbye."*

2. *Peter Weil and Jean Ross,* IT Governance: How Top Performers Manage IT Decision Rights for Superior Results *(Boston: Harvard Business School Press, 2004). The authors studied over 250 companies and found that those with formal IT governance processes performed better financially than companies without a formalized IT governance process.*

3. *Simon Goodall, Michael Ringel, and Peter Tollman, "Good Governance Gives Good Value: Rising to the Productivity Challenge in Biopharma R&D," BCG Focus, The Boston Consulting Group, July 2004.*

4. *Patrick Lencioni,* Death by Meeting: A Leadership Fable *(San Francisco: Jossey-Bass, 2004).*

5. *Obviously, the overarching answer to the question, "Who owns the data?" is that the corporation owns the data. However, this answer does little to address the issues of policy, authority, and problem resolution that usually accompany evolving data needs. The company indeed owns the data, but the data steward is the person ultimately accountable for its quality, protection, and meaning.*

7

Making Customer Data Integration Work

Customer data integration (CDI) involves an often complex combination of processing and technology. The obvious justification of CDI at most companies is to provide a consistent way of accessing customer details. Via CDI, these details are complete, integrated, and clean, thus freeing the applications to focus on their core functions. Of course, the information technology (IT) infrastructure around CDI will vary depending on the specific business needs, the functional requirements, and the actual technologies used.

This chapter examines how CDI technology works, reviewing the processing features typically associated with CDI hubs. We then relate that functionality to an overall systems architecture that delivers integrated customer data to your company's other applications and systems. The aim is to prepare you to implement CDI as part of your overall enterprise architecture while staying mindful of the capabilities specific to your CDI requirements. Thus armed, you can take a deliberate look at your company's IT infrastructure and know how CDI fits.

RESPONSIBILITIES OF A CDI ARCHITECTURE

Because CDI is so new, it's important to understand the functionality associated with retrieving, transporting, transforming, and delivering data between systems. So we'll start with a simple logical architecture, evolving it to introduce the different types of features associated with CDI. Once we've completed our logical architecture, we can turn to the various alternatives for physical implementation.

The goal of any architecture should be to:

- Provide a framework for addressing functions in a simplified and efficient manner
- Create an environment in which economies of scale and development reuse is the norm, not the exception
- Build an infrastructure that reflects overall system requirements, not just specialized application needs

The benefit of CDI hub technology is that it alleviates application systems from having to deal with complex data integration processing, particularly when the data integration requirements are highly specialized or apply to multiple constituents. Since the rules governing details such as household definition, customer identity recognition, or even address standardization can be complicated, it makes sense to address that processing in a single location. This should improve efficiency, improve accuracy, reduce overall costs, and decrease processing.

DATA INTEGRATION THE OLD-FASHIONED WAY

Accountability for providing integrated data to an application has traditionally been left to the individual application developer. Developers were forced to create custom code to retrieve the necessary data from each source system and then develop the logic to merge the data before it was available to the application. This required the developer to build an interface for retrieving data from *each* source system.

In the example in Exhibit 7.1, the customer support system is retrieving data from four other systems (service, billing, sales order, and loyalty). Supporting data integration across these systems required the developer to

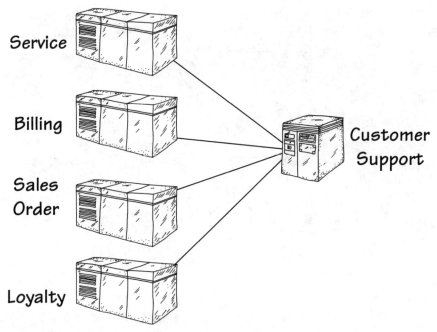

Service

Billing

Customer Support

Sales Order

Loyalty

EXHIBIT 7.1   **Retrieving Data from Four Systems**

understand the data and code interfaces between the customer support system and the other four systems.

The problem arises that if other applications require customer data from these four systems, they too need interfaces. Because of the potential number of interface combinations, more developers will be necessary to maintain the interfaces than were required to build the original applications. As Exhibit 7.2 shows, this can become unwieldy.

In this so-called point-to-point environment, the developers need to build and maintain twelve separate interfaces to support moving data from four source systems to three different client applications. Moreover, as the source systems change, code would have to be modified in each client application, a problem that will only grow more complex and costly as more systems evolve or are added. Consequently, maintaining these systems and ensuring their intercommunication is difficult and resource

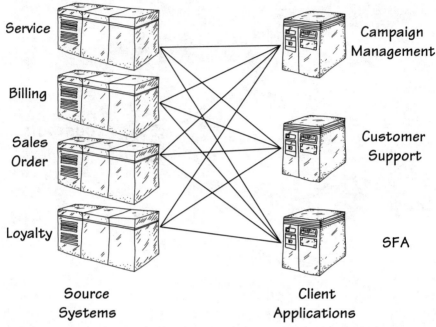

Service

Billing

Sales
Order

Loyalty

Campaign
Management

Customer
Support

SFA

Source
Systems

Client
Applications

EXHIBIT 7.2 Twelve Interfaces Connecting Seven
Systems

intensive, and the likelihood of keeping the individual interfaces synchronized is scant.

Indeed, the number of programs requiring maintenance and support can be staggering. Most companies rely on many more systems to share data than
we've shown here. In fact, in a point-to-point environment, the ongoing maintenance and support of
these interfaces can sometimes exceed the complexity of maintaining the application system itself.
Under these circumstances, it's not surprising that
application reporting details may differ between systems. It's rare that IT organizations have defined and
documented rules for merging data across separate
source systems—those decisions also are usually left
to the application developers. Point-to-point data

> *In fact, in a point-to-point environment, the ongoing mainte-nance and support of these interfaces can sometimes exceed the complexity of maintaining the application system itself.*

integration often creates inconsistent results where the numbers from two different systems don't match. In short, it's complex, expensive, and error prone.

DATA INTEGRATION VIA CDI

Customer data integration vastly simplifies the integration functionality necessary to support movement of data between systems. Exhibit 7.3 illustrates a simple CDI architecture. There are four source systems providing data to the CDI hub: service, billing, sales order, and loyalty. There are three client applications using the CDI hub for customer data integration: campaign management, customer support, and sales force automation (SFA).

In a real-life scenario, when a customer calls into the call center to request information about a recent order, the customer support representative retrieves the customer's order history from the customer support system.

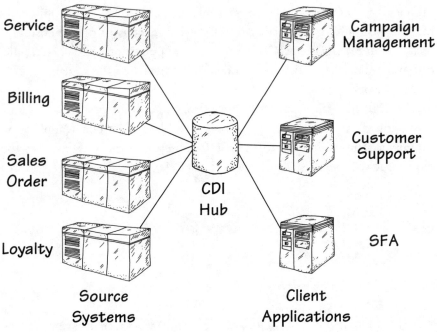

EXHIBIT 7.3   Seven Interfaces Connecting Seven Systems

Behind the scenes, the customer support system submits details to the CDI hub to identify the customer. The CDI hub interrogates the information and returns the customer ID details that match the customer support system's request.

In order to review the necessary concepts associated with developing a CDI architecture, let's start with a simple example showing one source system and one CDI client.

An Architectural Start

Exhibit 7.4 illustrates a simple environment comprised of three components: (1) the source system, (2) the CDI hub, and (3) the client application.

The source system is an operational system that contains detailed customer data. The CDI client is the application system that requires access to customer data. The CDI hub acts as an intermediary, retrieving customer data from source systems on behalf of client applications.

The source system can be as simple as a flat file of names and account numbers or as complex as a customer billing system. The client application may be as simple as a reporting tool or as complex as an online customer relationship management (CRM) call center application. The client application relies on the CDI hub to find and deliver the customer data it needs to do its work.

The CDI hub takes care of hiding all of the data integration and transformation details from the application developer. The client application submits a request directly to the CDI hub. When the hub receives the request, it will determine the specific data elements, their related source

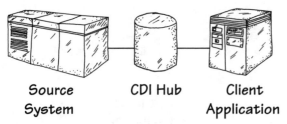

Source   CDI Hub   Client
System   Application

EXHIBIT 7.4   CDI Hub Connecting a Source System
and Client Application

systems, and the merge and transformation processing to create the data set necessary to respond to the client application request.

In order to integrate data from multiple data sources, the CDI hub is configured with details about each source system and the customer data details contained within it. These details are stored in a metadata dictionary contained within the CDI hub. As additional source systems are made available to the CDI hub, the metadata dictionary's contents are expanded to include the additional details of each source system. All of the rules necessary to address data transformation and merge processing are stored centrally within the CDI hub's metadata dictionary. This metadata dictionary is a unique feature that differentiates a CDI hub from the old-fashioned way of data integration: data integration rules are centrally stored and maintained within the CDI hub instead of being distributed (and maintained) within individual client applications. This allows the application developers to focus on building and maintaining business applications instead of having to build data integration solutions.

HOW IT WORKS: CORE FUNCTIONALITY OF THE CDI HUB

The role of the CDI hub is to deliver customer data to any system that requests it. While this sounds simple enough, there are several functions that are necessary to support the processing and delivery of customer data. They include:

- A single point of data retrieval
- Consistent value representation
- An accurate and repeatable means of merging data
- A repository of clean, reliable customer data
- Support of multiple data sources

Single Point of Data Retrieval

Among the CDI hub's most straightforward benefits is that it provides application developers with a single point of customer data retrieval.

Developers don't need to become experts on the multitude of operating systems, storage technologies, and data retrieval standards that are part of most IT infrastructures. They only need to understand the content and interface details of the CDI hub. After all, the number of interfaces associated with packaged and custom-developed application systems can be staggering (Java Database Connectivity [JDBC], Web services, proprietary application programming interfaces [APIs], Component Object Model [COM], Java 2 Platform, Enterprise Edition [J2EE], etc.) and impractical to track or manage. It becomes cumbersome, and sometimes downright impossible, to maintain a development team with the necessary combination of skills to build interface code that can tie together applications from dozens of disparate systems. Practically speaking, the CDI hub hides the complexities of data acquisition and integration from the various client applications and allows the application developers to focus on the more immediate responsibilities of system development and maintenance. In a registry-style CDI hub, the queried data is limited to the customer ID details contained within the hub. In a persistent-style hub, the queried data can include the customer ID details as well as the descriptive details relating to the customer.

Consistent Value Representation

Consistent value representation is a frequently overlooked CDI function. An example of consistent value representation is representing a Social Security number as a nine-character string containing digits separated by dashes (e.g., 123–45–6789), or representing days of the week as a string of three characters. While businesspeople may be in agreement about storing a Social Security number as a nine-character string, the confusion occurs when the data is exchanged across systems—for example, should the value be passed with or without dashes?[1] The format of the passed data should be consistent and understood across the systems that share it. We've seen this simple issue absorb large teams of developers as they put projects on hold to chase data problems and debug application code.

The importance of consistent value representation is that it ensures clarity of information meaning. This prevents confusion with details such as eye color (does the letter "B" represent blue or brown?) or date assignments (does day "2" represent Monday or Tuesday of a given week?). These decisions shouldn't be specific to the CDI hub; they should reflect the company's existing data standards as defined via a data governance process.

Accurate and Repeatable Merge Processing

One of the most powerful aspects of CDI hub functionality is merging multiple instances of data (either within a single source or across multiple sources). One of the benefits of providing centralized access to customer information is harnessing the rules and methods for merging multiple sources. The CDI hub contains configuration information (typically defined during the hub's installation and setup) that stores and manages the details necessary to merge data between various sources. While the functional capabilities of data matching and merging vary between CDI products (recall the discussion of probabilistic and deterministic matching in Chapter 4), the CDI hub will maintain a list of details necessary to merge the appropriate source data from different systems, as shown in Exhibit 7.5.

Merge processing occurs anytime the CDI hub merges multiple instances of the same customer. In Exhibit 7.5, the sales order system and service system each have information about the same customer, Rob Sands/Bob Sands.

As we described in Chapter 4, the merge process uses details from each of these systems to generate the index stored within the hub. In a registry-style hub, the hub will store only the necessary customer identification details and linkage information; any other descriptive detail (such as phone number, balance, or opt-in flag) will not be stored within the hub. In the persistent-style hub, the hub stores all of the details—both linkage details and descriptive details. The merge function is applicable only during hub update processing (or when new data is added to the hub); it isn't necessary to support search functionality.

Clean, Reliable Data

The CDI hub also acts as a reliable resource for clean, consistent customer data. It cleanses, reconciles, and transforms the data before delivering it to

192

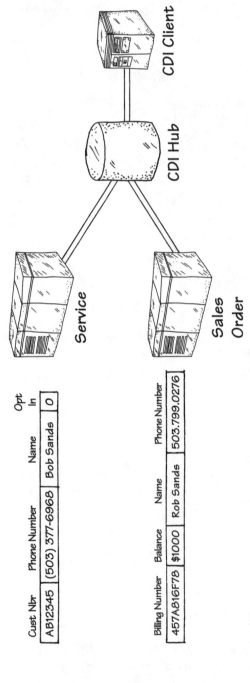

EXHIBIT 7.5 Merging Data Details

the CDI client. Some of the functionality associated with "clean" data may include:

- Value uniformity
- Value standardization
- Data certification

We've already covered data quality and standardization, but we'll briefly discuss these three functions, since they affect the processing (and thus the architecture) of CDI.

1. *Value uniformity* refers to the represented value of data. An example of this might be establishing that the height of the customer is represented in inches. The CDI system would ensure that any height information returned to the CDI client would be in inches—even if the source system represented height using a different measurement, like metric units or feet/inches. The CDI system would handle data transformation in a manner transparent to the CDI client so that height is consistently represented as inches.

2. *Value standardization* refers to data following standard formatting practices. The United States has a postal standard for address representation and a Federal Information Processing Standard (FIPS) for representing a state as a number code (for instance, Florida is represented as "12"). The CDI hub should support data value standardization where possible, leveraging existing standards where practical. The benefit is simple: applications communicating with the CDI hub can concentrate on their core business processing requirements.

3. *Data certification* is focused on *data accuracy*. This ensures that the data has gone through a series of acceptance criteria, usually determined by the business processes that need the data. One example might be the revenue numbers being generated by a sales system. It's not uncommon for a company's finance organization to *certify* the revenue numbers before they are distributed to the company at large. Data certification refers to the data's adherence to a particular set of rules or guidelines identified within a company or business process.

Supporting Multiple Data Sources

While much of our discussion thus far has focused on the robustness of CDI data delivery, it's just as important to focus on the number (and variety) of CDI data sources. The success of CDI adoption is directly proportional to the breadth and quantity of customer data attributes. The more data sources that contribute to building the integrated customer view, the more likely that applications will adopt the CDI hub as a reliable method of data access and integration.

Data source access can be handled in a number of ways. Depending on the circumstances, the CDI hub may rely on one of several established technologies to retrieve data from the multitude of data sources. The CDI hub solution may use enterprise application integration (EAI), Structured Query Language (SQL), enterprise information integration (EII), or even flat file access—the choice of which technology to use is typically determined by the CDI hub solution and its processing environment. We'll talk more about this later in this chapter when we review physical architecture alternatives.

EIGHT CORE FUNCTIONS OF HUB PROCESSING

Remember that CDI systems aren't geared to end users. Rather, CDI relieves applications from having to invent and manage the complex functional details of integrating customer data from multiple sources. CDI hub technology is targeted at offloading complex customer integration processing from other application systems. Exhibit 7.6 illustrates the core functions usually encompassed by the CDI hub. Each of the eight functions is described in the sections below.

Client Interface

The client interface enables connectivity between the CDI hub and the client application. This layer also determines or identifies the specific customer data elements being requested by the client application. The client interface:

- Supports client-to-hub connection
- Converts requests to data element details
- Dispatches request details to other CDI functions
- Returns CDI hub results to the client application

The first activity the client interface must perform is supporting a connection between the client application and the CDI hub. In most instances, there will be a series of parameters passed between both systems to establish a logon and secure connection. It's important that any security associated with the source data be retained within the CDI hub and maintained during the connection.

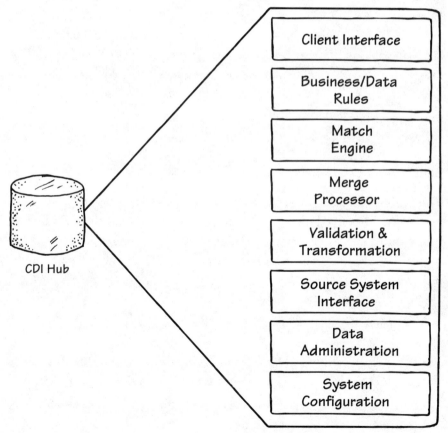

EXHIBIT 7.6   Eight Core CDI Functions

Once connected, the CDI hub will service the client application data requests. The request will consist of two general pieces of information: the operation and the data elements. The operation relates to specific query functionality: search, update (or insert), and delete. The second piece of information is the customer data elements associated with the request. The actual data might include customer name, ID number, or other customer details associated with the request. Where the operation is search, the data will include the search parameters. Where the operation is update or delete, the data will include all appropriate (or changed) details.

This function will convert the request into a component set of data elements and operation details that can be dispatched to the other functional components within the CDI hub. The client interface doesn't process the request; it just gathers the details and forwards them on to the other functions for processing.

Once the CDI hub is finished producing the answer set, the client interface will package the results and return them to the client application. The most common interfaces used are Web services and traditional language APIs. The most popular interface currently in use is Web services due to its portability and open standards.

Business and Data Rules

The business and data rule function provides metadata storage and reference capabilities for the other processing functions within the CDI hub. It stores and manages the business rules, definitions, equations, and other details required to support CDI processing. Some of these details might include:

- Data definition and derivation details such as "Profit = (price-cost) / cost"

- Storage location and access details for source data elements such as table/column name, database table or file location, system identifier

- Merge rules/algorithms for account number among sales, finance, and customer support systems

- Logic for identifying the preferred attribute when multiple instances exist
- Formatting details, like dashes in Social Security numbers

The term *business rules* frequently refers to rules and guidelines associated with the usage and processing of individual data elements. Business rules processing involves storing and retaining those details for use by other functions within the CDI hub.

Match Engine

The match engine determines (and identifies) where specific data records are referring to a particular individual. A simple example of this is the circumstance where an individual customer can be identified by different first names (e.g., Bob, Robert, and/or Rob). A more complex example is when the hub encounters multiple customer address and phone number details that may reference an individual customer.

Match engines differ among CDI products. Some feature highly sophisticated probabilistic or deterministic engines; others involve straightforward lookup dictionaries that contain simple matching logic. Regardless of the complexity, the match engine's goal is to identify where data references or represents the same information.

An important point for CDI is that the actual results of a match process may differ based on the needs of a particular application. For instance, the client application might request the most accurate (read: recent) customer mailing address. In this circumstance, the match engine evaluates the source data and returns the most recently updated customer mailing address.

In another example, a client application requests the customer's information, but—because the application requires a "raw" first name as it was entered by the customer—prefers the name details as they're stored in the CRM system. Thus, a CDI query result for an individual customer may actually differ from application to application based on the application's specific needs.

Merge Processor

The merge function concentrates on consolidating data from different data sources and establishing the linkages to support identification of customer data across multiple systems. The merge processor will analyze the details from each of the data sources and generate the results based on a series of rules. These rules may be stored within the CDI hub's metadata dictionary or identified by a specific client application.

Validation and Transformation

This function transforms and converts data retrieved from each of the source systems to enable further processing by the CDI hub. (The validation and transformation processing function implements the details associated with *clean, reliable data* we discussed earlier in the chapter.) An example of validation and transformation might include converting the customer's mailing address to a U.S. Postal Service standard or more complex transformation, such as generating a household ID from a series of customer addresses.

This component will also ensure that the resultant data passes certification and acceptance, such as ensuring that each state abbreviation is a valid value or that each U.S. phone number contains ten digits.

In situations where the CDI hub supports bidirectional data access to the data source, the validation and transformation function will also support converting CDI hub details into the native format of the data source in order to support writing data back to the data source.

Source System Interface

Similar in concept to the client interface layer, this function enables connectivity between the CDI hub and source system. The source system interface should support a wide variety of source systems, from flat files to databases to operational application systems. There are typically a variety of activities associated with maintaining connectivity and access to the source system, including:

- Supporting a CDI hub-to-source system connection
- Converting data element details to source system requests
- Retrieving source data results to other CDI components

The function first establishes a connection to the source system. This may include dealing with logon and security checking as well as determining the availability of the source system. Since a CDI hub gets data from multiple source systems, it's important that it supports situations where an individual source system isn't available. If the source system isn't available, it's up to the other CDI functions to determine how the client application's request will be processed.

Once the source system connection is made, a query will be submitted to the source system reflecting the type of request made in the client interface. If the source system is a packaged enterprise resource planning (ERP) system for instance, the request will be converted to the appropriate application message call; if the source system is a relational database platform, the request will be converted to an SQL request. In most instances, this function will communicate with a source system via a traditional transaction-based application interface (such as EAI, Web services, or coding API).

In situations where the source data is persistently stored content within the CDI hub, this component becomes a lightweight process and simply retrieves the data from the persistent storage system within the CDI hub.

When the query is complete, the source system interface will retrieve the results from the data source, package them for use by other functions, and forward them back to the requesting function within the CDI hub.

Data Administration

The data administration function provides an interface to applications and the hub administrator to support additional data adjustment and modification functionality. This function may also include details such as data access and security and audit control and access.

There will almost always be circumstances when data must be manually modified due to anomalies or problems (for example, the hub may have merged two customer records incorrectly). Most environments require a restricted means of data correction to address such circumstances.

System Configuration

The system configuration functions support the ongoing management and configuration of the hub infrastructure. This includes the functions and features associated with configuring the engines, storage management, integration parameters, and other resource details associated with the CDI hub product. The system configuration function also allows the hub administrator to configure (and load) new source system details, administer security, or address other hub access details.

SYNCHRONIZING THE HUB AND SOURCE SYSTEM

The initial population of the CDI hub requires loading detail from each of the source systems. This activity is typically performed as a bulk data transfer from each of the source data systems.

The actual logistics of the hub loading typically requires the construction of flat file extracts from each of the operational systems that in turn are loaded into the CDI hub. Exhibit 7.7 shows the loading of each data source in succession: (1) service, (2) billing, (3) sales order, and (4) loyalty. The CDI hub will integrate the individual customer records as it loads each of the sources.

For a registry-style hub, only those data elements required for customer identification are loaded into the hub. For persistent hubs, both the identification and the descriptive elements are loaded into the hub. The actual time required to perform the initial load and integration may span several hours (or even days, depending on the data volumes).

Once loaded, the CDI hub's data can be maintained or synchronized with source systems in a transactional manner. This typically requires custom development in order to capture any source system changes and ensure they are propagated to the CDI hub. (This is where leveraging an existing EAI infrastructure can simplify CDI hub implementation). As data

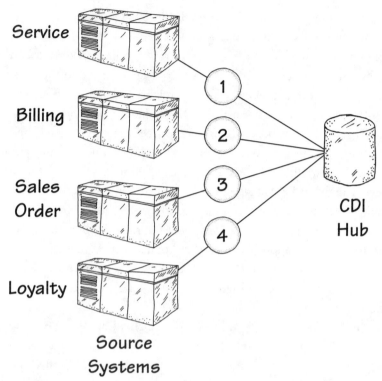

EXHIBIT 7.7   Loading Four Sources into the CDI Hub

is updated on a source system, a transaction can be applied against the CDI hub to update the customer's detail.

INTEGRATING MULTIPLE SYSTEMS WITH THE CDI HUB

Exhibit 7.2 illustrated seven systems interfacing to the CDI hub: the service system, the billing system, the sales order system, the loyalty system, the campaign management system, the customer support system, and the sales force automation system. In Exhibit 7.8, we've identified the two client applications, customer support and SFA, that use the CDI hub to retrieve customer details. And there are three source systems, service, billing, and sales order, that will provide customer data to the CDI hub. (For the moment we've left out two of the systems mentioned earlier, loyalty and campaign management, but we'll cover them shortly.)

As you can see in Exhibit 7.8, the CDI hub has been configured to work with each of the individual systems.

The characteristics of each source system are known only to the CDI hub; the source system interface function is specifically configured to the source system. If the source system is a relational database, the source system interface will understand the SQL characteristics and customer data elements required by the hub. If the source system is a packaged ERP application, the source system interface understands the programming interface (e.g., API, Web services, objects, etc.) in order to request and retrieve data from the packaged ERP environment.

Each client application interfaces to the CDI hub in much the same manner. The client interface will support interacting with the client application in a manner appropriate to that application. While the most common client application interface is Web services, many products support code that converts the individual client application calls to the hub's interface.

Exhibit 7.8 identifies a system as either a client application or a source system; however, it is possible for a system to interface to a CDI hub as both a client and a source. Exhibit 7.9 reintroduces the loyalty and campaign management systems into the environment. Each interacts with the CDI hub as both a client application and a source system.

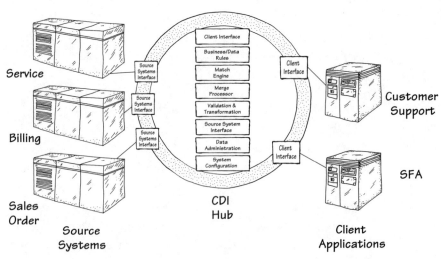

EXHIBIT 7.8   **Hub Connecting Sources with Clients**

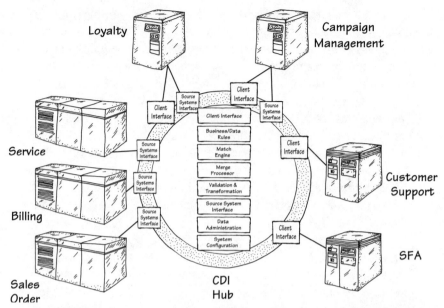

EXHIBIT 7.9   Applications Can Be Client Applications, Source Systems, or Both

The system architecture now supports seven individual systems interfacing to the CDI hub. You'll notice that each system interfaces to the hub via the source system interface, the client interface, or both. And the core functions—business/data rules, validation and transformation, and match and merge—are available to support integration processing of data from each of the systems.

CASE STUDY: AMGEN

When Nancy Lehrer arrived at Amgen as a lead architect in 2004, she already had plenty of data integration experience. Lehrer had worked for a federal government contractor building systems for organizations like the Air Force and the Defense Advanced Research Projects Agency (DARPA).

"When the Pentagon called, we were dealing with lieutenant colonels," Lehrer recalls. "These guys had immediate strategic needs. It wasn't practical to educate them about the data representation and structural complexities, and no one cared that their system had 1000 tables in the database. We needed to build a bridge to translate the data representation into clear terminology. There were important questions to answer." Lehrer and her team ended up accelerating the military's battle planning from more than three days to less than a day.

Fast forward to today, and Lehrer is still solving heterogeneous data problems. But this time, the enabling technology is CDI. Lehrer and her architect colleagues have built a solution to correlate customers from various systems and enable the integration of customer data across those systems.

In order to maintain the integrity and independence of its different source systems, Amgen adopted the registry style of CDI. An individual may have different relationships with the biotechnology company, and the systems themselves need to represent them correctly. Hence, the ERP system might only need customer data once a financial transaction has occurred, while the CRM system tracks physician interactions irrespective of purchase transactions. For instance, a physician group involved in purchasing Amgen medicines might not be the same physicians prescribing the medicine. Likewise, Amgen's contract relationship with a hospital will likely be different from the centers in that hospital (like the dialysis center), which will be different again from the individual physicians. The goal was to retain the different values about a customer, acknowledging that the "best record" was contingent on the business need for the data.

Parties represented by Amgen's CDI solution include prescribers of their medicines, wholesalers, specialty pharmacies, speakers, and researchers. Amgen's CDI approach supports the search and creation of new parties across Amgen's systems.

"Everyone who owned the various systems wanted to create their own version of the customer," Lehrer explains. "We needed to balance a consolidated view of our customers with flexibility and source system self-sufficiency." The system that first comes into contact with the customer defines the initial customer record. To do this, Amgen developed the Object Registry and Exchange (ORX), a hub that reconciles the parties across different Amgen systems and applications.

The company realized that it wasn't as simple as searching for an existing customer record. The ORX hub provides client applications with information about whether the customer data exists on other systems, alleviating systems from having to "fill in" specific details about that customer.

The challenge was how to build a solution to support a multitude of business processes from across a variety of data sources. "This system was built to be extensible to any application," says Victor Fehlberg, an Amgen architect responsible for deploying data quality as an enterprise service using a service-oriented architecture (SOA). "The standards-based SOA approach provides an interface that lets our systems interact with the hub regardless of the unique operating environments of the individual platforms." Amgen combined "build" and "buy"—implementing the hub within an SOA framework and compartmentalizing the data cleansing and standardization function-ality with a best-of-breed data quality tool.

"The maturity of existing data quality solutions enabled our approach," says Lehrer. "Buying a tool to leverage advanced cleans-ing and matching capabilities made all the difference. Otherwise, we would have had to become experts, and it would have taken a pro-hibitive amount of time."

When the client application wants to know if the customer exists, the hub searches its contents based on specific input criteria such as last name, address, or one of several other attributes. The hub main-tains a unique entry for the customer, along with the link from each of its client applications. The customer may have already been cre-ated by one or more Amgen systems and thus a record for that cus-tomer might already reside in the hub. In this case, ORX will return the hub ID, all descriptive details, and the system names and IDs for all systems that already contain data about that customer.

When Amgen's clinical system needs to create a new customer, it will ask ORX to search for the customer. The ORX hub compares its values to the application's, then—if the record exists in the hub—compares the standardized values with those already in the hub, and returns the record (or records) that match the search criteria. With this design, when other systems inquire about that same customer, the record already exists in the hub, and the associated customer details can be reused.

If the customer has been added via another system, ORX will add the clinical system's ID to the hub index and return the details. ORX links any customer detail within the hub already contained in other Amgen systems. "We wanted to limit changes to the source and appli-cation systems," Lehrer explains. "We didn't want to require either the source systems or client applications to embed any new functionality. The only requirement was to support hub communications."

Amgen is currently using the ORX system to correlate customer visits across sales and marketing activities and clinical trial activities. The company expects to add five more systems into the ORX framework within the next year. It's a testament to the benefits of providing customer data to a range of disparate systems. "It's not only about what works," says Nancy Lehrer, "it's about what works most efficiently, and what's best for the business."

SOURCE SYSTEM DATA: PERSISTENT STORAGE VS. REGISTRY ACCESS

It's clear from the overview of CDI hub functions that the technology is highly focused on data integration. We've used the term *integration* to mean all the details associated with creating a holistic and complete view of the customer: data retrieval, cleansing and transformation, value standardization, and merge processing. The actual integration process, however, can occur one of two ways within the CDI hub: data is either preintegrated and persistently stored or integrated "on the fly" and merged as it's retrieved from the individual source systems. We talked about each of these methods in Chapter 2, and will now cover the benefits and trade-offs of each approach.

How the Persistent Style Works

The persistent style of CDI hub stores both the identification details of the customer as well as the descriptive attributes. This information is retrieved and processed from each of the source systems, with the resultant details stored inside the hub. A persistent hub can process both identity-based and descriptive-based queries. An identity-based query requires only the identity details of a customer. A descriptive query includes both the identity and the descriptive details of the customer. Queries are processed by the hub without requiring any additional access outside the hub. All customer data lookups and value references can be handled locally on the hub.

In Exhibit 7.10, the client application, the customer support system, requests information for customer John Smith from the persistent CDI hub. In this particular example, the CDI hub was populated with information from both the sales order system and the billing system. When the customer support system requests the most recent order and billing details for John Smith (1):

- The CDI hub determines that John Smith is customer ID #123 related to sales order #894 and billing ID #756.
- The CDI hub retrieves order details (within the hub's persistent storage) on sales order #894 and billing detail #756.
- The CDI hub returns the result data to the customer support application.

The persistent CDI hub was able to process this request locally and didn't need to reference any data from an external system.

The trade-offs of the persistent-style CDI hub are in duplicate storage, data latency, and data synchronization. While having customer data stored physically in the CDI hub improves response time and simplifies query processing, it creates a circumstance where the source system data might not be completely current with the same data on the hub. This synchronization issue is addressed on the next update cycle; however, the problem returns the moment the source system is updated again. The fact is, the persistent style of CDI is only as accurate as the frequency of synchronization between the hub and its data sources.

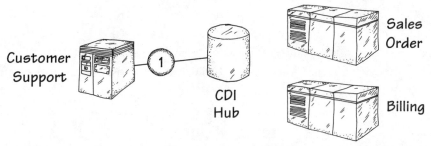

EXHIBIT 7.10   Requesting Information from a Persistent-Style Hub

How the Registry Style Works

With the registry style of CDI, the hub storage is limited to reference (or linkage) details. All other customer descriptive details reside outside the hub on the source system.

The benefit of the registry style is that data synchronization is handled; the latest data from the source system is made available to the client application. The registry style's strength is also its weakness: response time, since it requires access to additional data that's not resident on the hub. The data must be retrieved from the data sources and then processed for integration—you'll recall our discussions of data transformation, cleansing, value standardization, and so on. This takes time and

> The fact is, the persistent style of CDI is only as accurate as the frequency of synchronization between the hub and its data sources.

might make the client application wait for the results. Moreover, source system availability (and/or uptime) can influence the access and availability of data.

Which type of CDI is best? This really depends on the processing requirements of the client application. While there are always exceptions, there are a few guidelines to keep in mind.

The persistent style of CDI works well when data isn't highly volatile and the client applications are willing to accept data that isn't 100 percent perfect. While this might sound heretical, a common example is a customer master application that requires customer address and contact details. While the customer master undergoes daily changes, an individual customer's address and contact details change infrequently. While no one wants dirty data, the impact of having a few out-of-sync addresses is likely to be minimal. Given the exception processing with change of address at the post office, most mail is delivered if the address is clean and accurate. Persistent-style CDI involves frequent updates, and most systems can support regularly scheduled (e.g., daily) or event-based updates, so the persistent style tends to be a very good match for low-volatility data.

The registry style of CDI is usually preferred when the data is highly dynamic and changes often. An example is with a hospital's patient care details. While the patient's name and home address details aren't likely to

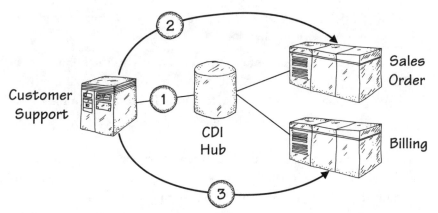

EXHIBIT 7.11   Requesting Information from a Registry-Style Hub

change often, her condition, symptoms, medication dosages, or admission status could change by the minute. The CDI hub tracks and manages the patient data across the continuum of her care, and thus across multiple systems, ensuring that the client applications get the data quickly and accurately. In this particular instance, a copy of data would become out of date very quickly, which could have significant implications.

Early versions of registry-style CDI products didn't support query federation. If the client application requests descriptive details relating to a particular customer, the early registry-style CDI products don't retrieve the descriptive details directly from the source systems on behalf of the client application. Any nonregistry details must be retrieved from the source system directly by the client application.

In Exhibit 7.11, a client application (the customer support system) requests information from the CDI hub to support an application process involving customer John Smith.

1. The customer support system requests the most recent purchase and billing details for John Smith. The CDI hub determines the customer ID from John Smith (#123) and returns the sales order ID (#894) and the billing ID (#756) associated with John Smith.

2. The customer support system submits a query to the sales order system to retrieve the most recent sales order detail for John Smith

(ID# 894). The sales order system returns the appropriate details to customer support system.

3. The customer support system submits a query to the billing system requesting the most recent billing information for John Smith (ID# 756). The customer support system now has sufficient information to complete its application process.

Some of the newer CDI products contain query federation functionality, which enables the CDI hub to service queries that require data contained outside of the hub. This enables the CDI hub to retrieve information directly from the source systems on behalf of the client application.

In Exhibit 7.12, the customer support system requests information from the CDI hub for customer John Smith. In this particular example, the CDI hub handles all of the query processing.

1. The customer support system requests the most recent purchase and billing details for John Smith. The CDI hub determines the customer ID from John Smith (#123) and as well as the sales order ID (#894) and the billing ID (#756).

2. The CDI hub submits a query to the sales order system to retrieve the most recent sales order detail for John Smith (ID# 894). The sales order system returns the appropriate details to customer support system.

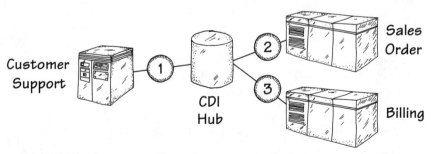

EXHIBIT 7.12   Query Federation from a Registry-Style Hub

3. The CDI submits a query to the billing system requesting the most recent billing information for John Smith (ID# 756). The CDI hub processes both query results, and returns the consolidated details to the customer support application.

> *The decision on which type to choose should be based on the requirements of the client applications that need the data, not on architectural preferences.*

There are other scenarios that compare the persistent and registry types of CDI. The point is that both provide a single, point-in-time, integrated image of the customer. The decision on which type to choose should be based on the requirements of the client applications that need the data, not on architectural preferences. Given the strengths of hub style, many CDI solutions (including both vendor- and custom-developed) have evolved into a hybrid solution persisting (or caching) frequently used data elements to improve performance and response time processing.

THE CDI HUB IN THE IT ARCHITECTURE

Up until now we've illustrated an architecture that's centered on moving customer data from source systems to client applications. Integrating a CDI solution into a production data center and the typical technologies that might already exist are also important considerations for selecting the right CDI solution. CDI technology can provide a significant amount of flexibility and performance improvement to an IT infrastructure if positioned correctly. Let's review some common technology components already in place in many IT environments and compare and contrast their functions with the CDI hub. In particular, the hub will have the most impact on an existing EAI message bus (otherwise known as enterprise service bus [ESB]), data warehouse, EII, and SOA environments.

CDI and EAI

Enterprise application integration technology has evolved significantly over the last few years. While it originally sprang from the need to manage transactions across multiple application systems, it has become a critical architectural component that can support business process automation and transaction management.

Not long ago, developers had to develop custom code to transport messages between applications. EAI and the advent of the ESB allowed developers to construct a utilitarian interface to support messages moving across numerous applications. This freed application developers from worrying about the details of message flow between systems. Managing message flow is quite complex. A business won't survive if it can't accept sales orders or process purchases.

Enterprise application integration technology has replaced most custom code contained in legacy operational applications and taken on the transaction processing management functions required by most modern application systems.

While EAI sounds similar to CDI, they have different roles within the IT processing infrastructure. The EAI system manages the flow of messages between applications; the focus isn't to integrate data between applications. It contains rules about message interaction, not data integration. Insulated from the contents of the messages, EAI simply ensures message transmission and delivery. It supports the migration of message and synchronization of systems to support business processes.

Thus, EAI isn't meant to integrate data across multiple systems. While CDI interfaces to systems based on a common subject area, customer, EAI interfaces to multiple systems based on common business processes, such as processing a supplier's delivery and payment detail.

Despite their differences, CDI and EAI can coexist and work together. Exhibit 7.13 illustrates how a CDI hub can leverage EAI technology, and vice versa.

In Exhibit 7.13, the CDI hub is attached to the ESB using EAI technology. This allows the CDI hub to access customer data on each of the operational systems—sales, support, billing, finance, and human resources. The ESB will allow the CDI hub to access customer-oriented application messages and data. As the operational systems add new customers (or place new orders or bill existing customers), the CDI hub will have access to that

> *EAI isn't meant to integrate data across multiple systems.*

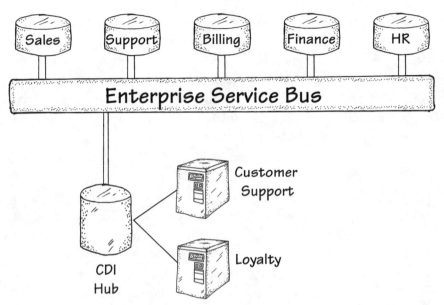

EXHIBIT 7.13   A CDI Hub with an Enterprise Service Bus

information to update its registry. The CDI hub can leverage an existing EAI environment to improve the quality and timeliness of customer data to other client applications.

CDI and EII

Enterprise information integration has emerged as one of the more promising technologies to support queries accessing data from different systems, known as federated query processing. In many companies there is a need for query processing that can extract and combine data "on the fly" from a variety of different data sources. Enterprise information integration technology provides the glue to connect multiple, disparate database systems so queries can be processed across different systems.

While there is overlap, the difference between CDI and EII centers on the individual strengths of each. With EII, the focus is on query optimization. With CDI, the focus is integration rigor.

An EII server offers developers a single point of contact for a multitude of subject area content. The goal is to provide an EII platform with dictionary details that enable access to a wide variety of subject areas and data elements. Data integration is usually handled using a rules-based method to merge data from disparate systems. In order to merge customer data from multiple systems, a linkage key must be identified. Integration is impossible without such a key to link records. While it lacks robust match/merge processing capabilities of CDI, EII focuses on query processing, determining the most efficient manner to process the results of each query.

Where EII requires specific linkage rules, CDI can function on fuzzy or probabilistic methods of data integration. It's quite common to see a CDI engine match data sources based on a multitude of rules and logic, sometimes even supporting highly complex "artificial intelligence"–type processing. Many of the CDI vendors have focused their products' strengths toward customer identification and management while leaving complex query processing to other technologies like EII. We fully expect to see these two technology areas align more closely in the near future.

Indeed, IT organizations can benefit from the coexistence of both CDI and EII technologies. Exhibit 7.14 illustrates this concept.

We've already discussed the benefits of tying the four application systems on the left together via CDI. The loyalty system will able to see an

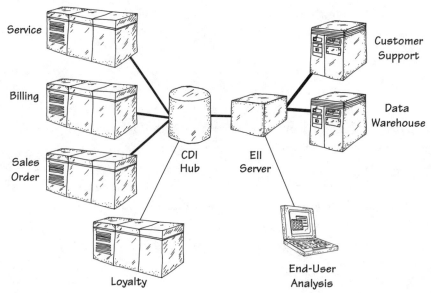

EXHIBIT 7 . 14   Coexistence of EII with a CDI Hub

integrated view of customer details from across the sales order, billing, and service systems. (Remember, the CDI hub is subject-area specific to customer detail.) The CDI hub will also support a highly complex method of merging customer details from across the different systems. Thus, if the loyalty system requires additional data not contained in the other systems, the EII server can deliver that data from, in this case, the customer support and data warehouse systems.

The advantage of this approach is that the hub can determine which (if any) details from the data warehouse and customer support system are necessary to provide a comprehensive view of the customer, and the EII server can deliver that data. Where there's content overlap, the CDI hub will determine the best solution.

If any of the systems attached to the EII server require additional customer details not already available within either the customer support system or the data warehouse, the CDI hub can enhance the content of the EII server. In fact, a CDI hub attachment may provide great value to an EII environment where customer data isn't readily available. As Exhibit 7.14 points out, the end-user analysis tool attached to the EII server will be able to merge customer service details with information from the CDI hub to avail business intelligence about customer support needs. Although there is some overlap regarding customer data access, there's certainly a significant amount of synergy between CDI and EII.

CDI and SOA

Without question, SOA commands a significant portion of mindshare with IT executives. The advent of SOA has truly challenged the fundamental structure of IT architectures. Where traditional system architectures focused on identifying application platforms to support individual business functions and processes, the SOA has emerged to enable architectural support of more detailed business processes or services.

Most application development processes (data infrastructure, processing, business rules and logic, among other functions) still require developers to build from scratch. The concept behind SOA is to enable a development framework in which programmers can leverage and reuse prebuilt services to simplify their application development responsibilities. As new applications are built, new services are constructed that can be leveraged by other developers. The end result is that applications comprised multiple services and ensure economies-of-scale in development. (Applications that rely on multiple services within an SOA are often called *composite applications*.)

Most of the current crop of CDI products support SOA. In fact, many of these products are constructed to integrate into a company's existing SOA architecture. Most CDI hubs provide SOA exposure or interfaces using standard Web services. The most common interface services include "search," "add," "update," and "delete." The actual values and parameters will differ across individual products; however, all of the CDI vendors realize that SOA is critical for CDI adoption and optimal for service and code reuse.

> *The concept behind SOA is to enable a development framework in which programmers can leverage and reuse prebuilt services to simplify their application development responsibilities.*

Indeed, the entire theme of this chapter has been reuse. We recommend that IT managers considering CDI adoption understand the type of processing and functionality required from a CDI solution so that they can leverage it across systems, development teams, and data elements.

WHAT WORKS: TIPS FROM THE EXPERTS

Brenda Kydd: "Leverage what you have."

"When we started this process, the vendor community wasn't really there yet. It taught us the importance of understanding what we already had in place. For instance, each of the operational systems within our various lines of business had its own customer information, each with its own unique key. If we hadn't understood that, or had tried to start from scratch, we would have overinvested or had to make huge resource commitments. It would have been disruptive, and probably wouldn't have survived. As it turned out, everyone supported us and it's been a major success."

BRENDA KYDD, Senior Manager, Information Management Infrastructure and Governance, Royal Bank of Canada

MANAGER DO'S AND DON'TS

Making CDI work involves a diverse set of technologies, standards, policies, and skills. As you embark on retrofitting new CDI capabilities into your existing IT infrastructure, here are some tips to keep in mind:

- **Do** establish your development goals before you engage vendors. Are you looking to reduce coding complexity for programmers? Do you want to centralize customer identification and management? Do you need to raise performance to online transaction processing–class speeds? Understanding your functional requirements, as we discussed in Chapter 5 as well as the architectural functions discussed in this chapter will take you and your team a long way toward having informed vendor conversations.

- **Don't** position the CDI hub as a replacement for a data warehouse or data mart. It's not about customer data reporting; it's about providing reconciled and authoritative customer data to other systems. While the CDI hub can offload customer data integration from a data warehouse or mart, it's not intended to replace the query and reporting functionality inherent in data warehouse and business intelligence environments.

- **Do** focus on leveraging the existing IT infrastructure to support CDI. If you've already invested in EAI or extraction, transformation, and loading (ETL) technology, review where you can leverage your team's current experience and existing technologies to simplify CDI implementation.

- **Don't** assume that CDI will release the development organization from having to understand the data sources. Your team will still need to research which customer data elements are needed and the sources from which they originate. This usually requires a source system data inventory to map out the data used by CDI client applications.

- **Do** conduct data profiling on all the candidate data sources to ensure the data contents are usable. A CDI hub won't work if 40 percent of the names are null or all address fields are blank. It's important to ensure that data sources contain usable—albeit sometimes imperfect—data.

- **Don't** expect architectural elegance in the first iteration. As the business requirements evolve and usage grows, be sure to reevaluate the CDI architecture to ensure that it continues to match your business requirements.

ENDNOTE

1. *For the record, we recommend storing and passing the Social Security number details* without *dashes.*

CHAPTER 8

Making the Case for Customer Data Integration

What can't your business do that it needs to do, and how can integrated customer data help? Understanding what's missing in your company's business and information technology (IT) capabilities is a great first step in pitching an initial customer data integration (CDI) project. However, as with most strategic IT endeavors, CDI requires a deliberate approach to explaining the problem, educating stakeholders, laying out the financial costs and benefits, and continuously communicating progress.

CDI's promise lies in its ability to deliver integrated customer information operationally. Where customer relationship management (CRM), data warehouses, custom applications, and even emerging technologies like enterprise information integration (EII) can provide a window into customer information, they usually rely on an incomplete view of the customer. CDI provides customer information as of right now. It serves a class of business problems in need of immediate, current, accurate, and complete customer data.

Justifying CDI can challenge even the most hardened manager, and will probably have as much to do with your organization's political environment as it will with formal business case development. This chapter provides some practical advice on how to make the CDI pitch and how to deflect the inevitable arguments from those in your organization that have a firm stake in the status quo.

BENEFITS OF CDI INVESTMENT

A 2005 article on SearchCRM.com called "CRM's ROI Answer" heralded a promising new vehicle for delivering return on investment (ROI) for CRM: CDI.[1] CRM projects, while increasingly successful at delivering operational efficiencies and customer retention, have largely failed to recoup their costs. According to Forrester Research, only 10 percent of business and IT executives surveyed strongly agreed that the expected CRM business results were met or exceeded.[2]

An integrated view of the customer has traditionally been an expensive proposition. Most CRM deployments focused on dashboards and reports, and never intended to deliver on-demand customer details with sufficient speed and accuracy. Some were nothing more than elegant databases with a portal on top.

Indeed, CDI has been embraced by many who, dissatisfied with their CRM outcome, consider it a necessary next step in CRM's evolution, and one that can provide the tactics and operational features that can (finally!) be quantified to justify the investment. The market has moved on, and we find many clients and prospects looking toward CDI and master data management (MDM) as a way to leverage the data they deployed for their CRM efforts, as well as other strategic IT programs.

CDI requires a different means of value measurement than CRM. Moreover, unlike with many strategic IT projects, senior executives may not actually know or care about CDI. Therefore, the pitch looks very different.

Solving the Need, Pain, or Problem

In Chapter 2, we discussed some of the business trends that are increasingly driving CDI adoption: the need to comply with legislative and regulatory edicts, to track and reduce fraud, to quickly react to attrition, to increase customer acquisition and retention across the customer life-cycle, to identify so-called persons of interest and enable master patient indexes, and to improve the company's brand through differentiated customer interactions. There's a near-universal need to tailor customer conversations and it requires a single, authoritative system of record—one that can respond to business and customer changes.

When clients and prospects invite us in to discuss CDI, we sound like the consultants we are, since our initial question is usually the same: "What's the need, pain, or problem you're trying to solve?" The answers aren't as diverse as you might think.

The initial entry point for CDI is usually represented by an immediate, tactical need. These needs often drive seminal conversations about improved customer master data and are often the pretext for meeting with a CDI vendor or engaging a consultant specializing in CDI. Here are the business needs that most often initiate discussions about CDI:

- **Customer preference management.** Most companies must collect and track a variety of customer details for multiple business reasons, from compliance to improved marketing programs. For instance, has a customer opted out of telemarketing? Has he provided us with his preferences for direct mail and e-mail marketing? Are there regulatory or legal mandates, like nonpublic proprietary information (NPI) or customer proprietary network information (CPNI), that require detailed data and data policies and that circumscribe who internally can see that data?

  Though many companies track these details, they are not usually well synchronized. A friend of ours completed a preference postcard from his bank allowing him to opt out of solicitations. When he received marketing mailings anyway, he called the bank to remind him of his opt-out status. The bank explained that they had the opt-out request—customer support had indeed updated its system—but our friend continued to receive sales pitches both online and in the mail. The bank's marketing department wasn't in the loop.

- **Customer data protection.** Currently, consumer data ownership is undefined and regulated and companies that have consumer data are the de-facto owners of that data. However, legislation may be coming that puts ownership of the data back in the hands of consumers and businesses; thus, companies might soon be asked to disclose who is accessing, touching, and updating individual customer records. It's not only about privacy—it's about managing access to personal information.

- **Customer identity management.** We've already introduced the concept of customer identity management as a core CDI capability. This means the alignment and consolidation of customer data across business units, divisions, subsidiaries, and sales channels—in other words, the integration of customer detail from different source systems. A critical aspect of customer identity management capabilities is maintaining the original value of the source data. This is important because the "real answer" may vary. A customer might like being called "Bob" by his sales rep, but prefers "Mr. Smith" when calling customer support. Customer identity management keeps the original source system values and determines their linkages. Identity management isn't about finding the "right" answer as much as it is linking various attributes, say, multiple addresses, to the same individual. In the telecommunications industry, for instance, the holy grail is to understand the products a given customer has purchased across diverse lines of business—wireless, local service, and long distance. In retail, companies need to understand customer purchases across Web, catalog, and brick-and-mortar channels. Insurance companies need to understand the breadth of products for an individual policyholder. The goal is to match the transactions and activities to the individual across business areas.

- **Simplified application access to customer data.** According to a Delphi Group report, business professionals spend 25 percent of their time every day simply searching for information. The same report found that 35 percent of respondents blamed "data changes" as the main impediment to knowledge gathering.[3] As we've discussed in other chapters, the number of sources of customer data has become downright overwhelming. Integrating data across the multitude of data sources is not only highly complex, but it frequently exceeds the skills of IT development staff. Add the sheer number of applications that require customer data to support their processing and it becomes obvious that the results are bound to differ from system to system. The reason is simple: every application integrates customer data in a different way. The effort that individual application development teams spend on locating, accessing, understanding, defining, correlating, integrating, and deploying data from various siloed systems for their applications is significant and multiplied exponentially by the number of development projects in need of accurate customer data. Customer data integration centralizes the integration processing—now spread across multiple applications—and understands which data elements are involved in each application's need. The integration is done once and is then available to everyone.

- **Customer data maintenance.** It's no secret that once programmers or data stewards identify data errors, it's next to impossible to convince a source system owner to change or correct the data. With CDI, companies finally have a way to correct and propagate customer data through the traditional application processing channels without requiring involvement from the operational systems. While the CDI hub finds data errors, operational systems seldom fix their bad data. By linking disparate data, CDI provides the mechanism to reflect consistent data across systems. It's important to distinguish that CDI provides the *means* for error identification and correction options—but the application must decide to make the fix.

CDI Drivers by Industry

Inasmuch as every company can claim the need for a single source of customer truth simply based on the business drivers described above, each industry has its own specific business drivers that can in and of themselves justify the CDI investment. Following is a brief discussion of CDI drivers for each major industry.

Financial Services

From banks to brokerage firms to mortgage lenders to credit card companies, financial services firms continue to focus on sales, marketing, and customer service. The motive of these firms is to tie customers together across multiple and often diverse sales and support channels. These channels can include credit card, standard banking, mortgage, insurance, and other services. Each of these channels not only has its own systems, but it's rare for all of the account details to be linked in a sustainable way.

A few years ago, we worked with a large national bank that didn't have the information necessary to identify all a customer's accounts. Some customers had personal accounts (deposits, mortgages, credit cards, and even investment accounts) as well as small business deposit accounts. A significant portion of these customers required lines of credit for what turned out to be business reasons. But the bank had been sending them offers for home equity lines of credit because it was unaware that these same customers were also small business owners. In what the bank thought was a successful campaign, these small business owners were responding to the home equity line of credit offers instead of the more profitable small business loans—which generated almost 50 percent more profit!

Another business driver for CDI in financial services is regulatory compliance. For instance, regulations like the Gramm-Leach-Bliley Act are forcing banks to not only individualize each customer across accounts, but also to provide opt-out options before they share information with their affiliates and partners. Financial services need to be able to identify NPI as part of Gramm-Leach-Bliley. Since a consumer can have multiple product relationships with a bank, the bank may unknowingly apply an opt-out flag to an account rather than an individual, thus risking the disclosure of customer details.

However, financial services firms are still very focused on managing customer relationships, and their ability to recognize customers as individuals and differentiate their treatment is still a high priority. Despite large investments in CRM and data warehousing, duplicate customer profiles are still rampant. Most banks say they want to be their customers' single source for everything from credit cards to banking to insurance to investments. One of the age-old problems in financial services is marketing products to existing customers—we've all received credit card solicitations for cards we already have. Improved cross-selling remains an important business driver.

Financial services firms continue to assume that their CRM and data warehouse systems can solve these problems. But these solutions simply ensure that certain data has been stored in one place. In order to improve cross-sell effectiveness and reduce marketing costs, banks and other financial services providers need to understand the true view of their customers across products and channels. CDI ensures that customers are identified correctly, that the data is matched and merged, and that different divisions can see the same customer in different but accurate ways.

Retail

In a business that's all about the customer, many retailers still aren't. Most retailers still have the classic marketing challenges of duplicate customer addresses (most catalog companies still send multiple costly catalogs to the same household), an inability to effectively cross-sell, and lack of knowledge about customers' cross-channel activities. In an effort to get closer to customers, retailers have invested in CRM and even advanced data mining technologies, but still have a hard time harnessing individual customer attributes.

According to a 2005 study by JupiterResearch, the shopping population is flattening, putting additional pressure on retailers to grab greater share of wallet from an ever more stabilizing number of customers.[4] Motivating existing customers to buy more will be retailers' new marketing mantra.

Despite this goal, few multichannel retailers are able to access a customer's consolidated account activities across all sales and service channels. Because so many retailers now have multiple channels—Web, brick and mortar, and catalog—it becomes even more difficult to tie together all the activities of a given individual or household. Retailers often operate these channels as separate business divisions, exacerbating the organizational and technical challenges associated with integrating data.

Retailing partnerships like Toys "R" Us with Amazon.com or Sharper Image with Bed, Bath, and Beyond are offering a new channel challenge, since their products are being sold through other retailing sites. Traditional retailers are taking on wholesaler relationships and thus may not have the access to customer details they once did. If a customer calls in for product support, the retailer might not even recognize him.

Meanwhile, their reliance on third-party data providers to support their data enrichment activities often means that duplicate records are regularly introduced into retailers' customer databases. Retailers—especially high-touch retailers like online, catalog, and specialty retailers—spend exorbitant sums on direct marketing. Whether internal or through third-party providers, data deduplication and integration are expensive. In addition to its potential for enhancing customer loyalty programs and other marketing initiatives, CDI could represent a successful solution for integrating customer data in a sustained and accurate way.

Communications

Competitive differentiation in the communications sector often lives or dies on customer service quality and efficiencies. Communications companies still have trouble linking the same individual across their wireless, long distance, and local service businesses. They don't always know the portfolio of products a single customer has. Until they do, cross-sell and up-sell activities will be hit or miss.

As with the other industries mentioned here, recent merger-and-acquisition (M&A) activities further muddy the customer recognition waters. With the recent acquisition of AT&T by SBC, the combined company (called AT&T) has an entire new population of customers to reconcile. Many SBC customers already had AT&T long distance services—or vice versa. The risk of offering existing customers competitive plans is high, since it means compromising profitability of existing products and services.

Telephone companies are increasingly launching MDM initiatives in order to track data lineage—so they understand the heritage of every data element, including the systems that currently process and store it, and where it originated. Product or segment managers often look at customer data in a vacuum, never knowing whether the customer originated in the long distance area, the company's broadband unit, or with a partner or subsidiary. Not knowing where in the business a customer originated can mean squandered sales and marketing efforts.

Regulations like the Federal Communications Commission's (FCC's) CPNI require phone companies to avoid sharing consumer data for marketing purposes. In March 2003, the FCC fined Verizon $5.7 million for marketing long distance services to customers before securing regulatory approval. Had CDI been available, automated business rules would have prevented such out-of-bounds solicitations. Likewise, in December 2005, the Federal Trade Commission (FTC) fined broadcaster DirecTV $5.3 million for calling consumers who had registered on the Do Not Call telemarketing registry. Had CDI been functional at DirecTV, the company could have integrated their marketing list with the Do Not Call registry.

Consumers have the right to opt out of marketing programs, but it's difficult for companies to propagate such requests across all the systems associated with individual accounts, products, and service channels. A customer might have multiple phone numbers, products (like call waiting and caller ID), and even digital subscriber line (DSL) service. To make matters worse, the different accounts might be under different names within the same household. Thus, a phone company may not be certain whether the customer is on a Do Not Call list somewhere.

Moreover, supporting commercial clients, often responsible for the majority of a phone company's profits, is increasingly complex. Because of their organizational structures and complex hierarchies, large commercial companies might have a diverse set of products and different contractual arrangements with a single carrier. The carrier has a hard time knowing that two purchasing groups exist within the same parent company; thus, sales, marketing, and billing problems are exacerbated.

Travel and Entertainment

From overbooked hotel rooms to crowded runways to frequent guests who must nevertheless provide their information anew, the travel and hospitality industries have problems practicing customer focus. Having failed to recoup their investments in expensive personalized e-mail campaigns and frequent guest programs, airlines, hotels, and casinos are looking for new ways to get and keep customers.

Aside from the marketing challenges, however, security, fraud, and risk management all play into the need for more robust customer recognition. For instance, casinos are now moving to CDI technologies, since customers have different entry points. From the casino to the hotel front desk to a high-end wine bar to a cabaret, a customer can have many mini-experiences with a casino. If a high roller enters a game of blackjack and hands the dealer his frequent player card, the casino might not be aware of how many hotel nights he's paid for, or how much he's spent in its restaurants. Without CDI, it's difficult for a casino to truly know a customer's wallet share.

Merger-mania is also taking its toll on the already disparate customer databases that litter the travel and leisure sector. Harrah's now owns Caesar's Entertainment, and MGM Mirage—already the product of a merger—acquired Mandalay Resort Group. The Caesars acquisition alone challenged Harrah's to add 20 million additional customer profiles to a customer database that was already 30 million strong.[5]

When Marriott International acquired the Ritz-Carlton, it added 1.4 million additional guests. Hilton Hotels actually reunified with its international namesake, while maintaining separate brands like Embassy Suites, Hilton Garden Inn, and Doubletree. Even the online travel sites like Expedia are being acquired. There are dozens of other examples of the M&A frenzy that requires hospitality companies to quickly integrate new customer data sources and identify customers more effectively.

> *The Caesars acquisition alone challenged Harrah's to add 20 million additional customer profiles to a customer database that was already 30 million strong.*

The airlines continue to merge as they add and eliminate cochair partnerships, constantly introducing and merging customer records. With the advent of the online companies like Priceline.com that let customers "name their own price" for airline tickets, air carriers can't always identify customers that come in through indirect channels that aren't linked to their frequent-flier systems. Identity management functionality from CDI vendors offers promising strategic hope for travel and hospitality firms.

Health Care

Health care would never be accused of being an IT early adopter. But that's changing. The main drivers of CDI in health care—patient recognition and payer-provider collaboration—are turning the industry upside down.

Because of the Health Insurance Portability and Accountability Act (HIPAA), patients must have access to their private health care records. Moreover, whenever patient data is stored or shared, the patient must be informed of such transactions. Thus, HIPAA legislation forces hospitals, providers, health maintenance organizations (HMOs), and insurers to track individual patient records across the continuum of care. This means a new sense of urgency around implementing electronic medical records, despite often reluctant physicians and high initial costs.

It also means that data quality and accuracy will get even more attention in a sector that is already investing heavily in its data. According to one study, nearly 99 percent of provider patient data had error rates that risked jeopardizing the accurate identification of individual patients.[6] HIPAA has been a paradigm shift for the health care industry, traditionally more focused on clinical workflow automation than on patient record reconciliation and tracking.

More important, the need to match patient records to identify individual patients could be a life-or-death proposition. So-called enterprise master patient index (EMPI) capabilities promise to help health care providers recognize patients as individuals by combining data across multiple hospitals, doctors' offices, clinics, laboratories, pharmacies, and other patient entry points, as well as across diverse systems. The vision is to have a consolidated, trusted view of every patient for every point of care or every system across the health care delivery network.

The impact is nothing less than patient safety. For instance, a pregnant woman sees her doctor, who diagnoses preeclampsia, a complication of pregnancy that includes high blood pressure and high levels of urine protein that could, if left untreated, be fatal. He prescribes bed rest and blood pressure medication. A few weeks later, the patient is rushed to the emergency room of a different hospital—just a block away from her doctor's office—with severe abdominal pain and headache, but the ER doctor has no information about the prior diagnosis and the patient has a seizure. There are hundreds of thousands of instances where missing or incomplete patient records have had tragic consequences for patients.

Discussions of national health care registries or federal patient matching capabilities have been amplified despite privacy concerns. "The data that we would use to match patient records is all on someone's driver's license," one health care provider told us. "The privacy concerns are becoming moot as the enabling technologies improve." For many health care providers, CDI is at the center of the solution.

> *There are hundreds of thousands of instances where missing or incomplete patient records have had tragic consequences for patients.*

Regional health information organizations (RHIOs) are networks emerging to tie various health care networks together to share patient information. Having patient details from individual physicians on a centralized hub is CDI defined.

Pharmaceutical

Pharmacies too are getting in on the act. With access to complete patient records, a pharmacist can prevent unforeseen drug interactions or call the right doctor for additional prescription detail. Likewise, doctors can research what medications their patients might be taking at or before the time of treatment. The aim of pharmacy benefit management is to bring data together from hospitals, care clinics, and other pharmacies to consolidate different prescriptions for the same patient.

In the pharmaceutical and biotechnology industries, a successful drug can generate $1 billion or more in annual sales. With potentially hundreds of drugs in the development pipeline, the potential for profits is huge.

So is the number of data sources. The rise of so-called electronic data capture in pharmaceutical firms has meant the proliferation of data from sources inside and outside these companies. A given pharmaceutical company might have a range of overlapping relationships with doctors, managed care organizations, researchers, patients, distributors, and hospitals. MDM projects, specifically those focusing on a "party reference system," are taking hold to enable pharmaceutical companies to recognize these expanded relationships and put them in context with one another.

Most pharmaceutical companies were early adopters of CRM systems to help them manage their sales contacts. Many have even automated their sales and research workflows, thus leveraging IT to standardize critical business processes. The proliferation of packaged applications in pharmaceutical and life science industries has meant the replication of critical data across these systems. In many pharmaceutical companies, each drug product may have its own system for clinical research and sales.

The main use of CDI in the pharmaceutical industry is the so-called single physician view, or physician master hub, providing the company with cleansed and matched data to help pinpoint different physicians and their attributes. Customer data integration enforces business rules pertaining to interactions with a doctor who may be affiliated with multiple care organizations, has multiple specialties, or manages a particular department. Reconciling doctors with their hospitals, offices, and accounts can help pharmaceutical companies more accurately determine sales compensation.

Integrating such diverse information across data sources from clinical trial systems, sales force automation packages, contract management systems, and enterprise resource planning (ERP) systems can represent significant cost savings and productivity efficiencies, as well as data quality improvements across the industry's diverse business processes. From a marketing perspective, this can help drug companies reach a universal goal of managing physician relationships and retaining physicians in their networks.

Compliance, globalization, and safety concerns are further driving the need to integrate data from these siloed systems. Customer data hubs can address data semantic concerns since in the pharmaceutical industry the term *customer* can mean many different things. Integrating many data sources to provide a single view of physicians, hospitals, and other care organizations—and pinpoint their relationships with one another—supports the continued operation of diverse transaction systems while offering considerable productivity benefits.

Insurance

Insurance is a complex industry, made even more so by the fact that independent agents and subsidiaries usually have their own data and systems. Consolidating individual customer data across these business boundaries isn't easy. Despite the fact that most insurance companies have implemented centralized customer databases or data warehouses—largely for claims analysis and other business intelligence work—many remain mired in paper-based enrollment forms and resellers resistant to sharing their data.

The customer life-cycle within an insurance company can be very complex, from the initial application for insurance through actuarial services through to underwriting, payment, and claims management. Some insurance companies are renowned for their delays in shepherding new customers through the policy enrollment process. Tracking customers at a point in time across customer-centered business processes is a key, but largely unmet, goal for insurers.

Indeed, at each point in a customer's interaction with an insurance carrier, his status with the firm can change. This workflow touches people and systems both inside and outside the insurance company, rendering the monitoring of current and accurate customer information difficult. Add to this the multichannel environment that may encourage a customer to purchase a term life policy at his agent's office while securing auto insurance online and his homeowner's insurance through a subsidiary. It's a tangled web of policies, forms, organizations, and payment details, and linking the relevant customer data is a complex and intricate task.

Individualizing customers drive smarter target marketing. While many insurance firms had initially relied on new CRM and data warehouse technologies to solve some of these problems, they linger due to an inability to perform effective customer matching across systems and business divisions.

Insurers share the classic marketing problems associated with the lack of a single, authoritative source of customer information. Some have actually begun acquiring CDI solutions and seeing the benefits. A friend whose roommate had switched auto insurance carriers received a postcard in the mail a week later. The postcard said, "A member of your household recently switched! If you switch too, both your rates could drop!" This isn't only smart target marketing, the ability to recognize individuals with different last names in the same household is CDI delivered.

Public Sector

The public sector can be split across federal, state, and local legislative areas as well as divided into dozens of smaller market segments. There are almost as many opportunities for CDI as there are government agencies. Pressure to share information across various government agencies is growing, but the emerging uses of CDI tend to involve recognition of individuals.

"Person of interest" recognition is paramount to law enforcement agencies worldwide. While a person of interest evokes the capture of terrorists, it also applies to crime suspects at the state or local level, and anyone whom law enforcement needs to be aware of, like deadbeat dads or prisoners on parole. CDI holds significant promise for law enforcement organizations from the Central Intelligence Agency to local police. With the spotlight on national security in the United States and abroad, recognition of individuals at the time of their entry into a country, purchase of a weapon, or detainment at a law enforcement location offers unfathomable benefits.

This also applies to welfare. The challenge here is to surmise the benefits a household—an entire family—is receiving. This means linking data about multiple members from multiple programs, from juvenile health care to food stamps, job training, or government-subsidized child care. Understanding a family across their spectrum of need can help government agencies to better serve their citizens while reducing fraud and cutting costs. For instance, New York City's Master Child Index consolidates patient records from its Citywide Immunization Registry and Lead Poisoning Prevention program, helping the local government to identify populations in need of immunizations or screening.

Voter registration is also an emerging area for CDI. The Help America Vote Act (HAVA) of 2002 represents the most significant voter reform legislation in recent U.S. history. The act requires states to create a statewide, centralized, electronic list of all registered voters. The implication is that these lists will reduce the instances of fraud and provide accurate and non-duplicated information about voters. The vision is for databases in state agencies like the Department of Motor Vehicles to "fill in" missing data about voters, rendering the electronic voter lists more complete over time.[7]

There is also an opportunity for CDI in the prison system. There is an acknowledged need for individual identity recognition in the justice system, particularly at the state level. We worked with one state prison system that struggled to tie together individuals and their criminal histories and was thus unable to understand the scope of their criminal records. This meant they couldn't be assured of seeing the individual's entire criminal past. Identifying suspected criminals was exacerbated by the fact that many used aliases and fraudulent or inaccurate identification, with repercussions on case management and criminal charges. Since the state had no access to individual history, it was possible for someone to commit a third felony that went undetected, thereby avoiding the "three strikes" law.

There are other industries where CDI is a latecomer. Currently, the management of product master data is a hot issue with manufacturers. Nevertheless, the concept of party reference data—across customers, distribution partners, and suppliers—is gaining traction. Although ERP systems have helped, they haven't integrated data from subsidiaries and suppliers across different lines of business. Where CDI can help here is in understanding and identifying entities within company hierarchies.

BUILDING THE BUSINESS CASE

Someone once said that, in justifying new technology investments, managers should be able to answer the question, "Why is this better than doing nothing?" CDI can solve a host of both business and technology problems, but explaining how isn't always easy.

Successful CDI requires a business case, but perhaps not in the classical sense. The business cases we recommend for clients who are adopting CRM, data warehouses, or other, more end user–focused IT projects emphasize both cost savings and revenue generation. At their most comprehensive, effective business cases can include discussions of:

- Revenue improvement
- New revenue generation
- Reduced costs
- Productivity gains
- Increased customer acquisitions
- Improved quality of service
- Reduced business risks
- Employee satisfaction and retention

As we've written elsewhere,[8] a truly effective business case covers both financial and nonfinancial benefits—also called "hard" and "soft" benefits—of the proposed IT project. For example, a hard benefit might be the sales uplift and associated revenues driven by better target marketing, achieved through the ability to pinpoint individual customers and their behaviors. A soft benefit might be improved customer satisfaction because of better customer lists and higher customer interest levels.

CASE STUDY: BELL MOBILITY

John Walker remembers his early days at Canada's Bell Mobility with a mixture of wistfulness and amusement. "We were in the early stages of our database marketing," he admits. Indeed, the company—Canada's leading provider of wireless voice and data services to consumers and businesses—was experiencing the classic marketing challenges associated with fast growth.

"The duplicate mailings were one thing," Walker says. "Some of our commercial customers were getting 10 to 15 different pieces of direct mail. And we were missing opportunities to engage existing customers. Sometimes we called the wrong people, like existing customers on prospect lists." Walker laughs, "Obviously, a customer doesn't appreciate it when we send them an invitation to be a customer. We also had no idea who was responding to our offers. There was no continuity of information."

Walker's no marketing novice, having worked at a number of direct-marketing powerhouses, including a stint at Kraft, where he worked on CRM. He understood that Bell Mobility needed to be able to track customers across their life-cycle with the company. "But we didn't have a marketing database outside of the billing system, and the Bell Canada side didn't have a database for us to piggyback off of—so we had to build our own."

By then, Walker knew there would be technical hurdles. Nevertheless, he decided to convince management of the business challenges that awaited the company if it didn't solve its marketing issues. He met with executives in marketing to pitch the solution in business terms.

"My proposal deck was eight pages about the kind of marketing we could do if we fixed our problems and only two describing the technical aspect of the solution. I explained how we were wasting cost-of-acquisition (COA) dollars and eroding customer satisfaction by calling existing customers with prospect offers. I showed how we were leaving money on the table. I talked about what could happen if we cleaned up the data to increase our contact hit rates. And I put it all in financial terms that they could understand."

Marketing bit. Now Walker and his team needed to focus on tactics.

The first order of business was to fix the data. The goal was to enable data matching and eliminate duplicate records. Walker's team acquired a data quality tool, and installed and started running it within a week. The resulting address standardization and data cleansing delivered almost immediate payback. "Our data quality solution yielded about 1000 percent ROI. We saw an incremental million dollars in revenue in the first year, and it only cost us around $50,000."

Once the initial data had been cleansed, Walker and his team turned their heads to the database. Their prospect history database delivered the basics: storage of the newly clean data on a Microsoft SQL Server platform, and a business intelligence tool to analyze the data. The team began loading and analyzing the data and measuring the associated improvements.

"Measurement is enculturated with me," Walker explains. "My past jobs have been analytical, and I've always loved direct marketing because you can monitor your successes and make adjustments based on what you learn. Measurement lets us test things to find out what works and what doesn't. It's really hard to get an executive to approve a project unless you can assure them it'll work. The results need to be measurable enough that you can prove the benefits."

And prove they did. At the end of the project's first year, Walker and his team conducted a postmortem, illustrating the before-and-after payback of the new system. They were able to show measurable improvements in:

- Sales uplift
- Right party contact rates
- Sales rates in the call center. "We didn't think that would move at all," Walker confides, "but the reps were actually motivated by the new lists they were getting. For the first time ever they were actually telling us the lists were great!"
- Cost of acquisition. "Essentially, we had to send out fewer pieces of mail to get the same results so our COA dropped."
- Revenue from incremental sales

"Every time I go out with a new communication, I want to be able to improve the results," says Walker. "And now we can do that."

Not only did the marketing organization notice, but so did Bell Mobility's parent company, Bell Canada. "We've always been the 'kid brother,' so it's sort of fulfilling that we've been able to drive some of these initiatives. Bell Canada's a big, established company with a 125-year history behind it. So it's cool that we can still be the personification of a small, nimble team getting things done quickly and cheaply, and delivering value to customers."

While estimates vary, in recent years a host of industry analysts and trade magazines have reported that integration absorbs between 30 and 60 percent of an IT organization's development budget. In 2001, a vendor white paper claimed that direct programming costs associated with data transformation constituted 20 to 30 percent of implementation costs.[9] In 2002, *PC Magazine* cited an estimate that 35 percent of IT activity in a typical enterprise was dedicated to application integration.[10] Also in 2002, two researchers reported that the average company had 49 different databases, and that integrating data from disparate source systems comprised 35 percent of the IT budget.[11] In addition, in a study conducted by The Data Warehousing Institute in 2005, 69 percent of respondents claimed that data integration was a barrier to new application development.[12] The numbers are getting worse as data volumes increase and new data arrives from additional sources both inside and outside your company.

One thing for sure: data integration is a routinely underestimated development task. Development organizations often make overly optimistic assumptions about the integrity of corporate data or about the accuracy of the data on a given source system.

Development Cost Savings

The best way to estimate the cost savings of CDI is what we call the pre-facto approach. When you look at the quantity of customer-centric applications on your company's radar for the next 18 months, it's likely that the integration development work for those applications will comprise 30 percent (a conservative estimate) of total development. The cost saving benefits of the aggregate value of 30 percent for each application make the payback promise of CDI relatively straightforward. This will likely be your best bet for financial justification of a CDI project.

If you don't have the facts about what your IT development pipeline looks like, consider the post-facto approach and extrapolate from past projects. Look at what your annual investment in application maintenance and new application development is

> *The cost saving benefits of the aggregate value of 30 percent for each application make the payback promise of CDI relatively straightforward.*

specific to customer-focused projects. Most IT organizations are hyper-aware of their budgets and can get their arms around past projects and what they cost. How much data integration and cleansing work has been involved to deliver your business intelligence, campaign management, and sales force automation projects? Apply 30 percent of those costs and you'll have a reliable idea of what data integration has cost you in maintenance.

You can also look at maintenance activities centered around customer data correction, data cleanup, and data reconciliation. Consider the maintenance associated with one-off data correction issues, data inaccuracies, and source system changes. This work is replicated across multiple applications and can be tied back to the lack of sustainable data integration. A business case can usually be made for CDI based on the maintenance cost savings alone.

It's worth noting that CDI represents a remedy for companies badly in need of integrated customer data that assume a data warehouse is their only option. "When you have 63 different data silos to integrate, loading all that data onto a single platform is pretty hard to explain to management, let alone to cost justify," one addled banker recently told us. In many instances, the integrated view of the customer doesn't require acquisition and loading of all associated customer data, but merely calls for the linkages to that data via the registry type of CDI or a homegrown "index" approach. This approach can address business problems such as:

- Discovering whether someone is already a customer
- Searching for the customer while she's on the phone
- Identifying a customer at an airline check-in kiosk
- Knowing how recently a customer has contacted the company

For instance, you don't need the customer's entire purchase history to understand his most recent purchase. Such business problems don't require exhaustive information about the customer—just the unique attributes that characterize that individual.

"The main driver for CDI is a shift in corporate strategy."

For a CIO to begin a conversation with the strategy angle is unexpected but refreshing. For David Gutierrez, chief information officer for ING Insurance Americas, his company's recent strategic shift was significant, both for the business and for the programs his IT organization is planning to deliver.

"Our corporate culture is changing to become more customer oriented, less product oriented," Gutierrez explains. "We're promising to treat our customers as individuals. Our main objective is to bring all of our customer data together so that when you call us, we know you."

When Gutierrez joined ING Americas he not only had deep IT and insurance industry expertise, but he brought 16 years of advertising background. All this added up to a vision for managing customers across a global landscape while supporting the company's brand integrity. "We're in 62 different countries," he says. "But we developed our overarching approach in the United States, since it represents one of the more complex business models. We figured if it could work here, it could work anywhere."

Add to that the fact that ING is comprised of many different companies, a product of a divisional organization and a global presence combined with an aggressive growth-through-acquisition strategy. Each of ING's subsidiaries and divisions has its own systems, its own data, and its own challenges.

Gutierrez and his team addressed these challenges with their Enterprise Information Platform (EIP) program, the foundation not only for integrated customer data, but also for re-use of other data across the various ING companies. The goal of EIP was to create business value based on three dimensions:

1. Delivery speed of data-enabled business programs

2. Minimization of risks around data usage and realization

3. Cost reduction through technology and data reuse

With EIP, Gutierrez's team took a "leave it where it is" strategy, providing federated query functionality and bidirectional updates of distributed customer data via a centralized hub interchange. The hub supports both distributed and centralized data from across ING's numerous data sources, including its ERP, mainframe, and document management systems.

The hub is flexible enough to store persistent information when it needs to, but extensible enough to support the addition of new data sources and client applications as they become available. "We toyed with the idea of just having a centralized data warehouse," Gutierrez explains, "but we realized that wouldn't be enough to support the real-time needs of our business. The hub interchange is really our engine for integrated customer data."

The results have been impressive. Before EIP, ING relied on custom-built extracts from siloed systems and latent information from dozens of legacy applications. Post-EIP, the company has seen dramatic improvements in data quality and data provisioning turnaround time. Customer survey data is available on demand and in near real time across all lines of business. The Securities and Exchange Commission (SEC) and insurance regulations can be more tightly managed, since policies can be more strictly enforced and tracked.

And the financial return is noteworthy. The company estimates savings of $450,000 for each application that requires customer profiles, and $1.2 million for each system requiring transaction details.

Moreover, EIP has a global reach for ING, serving as the foundation for diverse programs across different countries, including data migration in Brazil, a common information architecture in Canada, customer segmentation in Chile, and business performance management in Mexico. It's the intended standard for different development processes across the company, including data quality, data modeling, and knowledge management.

Gutierrez takes the benefits of EIP full circle, back to the company's strategy. His team mapped EIP's benefits back to several of the company's key strategic objectives, including maintaining brand integrity, achieving a reputation for regulatory compliance, and increasing marginal revenue and asset retention. "We just launched a campaign that celebrates how easy we are to do business with. ING wants to be a different kind of company. To be innovative with our customers, we needed to be innovative with our technology."

Mission accomplished.

The heart of CDI's value is the eventual eradica-
tion of redundant data integration processing across
a company's various application systems. Combined with increased staff productivity, these are the
two "low-hanging fruit" justifications of CDI.

But don't ignore other potential CDI benefits.
Many will be company or industry specific or solve
political issues like data ownership and processing
problems that have plagued development organizations for a long time.

> *Be ready to argue the conse-
> quences of not doing CDI. This
> will help you make a much
> more persuasive argument.*

For instance, as discussed in Chapter 5, mapping CDI to specific and
high-visibility company strategies is a legitimate tact, but probably more
difficult to quantify financially. Consider your company's culture and re-
ward mechanisms when requesting budget and support for CDI. Be ready
to argue the consequences of not doing CDI. This will help you make a
much more persuasive argument.

A riskier move is the "If We'd Had CDI . . ." approach, as in, "If we'd
had CDI before we launched the corporate compliance program, we
wouldn't have had to spend the $600,000 it took to research and profile
our existing customer data sources, and we would have saved $1.2 million
in data extraction programming."

The more effectively you can make the case for CDI, the better your
chances are for convincing management to fund it. Moreover, the more
thorough the business case, the higher the likelihood that IT management's
behaviors will match its claims of support, ensuring that CDI teams will be
adequately staffed and managed.

WHAT WORKS: TIPS FROM THE EXPERTS

Ted Brewer: "Extend client strategy beyond the department."

"We realized that once we built an authoritative customer view, our
business processes would have to change. This meant synchronizing
client interactions across our lines of business. So we determined at
a more global level what the client contact strategy would be. That

way, different companies and departments weren't stepping on each other's toes. You need to involve everyone and do this holistically. The meetings can get pretty lively at times, but it's for the greater good. If you're going to do it right, you need to be ready to extend the client contact strategy across the enterprise. "

TED BREWER, Vice President, Customer Information Management, Royal Bank of Canada

KEEPING THE SABOTEURS AT BAY

The organizational aversion to change has been cited throughout history. In 1829, Martin Van Buren, then governor of New York, wrote in a letter to President John Quincy Adams:

> The canal system of this country is being threatened by the spread of a new form of transportation known as "railroads." . . . As you may well know, railroad carriages are pulled at the enormous speed of 15 miles per hour by engines, which, in addition to endangering life and limb of passengers, roar and snort their way through the countryside. The Almighty certainly never intended that people should travel at such breakneck speed.

With CDI, too, there will be those who are uncomfortable with the adoption of a new—indeed, an authoritative—way to process and source customer data. After all, if CDI is done correctly, it will become the de-facto system of record for all the company's customer data. That can mean changes in job roles and responsibility for people who have had a hand in defining or acquiring customer data. These people are likely to include:

- **Application owners.** This chapter has already touched on how CDI can be a boon to developers. So why wouldn't they support it? Because many application developers have spent long hours doing the grueling work of writing data integration code from scratch. They have become reluctant experts on data integration, and it's now a big part of their jobs. An application developer might be suspicious of technology that claims to replace her specialized code. Or she may realize that so much of her time has gone into maintaining the data integration functionality that she needs to find something else to keep her busy.

- **Source system owners and developers.** The fear here is loss of control, and it's genuine. Often, these people build and maintain the systems that run the company, and the possibility that their data might be accessed or modified by a new development team makes them justifiably nervous.

- **Data warehouse owners and developers.** After all, they've already delivered integrated customer data. In fact, they may consider the data warehouse the company's de-facto single version of the truth! Any technology that usurps that role could be perceived as a threat to the viability of the data warehouse. (As we'll see below, it shouldn't be.)

- **Extraction, transformation, and loading (ETL) developers.** Programmers who have become experts in moving data around the company might perceive that a CDI hub could remove the need for ETL. This is especially true with the emergence of probabilistic or deterministic algorithms that can match data in a more automated and algorithmic way. For large-volume data migration efforts, CDI is not an appropriate solution, nor should it be applied to non-customer master data. Extraction, transformation, and loading remains necessary for subject-area content where business rules are more specialized or unique from company to company and thus can't be easily packaged. There's still a legitimate need for ETL skills and tools.

- **Business people vying for IT resources.** One of the truisms of IT is that the demand for IT services exceeds the available supply of resources. Probably the most valid reason for being "against" a CDI initiative is that it will take precious staff and system development time away from someone's pet project on the business side. Project managers can often link CDI's benefits with such an initiative, positioning it as a valid first step in the development of the future project.

Victor Fehlberg: "Start small—and don't overpromise."

"I'd encourage people embarking on a CDI project to start small and don't overpromise. You can solve world hunger after you successfully get your data matching solution up and working. A small pilot is a good way to get started."

VICTOR FEHLBERG, Architect, Amgen

Common Arguments against CDI

By now, you're probably picturing at least one person in your company who will take aim at CDI before the business case even sees daylight. It's helpful to understand the likely arguments against CDI and MDM adoption so you can be prepared to defend your proposal—or to fire back. Here's the ammunition they're likely to lob your way:

"We have a CRM system. We don't need CDI." A CDI solution provides an integrated view of customers across multiple systems. It's not CRM specific. In fact, a CDI hub can solidify and sanction customer information used by a CRM tool, finding and reconciling customer-related data across data sources without manual intervention. Conversely, CRM systems are not built for source system extensibility. They are usually limited to the data contained within the CRM system or data retrieved via preexisting keys or connections. A CDI solution can provide access to data from other customer data sources where those keys or connections don't exist.

"Our data warehouse already integrates customer data." Yes, but it can't determine data relationships across sources in a dynamic and accurate way. Because of its lower latency, CDI can make data available in real time, and all the processing of data cleansing and accuracy are baked in. The matching algorithms that are part of CDI are more robust than the standard transformation code involved in ETL programs. The CDI solution will identify where transactions and data are related to a particular individual. Identity functions like alias recognition aren't automatically processed by data warehouses or off-the-shelf ETL tools. Moreover, the data warehouse can't address data correction at the source. The CDI hub is more responsive to operational systems changes, so when data is updated on the sources, it's automatically updated on the hub. The CDI hub also addresses the issues of data privacy and data sharing that aren't part of data warehouse processing.

"We're building a real-time data warehouse." Be careful not to overinvest. So-called real-time data warehousing is an interesting step up from traditional data warehousing, providing the data is already resident in an existing and functional data warehouse. Nevertheless, a real-time data warehouse won't handle automatic customer identification and reconciliation—the ETL processing isn't as robust as the integration algorithms that characterize CDI products. The complex rules and functions inherent in most CDI hubs aren't utilitarian transformation functions but are rather highly specialized to customer data. A real-time data warehouse won't automatically provide the data lineage support—CDI will tell you which elements of operational systems are associated with an individual party. If you think about it, what's more efficient: moving all the data, or just the IDs? Most CDI solutions have been specially architected to support the dynamic changes of operational data. This is unlikely with a real-time data warehouse, and in any case it will probably cost a whole lot more.

"Our operational data store (ODS) does that." An ODS typically retains data in the native format and structure of the source system, so it's not providing an overall picture of a customer in real time. The CDI hub provides a picture of a customer at a particular time, with highly cleansed, highly transformed data, whereas the ODS is usually a quick and dirty way to access recent customer data that hasn't yet been integrated.

"We're extending our enterprise application integration (EAI) capabilities. We have a messaging infrastructure with an enterprise service bus." As we discussed in Chapter 7, EAI technologies manage application-to-application messages, enabling transactions to move between business applications efficiently. While EAI has no knowledge or intelligence about data, the CDI hub has inherent knowledge of the fields themselves. It knows that there are special rules about integrating multiple addresses. Plus EAI doesn't provide data integration and the entire picture of a customer at a point in time. While it can recognize a customer's purchase transactions when they occur, EAI doesn't provide all the details about that customer.

"We already have a customer data model for the enterprise; we don't need CDI." The data models that accompany most CDI solutions are, in reality, physical database schemas. Those from enterprise application vendors usually reflect the customer's transaction details, thus mirroring the application aspects of the customer, not the customer's identity. This is an "apples and oranges" argument, since a company's existing customer data model can be useful in CDI development, reflecting the company's view of the party or customer and their relationships and attributes. The CDI hub isn't only the single version of the truth; it also supports the data lineage—it knows not only what the data relationships are but where the data originated in the first place.

"There's no use. We'll never get people to agree on common data definitions." As we've mentioned, launching CDI as a consensus-driven, top-down effort can be risky. If a company can implement an EAI environment in which messages are shared across applications, the company should be able to establish the customer data elements that should be shared across systems. As the CDI hub supports additional applications, each application's data-sharing and standardization requirements can help a company develop sanctioned standards for customer data.

"We've just launched an MDM project. We're not ready for CDI." Maybe yes, maybe no. Master data management and CDI should be complementary efforts with significant overlap. Often, an MDM team insists on running the show. We don't believe that MDM can happen in a vacuum or that it should be a barrier to launching CDI. We recommend launching a CDI initiative to build the linkages to see which data is related across source systems, an effort that might help the MDM team understand key customer data. Such an approach provides subject area integration of customer master data to an MDM effort.

"We already have an accurate view of our customer through our packaged ERP system." This is the same issue as with the CRM scenario described above. While ERP vendors do offer MDM functionality, tying together like transactions about customers, they don't necessarily support the robust customer identification functions that allow access of customer details with nonintegrated data sources. The vast majority of ERP offerings were never designed to resolve customer hierarchies and relationships.

"We can already do all that with ETL." The fact is, CDI is smarter than ETL. It supports vastly more complex logic than a programmer can accomplish with an ETL tool. This is like comparing a computer to an abacus.

> *But the argument for CDI that gets the most traction with management is that the time to value is shorter than with comparable technologies.*

You and your team may well be the ones to educate other key individuals on both the IT and business sides about the value of CDI. When deflecting the arguments, remember that you're coming from a place of education that your audience is probably not. The CDI hub isn't a silver bullet, and shouldn't be positioned as a replacement for other technologies as much as a solution for discrete and potentially high-impact problems.

There are legitimate arguments to make that CDI has a lower total cost of ownership (TCO) and that development costs for CDI are lower than for the perceived alternatives. But the argument for CDI that gets the most traction with management is that the time to value is shorter than with comparable technologies. This can mean accelerating deployment of new applications—and, by extension, new business capabilities—that will be available more quickly and hopefully in advance of your competitors.

INTERNAL PUBLIC RELATIONS FOR CDI

Smart business sponsors and IT managers take pains to ensure that their CDI projects don't start with a bang and end with a whimper. If there is a business sponsor for CDI, he should not only help to pitch the initial CDI solution, but he should ensure that the project effort is "kept warm" once it's in development, especially with those who will eventually be using or benefiting from the CDI hub.

Like most highly visible IT efforts, the pitch should continue beyond initial project launch. Those responsible for developing CDI are often also saddled with "selling" CDI to other parts of the organization or business, either because those functions are unaware of CDI or because they need to be convinced of its value. This is ideally done by the business in collaboration with IT.

Indeed, a CDI project will likely have advocacy on the business side as well as support within IT. Gartner's John Radcliffe confirms that his advisory services involve both sides. "Business users are very often involved in our conversations," he says. "It's very common to have both business and IT on the phone together. Sometimes it's people who inhabit the 'middle ground'—they originally worked on the business side but now work in IT. It's fairly obvious that the organizations that have the strongest alignment with business drivers, have a high level of business sponsorship, and have a strong change management capability are going to be the most successful with CDI."

As we discussed in Chapter 5, the best way to implement CDI is incrementally. Beginning with a single "client" application and then proselytizing CDI's value to other applications, either successively or in parallel, ensures that your CDI team can have an informed and empirical discussion of the benefits, risks, and promise of CDI to other applications, and eventually to the company at large. Fostering these ongoing conversations is critical to CDI's adoption. We call this "internal PR."

With an initial project successfully completed, the CDI team can solicit additional applications over time to add to its portfolio. This is the best way to make the single version of the truth a reality for the entire organization.

There are several steps to building an effective internal PR campaign. Indeed, they mirror the steps of classic marketing efforts, but with a CDI flair:

1. **Name the "need, pain, or problem."** Developers of potential CDI client applications are one of several constituencies who can benefit from a CDI solution. These developers are often writing custom code or doing manual data profiling in order to capture customer data for their respective applications, and are prime recipients of the integrated, reconciled, and standardized data message. They'll likely be your biggest advocates. However, the business- and industry-specific problems listed above are all CDI drivers. Understand who owns them.

2. **Get face time.** The CDI team should meet with the application and systems architects as well as key businesspeople to explain CDI's value. Such meetings should be a little bit sales, but mostly content, and should include discussions of:

- The perceived value to the individual application or department in question
- The overall value proposition of CDI to the company
- The cost of CDI, as well as any cross-charging or funding requirements necessary to launch another CDI effort
- The risks involved (e.g., delayed projects or unavailable staff)
- What the CDI team needs from the application team in terms of time and resources

3. **Cultivate other opportunities.** Once people understand what CDI offers and how it differs from existing systems, they typically have other ideas about how a CDI hub can provide business benefits, realize strategic goals, and drive revenues. Track and record these ideas for subsequent CDI projects.

4. **Conduct regular review meetings.** The intent of internal PR is to keep CDI warm with constituents. This means the CDI project manager should establish a regular communications strategy with both the providers and the consumers of data, as well as with members of management who may benefit from the CDI project from a business perspective. Review meetings should include discussion of how CDI is conforming to its success measures.

5. **Create "leave-behinds."** One CDI project team retained the company's in-house graphics group to design a short "score card" that listed project milestones and success metrics. Each time a milestone was achieved or a metric was met, the team would distribute the revised scorecard to IT staff to let them know that progress was being made.

6. **Publicize the wins.** Unlike more user-focused IT projects, CDI doesn't get a lot of airtime with the business. The risk is that it gets "buried" as an infrastructure project. The CDI sponsor or project team nevertheless needs to share successes with the source and client applications teams, as well as with IT management and business stakeholders. A well-designed page on the company's intranet that illustrates shrinking development time frames or detailing the per-system cost savings realized since CDI was deployed will give the CDI hub—and the project team—the accolades it deserves and even ensure additional funding when the time is right.

The goal with internal PR for CDI is to elucidate the "total value of ownership," understanding both the total cost of ownership for CDI as well as the total realized and expected return. It's also to showcase CDI among the company's IT catalog of services, and to make clear why having the single version of the truth is such a clear benefit to IT as well as to corporate strategy. It's a tall order, but if you can do that, you're well on your way to success.

MANAGER DO'S AND DON'TS

In positioning CDI internally, it's important to start off on the right foot. After all, you're in the role of change agent, so tread carefully.

- **Do** realize that—if you're in the position of pitching CDI to your organization—you'll probably have to do some missionary work. Prepare some basic material about CDI, or use some of the concepts we've introduced here to educate constituents about CDI's potential value. And remember that the people you're trying to win over are probably passionate about the way they do their jobs today. Be mindful of the quote from psychologist William James, who said, "Whenever two people meet, there are really six people present. There is each man as he sees himself, each man as the other person sees him, and each man as he really is."
- **Don't** advocate replacing an existing application or system that is perceived as successful. It's usually more expensive to buy a new car than to fix an old one, and system replacement arguments usually involve more politics. The only time an existing application is fair game is when its maintenance work involves repeated resolution of data integration errors, and thus maintenance costs are higher than normal.
- **Do** focus CDI opportunities on new application development where integrating customer data will be a core component in realizing the new system's functionality.
- **Don't** limit your ROI options for CDI to cost savings opportunities. It's important to recognize that business growth often necessitates

revenue generation. Try to identify client applications focused on revenue growth, not just efficiencies.

- **Do** focus on problem resolution when discussing CDI with executives. Both IT and business managers are more interested in solving business problems and will welcome a conversation about benefits. Talk about the "whats" before the "hows."

■ ENDNOTES

1. *Barney Beal, "CRM's ROI Answer," SearchCRM.com, March 23, 2005. Beal quotes Meta Group (now part of Gartner) analyst David Newman, who explains that the reason companies have failed to quantify their CRM ROI is due to their failure to consider data management and data architecture.*

2. *William Bard, Jessica Harrington, Erin Kinikin, and John Ragsdale, "Evaluation of Top Enterprise CRM Software Vendors Across 177 Criteria," Forrester Research, 2005.*

3. *"Taxonomy and Content Classification: A Delphi Group Report," April 11, 2002.* See www.delphigroup.com/research/whitepapers/WP_2002_TAXONOMY.PDF.

4. *Patti Freeman Evans for JupiterResearch, "US Online Retail Forecast, 2005-2010," January 19, 2006.*

5. *Tony Kontzer, "High Rollers,"* InformationWeek, *September 13, 2004.*

6. *Michele O'Connor, "Data Quality in the EMPI,"* Advance for Health Care Professionals, *June 6, 2005.*

7. *According to the "Advocates Guide to the Help America Vote Act 2002."* See www.demos.org/home.cfm.

8. *Baseline Consulting white paper, "FindROI: Justifying and Re-justifying Strategic IT Programs," 2003. See* www.baseline-consulting.com.

9. *Contivo, Inc., "Introducing Enterprise Integration Modeling,"* www.contivo.com.

10. *Carol Levin, "Pulling It All Together,"* PC Magazine, *February 26, 2002.*

11. *Craig Knoblock and Subbarao Kambhampati, "Tutorial on Information Integration on the Web," presented at the 18th National Conference on Artificial Intelligence, July 29, 2002.*

12. *Colin White for The Data Warehousing Institute,* Data Integration: Using ETL, EAI, and EII Tools to Create an Integrated Enterprise. *Forty-four percent of study respondents ranked data integration as a barrier to new development as "High," and another 25 percent ranked it as "Very High." See* www.tdwi.org.

CHAPTER 9

Bootstrapping Your Customer Data Integration Initiative

One must be aware that there is nothing so difficult, more doubtful in its result, and more dangerous to do than to introduce a new state of things. The innovator has bitter enemies among all those who benefit from the old system, while he only has half-hearted defenders among those who expect to benefit from the new system.

This half-heartedness has its roots in man's lack of faith, because he does not really believe in the new state until he has experienced it.

—MACHIAVELLI

As we've discussed in every chapter throughout this book, from business drivers to functionality, customer data integration (CDI) is different from other technologies. This fact alone can result in confusion and inertia. The most common comment we hear from executives about CDI is: "I think we need it—but I'm not sure where to begin."

Information technology (IT) managers don't like surprises. Risk management is essential with any IT initiative, but particularly with one that proposes to be the customer system of record. This chapter discusses how to prepare for CDI and presents some checklists to ensure your success.

GETTING CDI RIGHT

Like so many other IT projects, the success of CDI depends in large part on setting the right expectations and being realistic about what success means. There are several basic rules to follow to ensure that your CDI project starts out on the right foot:

- Answer the question, "Why should we . . . ?" Is there consensus about the need for CDI? Is CDI really the best answer to the business problem? We've offered a host of different business drivers for CDI in this book, but often a company has already slated its existing technologies to address them. There may be a legitimate business issue of accessing timely and accurate customer detail, but that doesn't mean that another technology or platform can't deliver.

- Avoid overpromising. Lofty assurances of impossible functional gymnastics and data that's 100 percent clean won't cut the mustard long term if CDI is to stay relevant and useful.

- Be deliberate about the build-versus-buy decision. Homegrown systems like the one at Royal Bank of Canada often meet the specific needs of the business more quickly and directly than an off-the-shelf package. Just make sure that the decision to build is founded on research and not the personal ambitions of smart programmers looking for a fun experiment. (When Royal Bank of Canada developed its customer registry, there were no immediate CDI solutions on the market.) Likewise, a buy decision made too quickly could jeopardize the delivery of CDI functionality critical to business requirements. We recently watched a new client work with a CDI vendor with less-than-optimal results. They had been quick to take over ownership, but didn't have the staff with sufficient business and data skills to own the solution. Programming skills were not enough.

- Be sensitive to the feelings and experience of constituents. In the case of CDI, this means application developers, many of whom have spent arduous hours building custom code to integrate data and tuning that code so it works seamlessly with their applications. Although CDI means that the developer can free himself from the routine tasks of data maintenance and testing, he may still have pride of ownership in his code and thus be reluctant to relinquish it.

- Organize around applications and business processes. Many companies embark on new development projects based on geographies, product categories, or customer segments. That might work for other implementations, like CRM, but for CDI understanding the use of customer master data one business process or application at a time makes more sense and is more manageable in the long run.

- Find the right application. In order for CDI to start right, a team should convene to scope the effort and understand the applications that require integrated customer detail in order to work correctly. Find an application that needs customer detail quickly and show the application developers how CDI can help.

CASE STUDY: **INTUIT**

When you meet Marty Moseley in person, he strikes you as a smart guy who doesn't sweat the small stuff. But as chief architect at Intuit—the force behind the popular financial management software products Quicken, QuickBooks, and TurboTax—Moseley's had his share of challenges. Since he joined Intuit five years ago, he's been leading the charge to support an increasingly consolidating business model through integrated data.

With a market value of over $9 billion, Intuit has traditionally made heavy investments in research and development across its brands and treats technology as a significant strategic differentiator. "We've grown up as a portfolio company with separate products managed by separate groups," Moseley explains. "But our executives realized that we needed to function as a single company. We needed a well-managed technology infrastructure to support a dynamic set of business needs. And that meant laying a foundation that dramatically changed the way we integrated our systems. It was imperative that we eliminated the numerous point-to-point interfaces we'd built over time and replace them with a loosely-coupled information-sharing model."

Moseley, who reports into the chief technology officer's organization, was given his first assignment: fix the disparity around customer information and systems. Since one of Intuit's guiding philosophies is to be "highly available," Moseley knew that he'd have to deliver fast.

"Before PRS, we had data standardization, matching, deduping logic in easily half a dozen different systems—all implemented differently with different business rules. It took months to make changes, and data were moved around in batches for the most part. If a customer came to an e-commerce site to purchase a product, then wanted to change their privacy preferences, and then called a rep for help, the rep would have to enter the customer's data redundantly. Then the data had to be reconciled in batch. If the customer bought several products from us in different sales channels, the problem got worse."

"At one point I had a choice," he remembers. "I could have sat down in endless meetings with businesspeople and debated the difference between a lead and a prospect. Or I could build a solution that I knew would solve most of our problems." Moseley concluded that, given Intuit's speed and service philosophies, his solution should:

- Employ a service-oriented architecture (SOA) approach that was agile and make it easy to bring to new systems
- Leverage a hub-and-spoke architecture to decouple systems
- Scale to field real-time identity requests through all customer touch points

Almost immediately, Moseley ruled out Intuit's existing software packages. The enterprise application vendors the company used for its enterprise resource planning (ERP) and customer relationship management (CRM) operations had been highly customized. "Our CRM system was tailored to focus on small business customers, and was struggling to process fewer than ten million accounts" says Moseley, "and the new CDI system needed to support an order of magnitude more consumer customers." Likewise, the company's data warehouse had a database design that, while effective for analytic applications, would have been inflexible for customer identity management, and was not built to serve real-time identity needs.

The resulting CDI solution, the Party Reference System (PRS), integrates transaction-level detail about customers from all communications channels. As a hub-and-spoke architecture, PRS sits between products and Web sites Intuit customers use, and the IT systems that run the company. Due to the brand's appeal across consumer, small business, and professional constituencies, having four or five records for the same customer—including different credit card, privacy preference, and contact details—is not uncommon. "How many of our small business customers are also consumer customers?" Moseley asks. "How many of our customers license multiple Intuit products, but have used different personal information to register them over time?" Reconciled, accurate customer details make it easier and more effective in knowing their customers and in offering solutions that benefit both Intuit and their customers.

Moseley explains a hypothetical customer interaction. "Someone's using Quicken at home and then he connects to a Web site to purchase a new feature. During the download the dog pulls out the DSL cable and the customer has to call our tech support center. We want to be able to recognize them and say, 'We see you purchased a new feature a few minutes ago, but something seems to have happened during the download. How can I help?' We can connect these three touch points— the desktop, the Web, and the phone—to best serve the customer."

Moseley chose a packaged solution from Initiate Systems that specialized in highly scalable customer identity reconciliation. "We have a philosophy of 'buy what we can, build what we must.' We didn't want to build our own matching logic and looked at some of the big consumer data providers. Unfortunately, they either did batch-oriented processing or couldn't handle our volumes for real-time identity management. And we didn't want to outsource our customer data. Plus," he adds, "life is too short to build your own sophisticated transaction matching logic."

Moseley wove PRS into an already complex tapestry of IT and product-enabling solutions using an SOA approach, which supports loosely coupled technologies. This allows Intuit to add and replace new functionality and tools with its evolving business needs.

"We've been able to add new systems easily. We have over 20 different client applications that use PRS. That's because we've designed a robust standard data model in an XML (extensible markup language) schema. It doesn't matter what Seibel calls an account or what Oracle calls a customer—they all get mapped to a common schema. So we've really reduced our point-to-point complexity. Plus, we've been able to add new capabilities in a matter of weeks, where before it could have taken many months."

Although they chose a "buy" approach and made fast deployment a priority, Moseley and his team were hardly victims of the "build it and they will come" mentality. "Our different departments had different needs when it came to party data. Some just need customers, and others need employees and vendors. I'd advise people considering CDI to spend some time up front designing an information exchange format that will lead them into the future. You have to be deliberate in your approach so that CDI can be effective in the long term."

Despite its architectural elegance and quick delivery, the PRS system's real payback has been customer facing. "Our customers are having a better experience with us," Moseley says. "Our reps can go search on the data a customer has just provided and they no longer create a redundant customer record. We know the guy who bought the product five minutes ago." The PRS hub also centralizes privacy and data quality business rules for use by other applications.

Moseley acknowledges that PRS is a work in progress, but emphasizes that it now has full management support. "Party Reference System is known throughout the enterprise. It's an acknowledged part of Intuit's infrastructure. The CEO, CTO, and CMO are on board. They've seen it in action, and they know it makes sense."

Why CDI Projects Fail

As new as CDI is, we've already watched some CDI projects hit the skids. There are several reasons for this, and many of them invite the well-worn aphorisms of other strategic IT projects: IT didn't talk to the business. The vendor was chosen before the problem was understood. A skunkworks project never truly got off the ground.

We have also seen some issues that seem very specific to CDI. Listing them here is an attempt to warn you against the sins of those who have gone before you.

Fixing a Problem with the Wrong Tool

A hilarious cartoon shows two cavemen playing "Rock, Paper, Scissors." Both of them incessantly choose "Rock." The cartoon caption reads: "*Before the invention of paper and scissors.*"

As we discussed at the beginning of the book, the evolution of business has driven new strategies around customer focus, company branding, and knowledge management that have introduced brand-new business requirements. Customer identity management, for instance, was born from the need to understand and embrace the total customer relationship across subsidiaries, divisions, and contacts. Technologies to solve this problem have only recently come on the scene. Customer hierarchy management has emerged to help companies understand interrelationships between business parties.

But that doesn't stop system owners from trying to adapt old systems to new problems. "We can do that with our data warehouse or ETL vendor" seems to be the knee-jerk response to many problems that are best suited to bona-fide CDI technologies.

Companies that have tried retrofitting incumbent software products to new problems not only work harder, they overinvest. The resulting failure not only tarnishes the reputation of CDI but that of the system that was being adapted to fit the CDI needs.

Managers who approach their enterprise application vendors, many of whom now offer CDI as part of their product suites, shouldn't assume that their existing CRM or ERP tool can simply be "enhanced" to include CDI, data model or no data model. CDI is a different problem with different processing requirements, business rules, and business outcomes. It should be evaluated, adopted, and treated that way.

Failing to Profile the Data before Configuring the Hub

We've said before that CDI isn't magic. It requires hard work and specialized skills. However, like any IT project, there are shortcuts that, when taken, imperil the entire effort.

One such shortcut is the failure to research and understand the master data from the data sources. CDI development teams should take the time to go through the effort of profiling the source data at the element level before deciding which data elements are useful for generating an authoritative customer record.

We've seen inexperienced CDI project managers launch their data requirement activities by calling a meeting with source system owners. The meeting's objective is to identify the data sources and their key data elements. Operational system developers might bring along some record layouts.

The problem with this is that the source system owners might not truly understand their operational data well enough to advise the CDI development team on what's what. Source systems owners don't typically build robust data quality checking. Their focus is more on application functionality. So they might not understand which data elements are relevant for determining the customer's identity. Incorrect assumptions about important data or business rules can sabotage a merge process, resulting in faulty master records.

Developers should be ready to analyze and profile key data on each source system. Such an activity often requires more time than an organization expects to dedicate. Project managers typically underestimate the time and complexity associated with data analysis and integration research. CDI project teams need to work with source system data stewards to ensure that the right elements are used in identifying customers. They need to build use cases and test cases that reflect requirements.

Ignoring Hub Scalability Issues

It takes experience to know whether the CDI tool's underlying data model can handle concurrent access from multiple applications, or support the ongoing growth in customer data volumes. When configuring your CDI hub, remember to focus on both query performance and data update.

There are two different types of CDI hub processing: query search performance and ongoing data updates.

We recommend prototyping your CDI vendor tool to make sure it can handle your company's required functionality and expected transaction volumes. This means testing initial data load volumes separately from the incremental data enrichment process—add, delete, update, and so forth. It also means ensuring the hub's ability to support ongoing transaction volumes from the client applications, which could include search, add, or delete.

Ignoring Data Management and Data Quality

Introducing CDI to a company with immature data management processes and skills is a challenge. That's because the company hasn't yet agreed on common goals for good data, and hasn't yet established a vocabulary around accurate, available, and reconciled data. The risk is creating an application-centric CDI solution that can't be leveraged by the rest of the enterprise.

It's likely that the definitions and values of various customer data fields change and evolve over time. If a formal data management organization or established processes don't yet exist at your company, the CDI project team should be ready to respond to the evolution and introduction of new data.

Lack of Custom Development Skills

Many IT environments are so accustomed to buying packaged off-the-shelf applications that they lack the development skills and methods necessary to do from-scratch development. This isn't a value judgment—it's more of a skills issue. The skill differences between a packaged application developer and someone who can write Java code are diverse, and significant.

Falling Prey to Analysis Paralysis

Okay, this one's not unique to CDI, but we see it a lot on CDI and master data management (MDM) projects. There's an old maxim that says, "A good solution executed quickly beats a brilliant solution implemented slowly."

As we discussed in Chapter 5, top-down development of CDI is risky, since it relies on a level of organizational consensus that's often difficult or (depending on the company's culture) impossible to achieve. CDI should never follow a "big bang" implementation approach, since as the project moves forward customer data is always changing. Even with a top-down approach to requirements and analysis, the initial CDI deployment should be small and well scoped.

Beginning with a CDI proof-of-concept can mitigate arguments about "good" data and theoretical debates about the need for CDI. When people see CDI in action, its value becomes clear.

Leadership from the Top or the Bottom, but Not the Middle

We know, we know. Executive sponsorship is important for strategic IT projects. We say this ourselves in our writings and conference presentations. But any business sponsor worth her paycheck will be more effective communicating the value of CDI than she will be managing the actual development effort.

Likewise, we see many CDI skunkworks projects launched by a few smart technicians. These people not only see the business value, but they understand how they can deploy CDI functionality quickly and cheaply and they just do it. When they raise their heads and show people what they've built, they realize they have to educate them. Since CDI delivers data to systems and applications and not directly to end users, explaining its value to businesspeople who might end up supporting and funding it can be next to impossible.

Both approaches lack a sanctioned CDI project manager responsible for delivering and communicating the benefits of CDI back to the business. This "middle manager" is high enough in the organization to be credible, but low enough to understand the implementation issues and tasks. The CDI project manager will spend more time with the development team working out how to define the data requirements and integration design we discussed in Chapter 5. He will also likely communicate on a regular basis to senior managers about the CDI project's projected time frames, scope of functionality, and business benefits.

CDI for Its Own Sake

We've seen some organizations undertake a CDI project without first identifying the central business need or the target applications it's intended to support. Reasons for this include aggressive vendors—"Hey, they're *giving* us the software, let's use it!"—a poor understanding of the benefits CDI offers, or even bored technologists looking for a new tool with which to self-educate. (No one wastes more time at a company than an advanced technology group looking to kick some tires.)

Given the politics and personalities in your specific company, there will likely be other challenges. To manage risk, a good CDI project manager should kick off the project by articulating an awareness of the hazards that might accompany the project, with full knowledge of past project failures and organizational issues. Here are some other CDI challenges to be aware of:

- Application developers are too busy to help define data requirements
- The information returned to the CDI client application is wrong
- Lack of processes for tracking source system changes
- Application owners won't agree to use data from the CDI hub once it's built
- The data is too unreliable to be integrated, and the source system owners aren't responsible for fixing it
- Lack of expertise about customer data

CDI is different from operational systems development projects, yet shares many of the same project and implementation issues. As with every new technology, proceed with caution.

BUILDING THE CDI TEAM

The challenge in building a CDI development team isn't that the roles themselves are very different. In fact, on the surface the CDI development team might look like any other development team in the IT organization, with the requisite positions:

- **CDI project manager.** The CDI project manager ideally acts as both an administrative and a technical manager. She handles the communications and status reporting duties to management, tracks project progress, works with members of the development team to identify the necessary tasks within each main step (see Chapter 5), and ensures that the CDI development team is on track. The CDI project manager should ideally have experience managing other data integration development efforts in a multisource environment.
- **CDI architect.** A CDI architect determines the application or applications that need data from the CDI hub, identifies the sources those applications are accessing, and determines the best means of integrating data from those sources with the CDI solution or product. The architect should already be familiar with the company's overall architectural standards, ideally having worked in a broader IT

architecture function, and should have experience working hands-on with other data integration projects. The CDI architect should typically be familiar with a variety of data sources and other master data hubs in the company if they exist.

- **CDI developer.** CDI developers configure the CDI hub to work within the company's service-oriented environment. Alternatively, the developer will make the CDI hub resemble the prior application interfaces, for instance, an application programming interface (API) call set. CDI developers should understand SOA, as well as having experience developing interfaces to other applications systems. If the company has purchased a packaged CDI solution, development staff will need to train on the system developer's kit (SDK) and understand the vendor's underlying database schema.

- **CDI data steward.** The CDI data steward supports developer questions on accessing the hub and understanding the hub's various data elements. The CDI data steward is also responsible for documenting the business rules and data requirements of customer master data, and describing the services necessary to interface to the hub. (Depending on the scope and breadth of CDI, the CDI data steward can be the same person as the customer data steward.) This role is critical as IT adds new applications that need access to CDI data.

- **CDI administrator.** The CDI administrator configures the hub, working through how to load data into the hub and maintain consistent data integration. The CDI administrator also examines data error logs to identify and fix any data errors that have been flagged during CDI processing.

Most IT development teams focus on either implementing a package or automating a discrete business process. CDI does neither. It changes a fundamental infrastructure component—sourcing, integrating, and delivering customer data. Usually an IT project manager equips her team with people with specific skills. Application designers will need to analyze the appropriate business processes to understand where repeatable activities can leverage automation. For instance, a company finds that its legacy billing system is outdated and cumbersome, and identifies a series of updated requirements for the new billing system to support. These requirements are associated with the business process of billing.

The CDI development team doesn't automate new business processes, but rather focuses on providing data and functionality to specific applications. The challenge of putting a CDI development team in place for the first time is in ensuring that the skills are available. Managers in IT rarely hire developers for their data integration skills. But that's changing.

The other challenge with CDI development teams is ensuring their effective and structured communication with other organizations within IT, namely:

- **Data management.** As discussed in Chapter 6, support for data models, metadata management, and data requirements is often provided through a centralized data management organization.

- **Data governance.** The CDI project manager should be prepared to deliver regular status updates and communicate issues with data to the data governance council. This includes identifying any quality problems, interface issues, definitional questions, or acquisition issues confronted by the CDI development team.

- **Application development.** The CDI project manager and architect should conduct the initial data requirements activity with developers of the CDI client application to determine the right data, the acceptance criteria, and the test metrics.

- **IT architecture.** The CDI development team should involve the company's IT architecture organization in design review and code walkthrough activities, ideally obtaining sign-off. This ensures that the CDI development project conforms to overarching corporate development standards.

Exhibit 9.1 illustrates why CDI is bigger than the CDI development team.

As with other strategic efforts, the difference between a "core" team and a "support" team is an apt one for CDI. The CDI development team can leverage the design review and code walkthrough processes included in its IT development methodology of choice. The point here is to avoid insular,

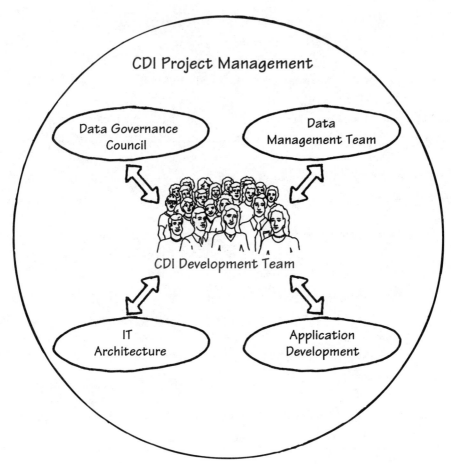

EXHIBIT 9.1   **CDI Development Ecosystem**

CDI-specific sign-offs and validate CDI development steps with a wider audience. Like the CDI hub itself, a CDI development process is broad and extensible.

For CDI, it's important for the team to be perceived as a "yes" organization. Many application development teams receive their marching orders in the form of requirements or a functional spec and never look back. Part of CDI means truly delivering a single version of the customer truth to anyone who may need it. The team needs a structured way to ensure that, once the word spreads, they can support a variety of applications to help the business evolve and grow along with its customers.

FIERCE CONVERSATIONS: TALKING TO CDI VENDORS

Some important questions need answering before you embark on your CDI journey. Ideally, you should be able to answer the following questions in an informed way, with an eye toward future business needs as well as current ones. Smart CDI vendors will ask you these questions, so knowing the answers up front will be helpful not only in choosing the best CDI solution, but even in negotiating the best deal.

Q. Do you have applications and reports unable to generate a consistent customer list?

A. Some managers believe that if you require users to get their information from a central repository, it will become the de-facto single version of the truth and data anomalies will simply be fixed with time. However, the data errors originate in the source systems, so the data stays dirty.

A CDI hub is an active integration system that monitors the values from individual source systems and determines the most accurate answer based on the values available. It doesn't rely on a static set of rules, but instead considers how recent the values are, the relative quality of data, and the best answer.

Q. Do you have more than one application requiring access to integrated, accurate customer data? What are those applications, and how do you know there's a need?

A. It could be overkill to implement CDI for a single application that might already have hard-coded data integration. The benefit of CDI is in its economies of scale. The goal is to centralize disparate customer data processing into a single location so the work is done once. For CDI projects, the greater the reuse, the higher value to IT and the business. The benefit of a centralized hub is that it's easier to check that the integration is done consistently and correctly.

Q. Are the applications operational, with response time requirements for data access?

A. CDI is really meant for online transaction processing applications. There are many lower-cost solutions if the need is for accurate reporting or simply query-based data access.

Q. How are you getting integrated customer data today? Does it come from an acknowledged system of record? From a data warehouse? Or is the data in use not integrated yet?

A. The goal of this question is to understand the level and complexity of data integration necessary. Extraction, transformation, and loading (ETL)-based integration might be too simplistic to support the application's specific needs. This also helps clarify whether the goal is to generate the golden customer record or simply integrate data from disparate systems.

Q. How are integration rules defined and maintained? Are they consistent across different applications? Is that an issue?

A. The issue here is how static or dynamic the integration rules are to support the applications. For instance, do we normally use the address from the customer service system, or do we try reconciling the most recent change of address across five different operational systems?

Q. Do you have an enterprise data management organization or data stewards who have defined data elements and the data sources of origin?

A. You should understand whether the details and definitions already exist or whether they need to be developed. Just because multiple applications use customer data doesn't mean they have consistent definitions and naming standards for customer data. The marketing organization could view a customer as anyone with a mailing address, whereas finance views the customer as someone with an account number. As discussed in Chapter 6, a centralized data management organization whose goal is to manage customer master data has thus likely defined customer and the details associated with the customer.

Q. Has the company already defined customer relationships in the customer hierarchy, or do they need to be defined? Do you understand interrelationships of customer data elements, as with multiple addresses for a single customer?

A. Understanding if the CDI hub needs to address interrelationships between various parties could affect your vendor selection decision.

Q. Should the CDI hub support specific business rules or policies?

A. Do you know if there are information-specific policies regarding what company staff is allowed to see and use? For instance, the CDI hub must respect the information-sharing policies of the company with regard to consumers who may have opted out of new marketing campaigns. Data usage needs to align with business policy, and it's impractical for businesspeople or IT developers to monitor business policies; the CDI hub can maintain them in a centralized and consistent way.

Q. Is the company responsible for meeting regulatory or legislative guidelines that affect the availability or use of customer data?

A. For instance, because of the Health Insurance Portability and Accountability Act (HIPAA), health care organizations must ensure that patient records remain private and that individual patient behavior can be tracked.

Q. Is there an existing and defined SOA environment?

A. Most CDI products leverage SOA technology. Understanding your readiness to implement SOA technology, and the skills necessary to do so, will help you understand how to prepare for CDI.

MANAGER DO'S AND DON'TS

> *If everything seems under control, you're just not going fast enough.*
> —MARIO ANDRETTI

As you embark on your CDI journey, here's a final list of do's and don'ts to ensure that you launch, sustain, and grow your CDI solution in the optimal way. Good luck!

- **Do** let application developers be the heroes. Successful CDI saves the company time, work, and money. As much as the CDI team has done, the application developers have accepted a new way of working, and it'll help the company in myriad ways. Give them the glory and they'll further the cause.

- **Don't** forget that even though CDI is a complex solution, its intention is to make things simpler. Realize that requirements will change over time and the initial project might require significant reengineering as new needs pop up. CDI can get hairy as it evolves toward an enterprise solution. But applications should get easier to develop and maintain.

- **Do** consider CDI a program. As new applications come online, the functionality and data supported by CDI will continue to grow. Leverage reuse, not only with data but also with development methods, skills, and tools. CDI is an ongoing process, and today's success could be tomorrow's failure.

- **Don't** forget the value of human capital. Success of CDI systems doesn't rely only on technical skills, but also intimacy with the company's data asset and a solid and evolving knowledge of its business. And those can't be outsourced.

Glossary

Agile development An IT development philosophy that argues in favor of quick, incremental implementations that focus on small, combined teams of users and developers, and quick turnaround of small slices of functionality. See **Bottom-up development**.

Analytical CRM The analysis of data originating front-office or operational CRM combined with other organizational or external data in order to evaluate key business measures such as customer value, purchases by segment, or customer profitability.

Analytical systems Technology that accesses and presents detailed information for the purposes of operational and strategic decision making. See **Business intelligence**.

Application programming interface (API) A set of routines that an application uses to request and carry out lower-level services.

Automated workflow The automation of business processes that have been optimized through business process modeling. Workflow systems usually involve moving data through a process, such as order and fulfillment, in which the data is touched multiple times by various systems and individuals.

Basel II Also called Basel Committee on Banking Supervision, Basel II is a set of international regulations aimed at standardizing the way the banks and banking regulators approach risk management across international borders. The regulation weights loan risks differently depending on the type of borrower, and lays down guidelines for determining the minimum solvency requirements.

Bottom-up development The process of incremental delivery of small pieces of technical functionality. Bottom-up development implies short projects, small teams, and an emphasis on refining requirements as new functionality is introduced. The goal is often to deliver new functionality or data every 30 to 90 days, and many advocate it as the preferred method of CDI implementation.

B2B The common abbreviation for business-to-business.

B2C The common abbreviation for business-to-consumer.

Business intelligence (BI) A category of applications and technologies to guide the analysis and use of detailed business data for improved business decision making. The term is sometimes used synonymously with *decision support*, though business intelligence is technically much broader.

Business process execution language (BPEL) An XML-based language that allows programmers to describe a business process that may take place across the Web in a service-oriented architecture environment. BPEL extends the Web services model to support business transactions.

Business process reengineering A business term made popular by Michael Hammer and James Champy in their 1993 book *Reengineering the Corporation*, business process reengineering is the practice of redesigning core business processes to drive organizational and technological efficiencies.

Business rules A set of methods or guidelines associated with a company's data and business processing that reflect its methods of conducting business operations. A business rule might stipulate that no credit check is necessary for an existing customer. CDI uses business rules to determine records in common.

Business sponsor A manager or executive who can articulate how CDI (or any business-enabling technology initiative) can drive improvements. This person helps establish the "need, pain, or problem" that CDI will solve, serves as a tiebreaker for issues during the project, and may actually fund some or all of CDI development.

Call center The organization charged with direct customer support interactions via a variety of channels. Also the description for the physical location where customer service represen-tatives handle inbound and outbound customer calls.

Call center automation The use of typically advanced technologies to facilitate communications to, within, and out of a call center. Automatic routing of calls to specific agents is one example of call center automation.

Campaign management A marketing practice that involves analyzing data for the purposes of launching a marketing campaign, then monitoring that campaign and tracking its results in order to determine the campaign's value. The term *campaign management* can also refer to the technology that automates the campaign management function.

Channel The means and media by which a customer prefers to communicate with the company—the "inbound" channel—or to receive communications—the "outbound" channel.

Channel optimization The practice of determining the best channels by which to communicate with customers, especially when they have not made these preferences clear, and availing these channels to the right customers. For example, a bank might want to install a grocery store kiosk in an area frequented by high-value customers who use other banks' automated teller machines (ATMs), thereby providing a desirable channel that encourages direct interaction.

Chief customer officer (CCO) A relatively recent addition to the executive ranks, the chief customer officer is a frontline executive focused on external customer communications. The CCO can have a variety of responsibilities, from analyzing customer surveys and overseeing the resulting product improvements to communicating with key customers on a regular basis about new product developments or service offerings to making on-site customer visits to monitor product usage and obtain firsthand customer feedback.

Chief information officer (CIO) The job responsibility of managing the information technology and computer systems that support enterprise business goals.

Chief privacy officer (CPO) The job responsibility of overseeing the company's privacy policies and practices, monitoring how the company uses confidential information about customers and employees.

Churn The phenomenon of customers leaving your business to go to a competitor. Churn implies the customer might or might not return. "Churn reduction" is another way of saying customer retention and is a major goal of CRM programs. Churn is most often used in conjunction with commodity businesses such as telcos, utilities, and airlines.

Clickstream The series of transactions executed by a Web site visitor while navigating through the site. The analysis of clickstream data can help a company understand which products, Web content, or screens were of most interest to a given customer. The company can then determine which site features are most effective, as well as personalize content to given customer segments and individuals.

Client application One of potentially many systems that rely on the CDI hub to provide access to integrated customer information. A CDI client application is typically a business application such as a sales force automation system or a call center system.

Closed-loop campaign management The practice of using the results of past campaigns to refine future campaigns, the goal of which is to hone customer knowledge while improving campaign response rates over time.

Component Object Model (COM) A software architecture developed by Microsoft to build component-based applications. COM is used to communicate between components on the same computer. It's part of a strategic building-block approach for developing application programs.

Composite application Composite applications combine functions and data from multiple systems via standardized messaging. They maximize reuse of business services within a service-oriented architecture. Components can be individual Web services, functions from other applications, or entire systems whose outputs have been packaged as Web services.

Composite view Usually used synonymously with the "golden record," a composite view is a record that combines data attributes from different data sources.

Contact center See **Call center**.

Contact management The area of sales force automation that allows salespeople to record key customer information such as names and addresses, as well as organization charts and decision-making authority. This prevents a salesperson from having to remember who's who at each of his accounts.

Common object request broker architecture (CORBA) A language-independent object model and specification for a distributed application development environment. Unlike COM, which is specific to Microsoft, CORBA is vendor independent.

Cross-functional   The description for a technology that serves more than one business function (e.g., financial analysis and sales analysis) or organization (e.g., human resources and accounts receivable).

Cross-selling   Selling a customer a product or service as a result of another purchase. The best cross-selling is done when a company understands the relationship between two products, and which product might "pull" another.

Customer data integration (CDI)   The combination of processes, controls, automation, and skills necessary to standardize and integrate customer data originating from different sources.

Customer data management (CDM) The set of practices and policies specific to managing customer data. CDM is a specialized subset of *data management*.

Customer interaction center (CIC)   The evolution of the operational call center into the locus of all inbound and outbound customer communications, with a special focus on customer satisfaction and multimodal customer access.

Customer proprietary network information (CPNI)   The data collected by telephone companies about consumer telephone calls. The data includes date, time, and destination telephone number, as well as the other information that is included on the customer's phone bill. CPNI data is regulated by the Federal Communications Commission (FCC).

Customer relationship management (CRM)   The infrastructure that enables the delineation of and increase in customer value, and the correct means by which to increase customer value and motivate valuable customers to remain loyal, indeed, to buy again.

Customer segmentation   See **Segmentation**.

Customer service representative (CSR) A member of the company's customer support staff (or a third-party call center agency) who takes phone calls and participates in Internet live chat sessions in order to answer customer questions, lodge complaints, record trouble tickets, or instruct customers on product usage.

Data accuracy   A data element's degree of conformity to an established business measurement or definition. Data precision is the degree to which further measurements or definitions will show the same results.

Data administration   The process of managing a company's data to ensure that it fulfills business requirements, and to provide the data in an accurate, secure, and accessible way.

Data certification   The formal process whereby data is evaluated, validated, and approved by data stakeholders for one or more business purposes.

Data czar   An executive position charged with the management of data as a corporate asset. The data czar may lead the data governance council, direct data management functions, and spearhead company data policies and practices.

Data governance   The infrastructure, resources, and processes involved in managing data as a corporate asset.

Data governance council   A steering committee charged with designating data policies, processes, and standards on behalf of an organization or enterprise. The data governance council is usually comprised of a mixture of managers on both the business and IT sides, and ensures accountability, ownership, standards, and metrics for corporate data.

Data hoarding   A phenomenon at many companies where owners of applications or databases will not avail their data to people in other organizations. Usually, the cause of data hoarding is fear of accountability for poor data quality or missing data.

Data management   The day-to-day tasks necessary to tactically manage data, including overseeing its quality, lineage, usage, and deployment across systems, organizations, and user communities.

Data mining   A type of advanced analysis used to determine certain patterns within data. Data mining is most often associated with predictive analysis based on historical detail, and the generation of models for further analysis and query.

Data mart   A platform that maintains data for analysis by a single organization or user group for a specific set of business purposes.

Data source   A system or application that generates data for use by another system or by an end user. The data source may also be the system of origin for the data.

Data supply chain   The concept that data has a life-cycle in a company that corresponds to a company's enterprise business processes. The data supply chain most often reflects the order-to-cash process. The fact that data flows across organizations, geographies, and systems is part of the rationalization for master data management (MDM).

Data transformation   The process of reformatting data based on predefined rules. Most often identified as part of ETL (extraction, transformation, and loading) but not exclusive to ETL, transformation can occur on the CDI hub, which uses one of several methods to transform the data from the source systems before matching it.

Data validation   The process of ensuring accurate data based on data acceptance and exception handling rules.

Data warehouse   A technology platform that stores business data for the purpose of strategic decision making. Data warehouses are normally the central integration point for large amounts of detailed, historical data from heterogeneous systems across the company to avail data for business intelligence.

Decision support   Data analysis with the purpose of fuelling accurate and effective business decisions. Known by the acronym DSS for decision support systems. See **Business intelligence**.

Deterministic matching   Deterministic matching algorithms compare and match records according to hard-coded business rules according to their precision. For instance, a rule can be set up that stipulates that every "Bill" be matched with a "William."

Direct marketing   The classic marketing practice of communicating directly to consumers. Traditionally associated with mail campaigns, direct marketing has evolved to encompass a range of media, from e-mail to banner ads to wireless messaging services.

Enterprise application integration (EAI) EAI enables data propagation and business process execution across separate applications as if they were a single system.

Enterprise information integration (EII) An integration technology that enables the access of disparate data from different data sources "on the fly," thus eliminating the need to store data in a single database.

Enterprise information management (EIM) A term used to distinguish global data management practices and policies, EIM is often mistakenly used synonymously with master data management or data governance.

Enterprise master patient index (EMPI) One of the major drivers for CDI in the health care industry, EMPI is the capability of tracking a patient across the continuum of his care, regardless of the care provider.

Enterprise portal An enterprise portal is a user interface, usually Web-based, that provides a virtual window into different data sources and subject areas. Enterprise portals provide a common look and feel across the company for various business data, but can nevertheless be customized to provide user-specific information at various levels and from various sources.

Enterprise resource planning (ERP) A system that ties together and automates the diverse components of a company's supply-chain operations, including the order, fulfillment, staffing, and accounting processes.

Enterprise service bus (ESB) A layer of middleware that enables the delivery and sharing of services across and between business applications. ESBs are typically used to support communication, connections, and mediation in a service-oriented architecture.

Event-based marketing The practice of detecting a key event that triggers a business action or custom marketing communication designed to increase customer loyalty or profitability. An example of event-based marketing is when a customer makes an inordinately large deposit, the bank offers a high-interest certificate of deposit.

Extensible markup language (XML) Facilitates the assignment of meaningful structures and definitions of data and services for use by multiple systems. XML simplifies the ability to transmit and share data.

External data Data acquired from a third-party data provider. External data usually involves consumer data that has been cleansed, formatted, and updated with current information, but may also include market research, demographic statistics, and business and industry information.

External reference style The type of CDI that leverages external bureaus such as consumer data or credit reporting agencies for data matching and reconciliation.

Extraction, transformation, and loading (ETL) A process for acquiring data from source systems, reformatting and cleansing it based on business requirements, and loading it, usually into a data warehouse. The term is more generally used as a means of moving data between systems.

Extranet A secure Internet site available only to a company's internal staff and approved third-party partners.

Extranets are flourishing in B2B environments where suppliers can have ready access to updated information from their business customers, and vice versa.

Federated query   The process of querying multiple data sources as though they were a single platform.

Flat file   A data structure that contains records with no inherent relationships.

Global data synchronization (GDS)   The concept of synchronizing common master data irrespective of where it resides geographically or what systems it affects. GDS is a concept used primarily in the context of aligning participants in a supply chain (e.g., retailers and manufacturers) around the use of common data.

Golden record   The single, authoritative record about an individual customer.

Gramm-Leach-Bliley   U.S. legislation (also known as the Financial Modernization Act of 1999) that protects consumer privacy by limiting the collection and disclosure of customer financial data by financial services firms, and mandating corporate programs to protect the data. The act also requires firms to notify customers of their data protection policies.

Health Insurance Portability and Accountability Act of 1996 (HIPAA)   Establishes national standards in the United States for electronic health care transactions and mandates privacy rules for patient data.

Help America Vote Act of 2002 (HAVA)   The aim of HAVA is to eliminate punch cards, which have historically been fraught with error and fraud, providing federal funding to states in order to create statewide computerized lists of voters.

Householding   The process of consolidating customer data in order to organize individuals into the households in which they live. Grouping customers within a household allows a company to be more prudent with its communications while at the same time enabling it to more accurately profile individuals in relation to one another.

Hybrid style of CDI   The hybrid approach combines both persistent and registry styles. It's a registry-style CDI system that stores additional descriptive details to improve performance and increase flexibility.

Infoglut   A term used to connote the phenomenon that information is generated faster than humans can search or analyze it. Also referred to as the "data explosion."

Interactive voice response (IVR)   Telephony software that recognizes the pressing of numbers on a keypad or human voice instructions in order to route customer calls to the appropriate call center or agent.

Iterative development   Iterative development implies going through small, repeatable development steps in order to speed up software implementation and deliver small amounts of functionality more quickly. Iterative development reduces risk and allows for adjustments, enabling technical staff to refine the development plan as they go.

IT governance   The processes, policies, relationships, and mechanisms that ensure that information technology delivers business value while balancing risk and investment decisions. IT governance ensures accountability and provides rigor for managing IT capabilities in the context of a larger corporate governance framework.

Java 2 Platform, Enterprise Edition (J2EE) A version of Java for deploying enterprise applications.

Knowledge Management The field of study that relates to the centralized management of a company's corporate knowledge and information assets in order to provide this knowledge to as many company staff members as possible and thus encourage better and more consistent decision making.

Knowledge management (KM) system A knowledge management system centralizes a company's knowledge assets, normally via an enterprise knowledge management portal. KM systems offer the ability to not only access information in the system, but supplement it with new or additional information as it's created.

Lead management A sales force automation capability for tracking and monitoring sales prospects and a company's interactions with them, as well as enforcing sales tactics and automating key tasks.

Life stage marketing The practice of targeting consumers based on where they are on their life continuum. For instance, a bank might e-mail a promotion for a new credit card to a recent college graduate, but might market a home equity line of credit to a recent retiree.

List generation Automatically generating a list of customers for a marketing campaign based on specific customer characteristics. List generation is a core feature of most campaign management products.

Logical data model A logical data model is a convention for representing data entities, relationships, and attributes in order to reflect business requirements. A logical data model is intended to facilitate an understanding of data's ability to support business needs, and does not reflect the physical implementation of data.

Loosely coupled Describes an architecture that supports multiple systems intercommunicating while remaining independent of one another. Loosely coupled architectures reduce the risk that changes in a particular system will create unanticipated changes in other systems.

Mass marketing The traditional practice of marketing a product to an undifferentiated group of consumers. Also known as "spray and pray" and "batch and blast."

Master data Master data is another term for *reference data*, which is descriptive data about a business subject area (like customer). Master or reference data contrasts with transactional data, which represents a specific business event.

Master data hub Hubs aren't limited to customer data. There are other types of hubs for other types of master data, for instance, product data or patient data. Master data hubs may intercommunicate for the purposes of supporting business processes.

Master data management (MDM) The set of disciplines and methods to ensure the currency, meaning, and quality of a company's reference data that is shared across various systems and organizations. CDI is a technology that supports the management of master data for the customer subject area.

Master identity The version of the truth about an individual customer created by the reconciliation and synchronization of diverse customer records, resident on the CDI hub.

Match engine   A program or process that compares disparate data elements to determine those that relate or match.

Member relationship management (MRM)   A version of CRM for non-profits, insurance companies, and other organizations whose constituents are considered members.

Metadata   Metadata usually refers to definitions and business rules that have been agreed on and stored in a centralized repository so that the business users—even those across departments and systems—use common terminology for key business terms. Metadata can include information about data's currency, ownership, source system, derivation (e.g., profit = revenues minus costs), or usage rules.

Metadata dictionary   A repository of often diverse metadata, allowing its centralized storage, management, and access.

Mixed workload   The combination of small, discrete pieces of work and large, complex processing activities occurring at the same time. From a CDI perspective, this means the ability to support a diverse set of processing requirements, including data loading as well as simple and complex searches.

.NET   A Microsoft standard to leverage Web services in order to run various business applications across multiple platforms.

Nonpublic personal information (NPI)   Usually regulated in financial services firms, NPI is information that financial services collect about consumers in the process of providing financial services (bank accounts, loans, insurance poli-

cies) to them. NPI includes information from loan applications or other forms, banking transactions, and data from consumer reporting agencies.

Online analytical processing (OLAP)   The ability for a user to "drill down" on various data attributes in order to gain a more detailed view of the data. Such analysis enables a user to view different perspectives of the same data in order to facilitate decision making. OLAP is part of the broader category of business intelligence.

Online transaction processing (OLTP)   The operational processes for executing a business activity while the customer or end user waits for the execution to complete. One example of OLTP would be an automated teller transaction.

Operational CRM   CRM systems that involve customer-facing business functions, usually involving real-time customer interactions such as customer service.

Operational systems   The IT systems that run the business on a day-to-day basis, typically OLTP systems.

Partner relationship management (PRM)   The practice of qualifying, tracking, and allocating leads to third-party sales partners (e.g., resellers) in order to understand how to price, market, and compensate channel partners.

Parsing   The use of a program to deconstruct the syntactic structure of a phrase or string of symbols. CDI hubs often parse data values, such as an address, to determine their individual components.

Party   A category for an individual or collection of people that share a common trait. For instance, a drug company might consider a party to be comprised of doctors, hospitals, and pharmacists. *Party* is usually used for complex businesses when the term *customer* is insufficient to describe constituent relationships.

Permission marketing   The term used to describe a customer's implicit or explicit agreement to be communicated to or to communicate to a company. Permission marketing usually implies that the customer perceives there to be value in the relationship, suggesting a *quid pro quo* between the customer and the vendor.

Persistent-style CDI   Persistent CDI involves the hub containing both linkage and descriptive details and physically storing those details.

Personalization   A company's ability to recognize a customer or prospect as an individual and differentiate its interactions with her. While personalization usually means individualized content delivered on a Web site, it can also involve target marketing, tailored e-mail campaigns, or customized banner ads.

Person of interest   An individual cited by an organization or agency for further scrutiny or understanding. The term is most frequently used by law enforcement agencies when announcing the name of an individual who has not formally been accused of a crime.

Physical database schema   The design of the physical database that defines the tables in the database that correspond to physical data objects. The physical database schema is often referred to by CDI vendors as their data model.

Point solution   Refers to a piece of software used for a specific business purpose.

Point to point   Usually refers to the direct interaction between two different systems. Point to point becomes an inefficient way for systems to communicate as individual systems proliferate.

Private portal   See **Extranet**.

Probabilistic matching   Uses statistical algorithms to deduce the best match between two records. Probabilistic matching usually tracks statistical confidence that two records refer to the same customer.

Product information management (PIM)   The management of product master data, usually via a PIM hub, to avail a single version of the truth about product data to the business.

Proof of concept   A software trial that allows a prospect to test the product before buying it, while at the same time delivering a realistic slice of functionality.

Pure play   A noun or adjective referring to a dot-com company without a brick-and-mortar presence.

Radio Frequency Identification (RFID)   RFID allows data be transmitted based on the placement of a microchipped tag. When read by a specialized reader, the RFID tag can transmit information about the item on which the tag has been placed. The information might include descriptive information about the item as well as price and manufacturer details. RFID technology accounts for the explosive growth of data volumes in businesses—particularly manufacturers and consumer packaged goods companies.

Recency, frequency, monetary (RFM)   A formula used by marketing to determine the relative value of customers. RFM connotes how recently and how frequently a customer has interacted with the company, usually through purchase transactions, as well as how much money they have spent. RFM represents the precursor to more robust customer value measurement.

Relationship marketing   The practice of marketing to customers based on specific understanding of their behaviors and preferences, which ideally drives relevant and timely interactions.

Reference-style CDI   See **Registry-style CDI**.

Registry-style CDI   The type of CDI where only the linkage (or indexing) details for customer information are maintained by the hub, referring back to the data sources where the customer details originate.

Retention   A company's ability to keep a customer by offering her products and services—and, by extension, the right messages—to keep her satisfied and avoid losing her to a competitor.

Return on investment (ROI)   The ability to measure a program's contribution to the bottom-line versus its cost. ROI analysis is most accurately performed once CDI has been put in place and improvements can be measured.

Return on relationship (ROR)
Sometimes used in conjunction with customer satisfaction increases, return on relationship applies to the overall value of a relationship and how it's paid off. It is sometimes used to describe B2B relationships, for instance, in measuring the uplift in sales triggered by certain partnerships. ROR can also imply a superset of a customer's financial value to a company, specifically in cases where a customer might refer other customers to the company.

Scripting   Automatic "scripts" generated for customer service reps based on an individual customer's segment and/or customer profile contents. Scripts remove the guesswork from determining how to respond to a customer query or complaint, guiding the rep through a dialogue with the customer.

Segmentation   The process of grouping customers (or products or cities or other business metrics) together in order to analyze the behaviors of the groups themselves with an aim toward target marketing the group-specific products and services.

Self-service   The ability of customers to ask their own questions or resolve problems without the intervention of a live person. Usually performed over the Web.

Semantic reconciliation   The automation of determining and comparing the definition of one or more data elements. Usually refers to the ability of different business applications to understand one another's terminology in their own native contexts, thus facilitating system intercommunications.

Service-level agreement (SLA)   A contract with a service provider, be it an internal IT organization, application service provider, or outsourcer, that specifies discrete reliability and availability requirements for an outsourced system. An SLA might also include other requirements such as support of certain technology standards or data volumes. An outsourcer's failure to adhere to the terms laid out in an SLA could result in financial penalties.

Service-oriented architecture (SOA)   A technology framework to support the design, development, and deployment of diverse business applications in a loosely coupled way. The goal of SOA is to encourage reuse of both data and functionality via the use of units of work (services) that are made available to different business processes across the enterprise.

Skunkworks project   A project that is being developed "under the radar," apart from the sanctioned integration projects that might be under way.

Source system   A system that provides data to another system is the data source for that system. A source system may also be the origination point for a data element.

Source system interface   The function within the CDI hub that supports the connection and data exchange with the source system providing the data.

Subscription services   The use of a paid outside provider for data reconciliation or provisioning.

Suite   A software package comprised of a range of functional modules that interact with each other.

Supply-chain management (SCM)   The integration and optimization of a company's supply chain, usually involving the automation of business processes that bring a product or service to market. SCM technologies can help to tighten integration and communication between a company and its suppliers and partners.

Target marketing   The practice of dividing the sum of the customer base into discrete subsets. These subsets can range from large—dividing customers based on whether or not they own a product—to small, even individual "segments of one."

Top-down development   The process of software development that factors in business requirements analysis as a first step in deconstructing functionality and data. Top-down development is usually a linear approach driven by consensus among stakeholders and managers, and mandating business involvement.

Trouble ticket   A record of a customer's call into the call center. A trouble ticket usually contains identifying features such as the reason for the customer's call, the status of the problem, and the ultimate resolution of the call. Trouble tickets allow a company to track and monitor the superset of customer calls into the contact center in order to summarize the main reasons for inbound customer contacts, be they problems, questions, or service requests.

Unstructured data   Data that does not neatly fit into a tabular structure with well-defined and bounded definitions. Examples of unstructured data are e-mail messages and video streams. Many customer databases contain comment fields where customer service reps put in additional notes about customers.

Up-selling   Motivating a customer to trade up to a more expensive or profitable product. The logic is: now that I know what this customer wants to buy, perhaps we can motivate him to buy a more profitable version or model. A jeweler might convince the buyer of a diamond tennis bracelet to go for larger diamonds at a higher price.

Value standardization   Refers to the establishment and adherence of data to standard formatting practices, ensuring a consistent interpretation of data values. CDI hubs should support data value standardization.

Virtualization   The concept of letting data stay "where it lives" and developing a hardware and software architecture that exposes the data to various business processes and organizations. The goal of virtualization is to shield developers and users from the complexity of the underlying data structures.

Waterfall development   A methodical and linear approach to technical development. While rigorous, waterfall development usually implies going through an entire development lifecycle before deploying functionality to end users, and usually begins with business analysis. See **Top-down development**.

Web services   The programmatic interfaces that enable different applications to communicate and process data via the Web.

XML   See **Extensible markup language**.

Index